ESCAPE WITH ONE'S LIFE

LEARNING TO LIVE WITH SURVIVAL

MR. CURTIS REED SCHAEFFER

ISBN: 1500520314
ISBN 13: 9781500520311

ACKNOWLEDGMENTS

This is the first book I have written and frankly I had no idea how time consuming and challenging the experience would be. I started very innocently by attending a class on writing at the Atlanta College of Arts and then had an article published in the Atlanta Journal-Constitution that described my experience surviving the plane crash. My initial goal was to simply document the survival experience, but after numerous interviews in Central America, I became hooked on the idea of actually writing a book. Throughout the close to five years of writing, I had to keep convincing myself that it could be done. The fact is that I could never have written this book without the support of many people who willingly gave of their time, their information, their affection and their love.

None of this would have been possible without the support of my wife, Magaly, who stood by my side throughout the crash experience and over the many years of writing this book. The encouragement of my daughter Alexa, my mother Paula, my brothers and close friends regularly motivated me to continue. The willingness of other survivors and family members of deceased passengers to talk to me and contribute to this book made my journey more meaningful and easier. I am grateful to you all.

From the first creative writing class when I wrote a short paragraph about the crash and read it out loud, the Professor and published author, Teri Holbrook, was a believer in my writing ability and the notion of documenting my experience in some fashion. A follow up class with

Teri for writers who wanted to be published provided me with invaluable weekly feedback and constructive criticism. This group forced me to learn to write. This was followed by the coming together of an informal group of writers with different interests. We met weekly and hammered each others' work in a constructive, honest manner. My fellow writers included Elizabeth Vantine, John Bunting, the now deceased Libby Mohr and Bill McGuff, Emily Paile, Wendy Worth, Christen Bryan and Larry Wills.

Two different book clubs in Atlanta, Georgia and Tegucigalpa, Honduras read and critiqued my manuscript. The Twelve Oaks group led by Darlene Schultz and the Tegucigalpa Book Club in Honduras led by Barbara Jackson were enormously helpful in their candid review of my work.

My brothers Mike, Alan and Doug read the manuscript and gave me feedback along with my good friend, Tony Gerlicz. Jumana and Greg Rosshandler motivated me throughout the process and provided useful suggestions. Mil gracias to my sister-in-law, Mayira Bunting, who helped with the layout and formatting of the book and her older sister Maigualida Matos who translated the book to Spanish.

Former colleagues from CARE USA, Bill Novelli and now deceased Peter Bell were gracious enough to read the manuscript and contribute to the book. Fellow plane crash survivors (on the same plane in Bolivia) were willing to write comments from their experiences for the back jacket-Samuel Doria Medina and Carlos N. Melo.

Houston attorney John Grayson, who successfully represented Honduran families of deceased passengers and two flight attendants, was generous with his time and information.

The list goes on and on but there are others I want to recognize. My astrologist Jo Barguinear, Lewis Marshall who informed me of the history of TAN Airline and whose father, Hugh Marshall, was an early TAN pilot; my friend and former colleague from Honduras, Gloria Manzanares; the former President of the Associated Press,

Sally Stapleton, who found and provided me with numerous photos; former CARE colleague Scott Solberg who helped set up initial interviews in Honduras and encouraged me to pursue this effort; John Thabes who both represented me and helped me understand the Warsaw Convention. Staff from my office in La Paz, Bolivia Emilie Salinas, Freddy Lemus and Gonzalo Gutierrez, were always there when I needed their help. Thank you all.

Dedicated to My Good Friend and Dear Mother-Paula

TABLE OF CONTENTS

PREFACE

I first met Curt Schaeffer when I joined CARE, the international relief and development organization in 1990. Even among CARE's many interesting and unique people, Curt stood out.

Although Curt seemed carefree and almost happy-go-lucky, he was serious about his work and was the well-respected director overseeing CARE's Latin American operations. As with the other regional directors, Curt traveled a great deal to communities in Central and South America, and, although I didn't know it at the time, to a difficult place for him to go: Honduras.

When he left CARE for a while to be a stay-home-dad, I admired his decision. I had come from a corporate existence, where that sort of behavior was exceedingly rare. Curt was just a different kind of guy.

I noticed that he wore elastics on his arms and wondered what that was about. Someone said that he had been in a plane crash and had been burned. I didn't bring it up in conversations with Curt, didn't know much about the details and didn't think much about it.

Then I learned more. Someone told me that he had been though a horrific ordeal, a terrible plane crash in Honduras. As the story went, it had been a miracle that he made it through, and the CARE people had rallied around him to get him home and into intensive care. It was a story almost as much about the CARE family as about Curt's incredible ordeal.

After reading Curt's book, I realize that his nonchalance was all an act, or perhaps more accurately, a coping mechanism to conceal the immense pain he was suffering, both physical and psychological. All the demons he was fighting, described in intense detail in this book, were unapparent to me.

Escape With One's Life-Learning to Live with Survival is an inspirational story of a senseless tragedy. This is a book about courage, written by a very courageous man. As I read the book, I found myself wondering whether I would have been able to do what he succeeded in doing. I suspect every reader will ask this same question.

What Curt achieved is both extraordinary and at the same time very human. He discovered how to survive... to be a survivor and wonder why. Curt learned how to continue flying, to forgive the pilots who caused the crash, to forgive those Hondurans who were so casual and inhumane, and to write this fascinating book.

In the end, it was his courage, the support of his wife, Magaly, and his family and friends, combined with his innate sense of decency- which is what led him to humanitarian work at CARE in the first place- that helped him through it all.

At CARE, nobody said, "There goes Curt Schaeffer, a real hero." But as I look back on it, that's just the sort of quiet kind of pride that people felt about him. In fact, that's how I think about him now.

In this day and age when we all seem more susceptible to senseless tragedy, *Escape With One's Life* is a compelling story. None of us really knows how we would react in such a situation, but as this story demonstrates so dramatically, we can learn to live with survival, Curt Schaeffer did.

William D. Novelli
Former President and CEO
American Association of Retired Persons (AARP)
Washington, D.C.

INTRODUCTION

I grew up in the birthplace of aviation just blocks away from the home of Orville and Wilbur Wright. Dayton, Ohio in the 1950's was as unfamiliar with air travel as anyplace in the country. The industrial town boasted a tiny air terminal with one gate for the few flights that went in and out each week. My parents said it was a disgrace to the legacy of the Wrights. The brothers Wright were deceased by the time I was born, but the big hill below their landmark home was our favorite sledding spot.

My Midwestern childhood benefited from a functional family. We actually sat down and ate dinner together every night. My father was a conservative attorney with a strong sense of ethics. He regaled us at dinner with stories of his favorite clients. They were humble people he made no money from, but they were real people, who struggled to get through each day and they depended on him for legal assistance. Payment for a year's worth of legal advice often came in the form of a bottle of whiskey. My mother lectured us on moral behavior after Dad was finished talking about his clients. Mom took on one crusade after another—civil rights, the Vietnam War and spiritual development. Both parents were role models, and they taught me honesty and fairness.

From an early age, I had a strong sense of adventure and became interested in learning Spanish from listening to my mother's tales of living in a small village in Southern Ecuador in the 1920's. My grandfather was a mining engineer and after graduating from the Mackey School of Mines at the University of Nevada at Reno in 1912, my grandparents set out for Ecuador on a steamer. They spent the better part of 15 years in a mountain village working a productive gold mine.

My mother was born in California and carried into the mining town on the backs of campesinos. Her strong, independent spirit comes from her parents and her frontier-like upbringing. I was the only brother who took Mom's bait, learned Spanish and found my future in South America.

I was a sociology major in college and found more practical education outside the classroom. I worked throughout my college years in a variety of jobs from a resource coordinator in a prison to a VISTA volunteer in a community mental health center.

My motivation to work with other people came from my extroverted nature and a genuine interest in making my little piece of the world a better place. I liked people, liked being involved with people and groups and pursuing a career in the helping professions was attractive. I was a child of the 60's. Making money and accumulating material possessions were not on my mind. Following my interests and forsaking conventional career paths guided my decisions.

After graduation from Pitzer College in Claremont, California, I worked for a Public Defender's office in Portland, Oregon. It was an ideal job for a sociology major. I assisted in diverting young offenders out of the system and into community programs that more adequately dealt with their problems than did the county jail. The work was compelling, but two intense years of daily encounters with lawbreakers was plenty. I had saved enough money to travel to South America, my lifelong dream.

Most of my friends were headed to Europe, but I had a burning desire to travel through Latin America--to see the places that I had heard about all my life. Starting at the Mexican border, I crossed from Laredo, Texas to Nuevo Laredo, Mexico. Once I passed into a new world of different sights, sounds, smells and language, I was hooked. For the next six months, I traveled by bus, train and hitchhiked through Central

America and down into South America before stopping in Bolivia to visit a friend.

I was lonely and scared at times, but always challenged by the newness of it all. I sensed that this was where I belonged, and certainly where I wanted to be. I was able to get a job teaching at an international school in Cochabamba, Bolivia and stayed for two years.

From that point on, my life was inextricably linked to Latin America. I eventually married a Venezuelan and much of my professional career was involved in the region through work with international relief and development organizations. The plane crash in Honduras in 1989 further strengthened my bond with Latin America and Latin Americans.

After my teaching experience in Bolivia, I returned to the United States and was accepted into a masters program at the School for International Training in Brattleboro, Vermont where I received a degree in international administration. The degree was my foot-in-the-door to working overseas. For the next five years, I enjoyed a series of management jobs in Peru and Bolivia with international non-profit organizations and the U.S. government.

During this time, I fell in love with Magaly Quintero Marquez from Caracas, Venezuela and we married. For the first three years of our marriage, we enjoyed the rarefied air of La Paz, Bolivia where I managed a national primary health care project and Magaly was the office manager for the World Health Organization. At this time, Bolivia was suffering from hyper-inflation which, at its height, reached 29,000% annually. Paper currency couldn't be printed fast enough to keep pace. Magaly and I sharpened our management skills as the country functioned close to anarchy. Every day brought a new challenge: strikes, blocked roads, no gasoline and consumer prices that increased as you shopped.

In 1988, we moved to New York. I went to work for CARE, the international relief and development organization, as the Deputy Regional

Manager for Latin American Operations. The crash occurred a year later. I returned to CARE three months after the crash and remained with the organization until 1998.

In the intervening years, I had a variety of management positions and we moved with a sizeable portion of the CARE organization to Atlanta. My most satisfying career move, though, was to take a leave of absence from CARE in 1992 to raise my daughter. Magaly returned to work with International Planned Parenthood Federation, and I took a break from my demanding job.

I quickly found out that staying home with an infant is far more challenging and exhausting than working in an office. Hanging out with my daughter and watching her develop on a daily basis was gratifying. After eleven months of being Mr. Mom, I was ready for a normal, less demanding job and returned to CARE.

When I finally left the organization that had meant so much to me personally and professionally, I realized that my departure had little to do with CARE and everything to do with initiating this book project. Nine years after the crash I still had too many unanswered questions, nightmares and unsettled feelings. Years of therapy helped, but I was driven to do something on my own. I had to act, and documenting the experience was the only thing I knew to do.

To pay the bills and help maintain my family during this period, I took on consulting jobs. Some of the jobs were home based but others took me to far-flung places like Bolivia-where I evaluated a grant supporting small farmers for Heifer Project International; India-where I was part of a team evaluating a government development program for children that reached over 100,000 villages; North Korea-where I managed a group of monitors responsible for ensuring the receipt and distribution of commodities donated by the U.S. government in response to a famine.

For the last three months of the job in North Korea, my wife Magaly and daughter Alexa accompanied me. We were the first American family to live and work in North Korea since the Korean War Armistice in 1953. It was an amazing experience that one can only have in an isolated, Stalinist country where Americans are truly hated. Magaly had just become a naturalized U.S. citizen, which along with her masters in business administration qualified her to work as the administrator for the team. Alexa was prevented from attending the international school in Pyongyang because she, like all Americans, was considered the "sworn enemy."

I have been asked many times since the crash if I am afraid of flying. I made a point of getting back on a plane within months of my mishap and remain a frequent flyer to this day. Each time I step on a plane, my emotional side tells me it may be my last flight, but my rational side says the odds of being involved in another air crash are slim to none. There is always an underlying discomfort during a flight.

Airplanes remain the safest means of travel. During the last twenty years of the 20th Century, there was an average of 125 deaths per year in air related accidents in the United States even though the number of flights doubled. The risk of dying in an air crash during the 1990's was 1 in 9.2 million. From 2000 to 2005, the odds of a passenger dying on a domestic U.S. airline flight was 1 in 22.8 million. These are astounding figures if you consider that in the United States more than 40,000 people die annually on the highways.

My journey to document the crash experience included annual forays to Central America to interview people who were directly or indirectly affected by this tragedy. For several years I attended the anniversary mass at the crash site, which is now a park with a beautiful monument honoring the deceased passengers.

In the process of confronting my own pain and the anguish of other survivors and family members of deceased passengers I interviewed, I was able to let go of my hatred toward those I blamed for my fate. I now have fewer unanswered questions.

The plane crash was an event in my life. Learning to live with survival has been an on-going process. Writing this book has been an essential part of the process, and I am thankful for the opportunity to share the experience with others.

Curt Schaeffer
La Paz, Bolivia
June, 2006

POSTSCRIPT

I self published this book in Spanish in 2005 and in English in 2006 collaborating with Artes Graficas Sagitario in La Paz, Bolivia. I sold more than 600 copies in Bolivia after presenting the book in different venues of importance in that country including Portales (Simon Patino residence) in Cochabamba, La Moneda (National Mint of Bolivia circa 1572) in Potosi, the Archivo y Biblioteca Nacionales de Bolivia (National Archives and Library of Bolivia) in Sucre and the Gran Hotel Ambassador in El Alto. It was an honor and a great satisfaction to share the Spanish version of the book with so many Bolivians in a country that has always been close to my heart.

The English copy was never promoted nor presented other than to a few book clubs in Virginia. I sold or gave away close to 800 copies after returning to the United States from Bolivia in 2007. Magaly and I did travel to Managua, Nicaragua and Tegucigalpa, Honduras on an October weekend in 2007 coinciding with the anniversary of the crash and presented the book in Spanish in book stores in the respective capitals. We also attended mass at the crash site outside Tegucigalpa.

After this weekend, we decided to back away from the book and the experience.

Curt Schaeffer
Falls Church, Virginia
October 21, 2014

FLIGHT ROUTE

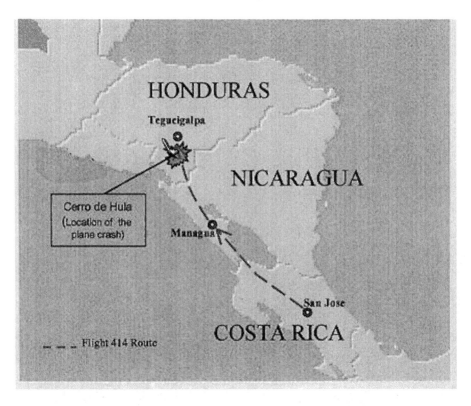

October 21, 1989 Flight No. 414 TAN SASA
6:00 Departure from San Jose, Costa Rica
7:25 Departure from Managua, Nicaragua
7:53 Plane Crash with Cerro de Hula, Honduras

CHAPTER ONE

A ROUTINE
CENTRAL AMERICAN FLIGHT

*Either we live by accident and die by accident, or we
live by plan and die by plan.*
-Thornton Wilder, The Bridge of San Luis Rey

Flight #414 was the first plane to leave Juan Santa María International
Airport in San Jose, Costa Rica on October 21, 1989. The Boeing
727, which was leased by TAN-SAHSA from Continental Airlines, was
initiating a routine Central American flight scheduled to stop briefly in
Managua before continuing on to Tegucigalpa, Honduras. I was one of
the first to reach the gate area about 5:15 A.M. and killed time reading
the morning paper and dozing. Other passengers slowly assembled.

Across from me sat a middle-aged couple. They were holding hands with their eyes shut, leaning on each other, looking content. The flight crew ambled past us and onto the plane. No one seemed to be in too much of a hurry. We departed close to 5:55 A.M.

I had spent the week working for CARE, the international relief and development organization, in San José and was on my way to the office in Tegucigalpa. As Deputy Regional Manager for Latin American operations, I was based in New York and had worked for the organization for one year. I was visiting country offices to become familiar with staff, operations and field programs.

My week in Costa Rica had been interesting but uneventful until Thursday night, when I tuned in the little black and white television in my hotel room to watch the third game of the World Series between San Francisco and Oakland. As the picture came on, the screen began to shake and the audio portion of the telecast was lost. I wasn't sure what had happened until a local announcer came on and explained that the San Francisco Bay area had just been rocked by the Loma Prieta earthquake. I knew from the reported Richter scale magnitude of 7.1 that this could be a real disaster for people in that area.

My wife, Magaly, was going to meet me in Tegucigalpa. She was scheduled to work the next week for her employer, International Planned Parenthood Federation, in Honduras. October 20 is her birthday, and we had planned to meet and celebrate over the weekend. I attempted to call her in the Dominican Republic to wish her a happy birthday, but was unable to get through. I faxed her a congratulatory message instead.

Thirty-eight of us boarded the Boeing 727-200 in San José. I had questioned the booking of the flight with the CARE travel agent in New York before leaving my office. My flying experience in Central America had been limited. I preferred a U.S. carrier, but was told that none flew this particular route. Air travel in Central America had been limited for years because of low demand, and TAN SAHSA was one of the few airlines flying within the region.

Upon boarding the plane, I headed for the rear of the craft. It was open seating, and we were free to choose. A young, attractive flight attendant approached me and encouraged me to sit in one of the more comfortable seats in the front. The plane had no first-class passengers, but did have a first-class section separated from the rest of the aircraft by a bulkhead. I sat in the fourth row on the aisle on the right side of the plane.

The flight from San José to Managua, Nicaragua, was a short 172 miles, and was smooth and comfortable. The sun shone brightly on the tarmac as we arrived at the Augusto Cesar Sandino Airport. From my seat I could see a sign that read *BIENVENIDOS A LA TIERRA DE SANDINO* (WELCOME TO THE LAND OF SANDINO). I was tempted to get off the plane to stretch and see if I could catch a glimpse of the Sandinista influence on the country. My desire to fall back asleep won out, though, and I stayed on the plane and dozed.

The 1980's were a volatile period in Central America and Nicaragua was on center stage. The country was ruled by the Sandinistas, a revolutionary group that had seized power from the despotic Somoza family in 1979 after a violent revolution. The U.S. government had imposed an economic embargo on Nicaragua because of the leftist leanings of the Sandinista government and its alleged connections to Cuba and to the revolutionary forces in El Salvador. The result was that the Nicaraguan national airline, Air Nica, was prohibited from flying into the United States. The embargo created more business for TAN SAHSA, a Honduran airline.

Flight #414 was a continuation flight to Miami after a stop in Honduras. While waiting for the journey to continue, I glanced down at the fuel truck next to the plane and saw a seemingly endless procession of passengers filing onto the aircraft.

The plane departed after some delay, and the routine nature of the flight continued. The next leg of the trip from Managua to Tegucigalpa was only 134 miles or thirty minutes by air. I expected to reach my destination by 8 A.M.

As the 727-200 climbed to eighteen thousand feet, weather conditions changed and the day took on a more ominous feel. Strong winds, thick clouds and occasional rain pelted us as we flew over a series of mountains between the two capital cities. I eavesdropped on several Americans sitting in front of me, employees of the United States Agency for International Development (USAID). I was curious about what little I could snatch of their conversation. The aircraft continued to fly in and out of clouds, and the plane was quiet. Given the early morning hour of the flight, many of the passengers were sleeping or dozing as the aircraft approached Tegucigalpa.

After visiting the restroom, the flight attendant's voice boomed out of the intercom, "We are preparing to land in Tegucigalpa. Raise your table, put your seat in an upright position and fasten your seatbelts." Visibility was poor, and I had tired of looking out the window at clouds. Suddenly, I noticed a flash of green out of the corner of my eye.

"No, No, No-We're going to hit!" one of the Americans sitting in front of me screamed.

The impact was immediate as the 170,000 pound behemoth careened across the mountainous terrain at an approach speed of close to two hundred miles per hour. We were thrown into darkness. I heard the grotesque sound of metal scraping on earth while people screamed hysterically. My first and only thought was that this was it. I was surely going to die.

I put my arms over my head as I was thrown forward. In a matter of seconds I passed through a wall of flames. I covered my face with my hands to protect it from the intense heat. There was a dream-like quality to those seconds; I was aware of moving and burning, with no discomfort or any control over what was happening. I lost consciousness.

I came to in a field. I was still belted into my seat. Miraculously, I was sitting upright as I had been inside the plane. My aisle seat had separated from the window seat next to me, and I was ejected from the plane. A short distance to my right was the blazing inferno of the exploding 727. High winds whipped the flames away from me.

I felt numb. I looked down at my hands and arms and noticed a pale, lifeless quality. The skin had been burned. I was still in a stunned state but was regaining my senses. I seemed to be the only one in this field--no other survivors, no dead people, no locals, nobody else but me! The odd sight momentarily struck me as being surreal until I felt chills course through my body.

I was in a state of shock, and it did not occur to me to try to rescue other passengers, as the plane was an inferno. I assumed that they had escaped on the other side of the fuselage but really had no idea what had occurred just minutes before this.

I looked down at myself and realized that my left shoe was missing. My pants were torn, and my clothes reeked of fuel oil. I knew that something amazing had just happened, but there wasn't time to give thanks to anyone or celebrate my good fortune. My body hurt. I was cold, and the plane I had just been in was burning.

I looked around for help. To my left, away from the plane, I spotted a small group of four to six Honduran laborers, working on another hillside no more than a hundred and fifty feet away. It looked as if they were harvesting corn. My first thought was that these guys could help me. It seemed odd that they were working at all, considering the crash. The more I watched, the more I realized that they were absorbed in their work and paying no attention what so ever to the startling carnage on the hillside adjacent to them. It was as if this sort of thing occurred regularly in the area, and they were accustomed to it.

After a couple of minutes, I unbuckled the seat belt and stood up, a bit groggy and unsure on my feet, but able to walk. I took a few steps towards the farmers. I waved my arms and shouted at them.

They continued to work, completely indifferent. Perhaps it was cultural avoidance of something they did not understand and had no desire to become involved with. Perhaps they were paralyzed from shock. My instinct told me not to waste any more time on them.

As I looked down the mountainside, I spotted a small adobe house a couple of hundred yards below me. I made my way down, fighting through thick shrubs and repeatedly falling in the mud. It was early morning and the grass and plants were dripping with dew. I felt like I had little control over my movement but was determined to get off that mountainside.

As I staggered away from the crash site, I was coughing from the smoke I had taken into my lungs and feeling nauseated from the stench of the fuel oil that covered my clothes. I promised myself that I would never smoke cigarettes again, a habit I had struggled with for years. It struck me too that this was a strange time to worry about a silly habit. I muttered to myself, 'Stay focused Schaeffer, just stay focused.'

I finally reached the adobe house and walked into a smoke-filled room. Something was cooking on an open hearth, and an older woman emerged from the thick air that felt like it was going to choke me. She cowered at the sight of me, and I was puzzled by her reaction. I was cold and asked her in Spanish for a blanket, but it did not materialize. Instead, the lady handed me a glass of water. I took it and looked into the glass. Dirt was swimming in the cloudy liquid. I knew that if I drank the water, I would be sick within hours.

"*No gracias,*" ("No thanks.") I said to the woman. I handed the glass back to her and walked out of the house. I needed help, not diarrhea.

To my surprise, a *camino vecinal* (dirt road running through the area) ran in front of the house. A small truck had stopped on the road, and for the first time I saw other survivors. A man and a woman were climbing into the front seat of the truck. I walked around to the bed of the truck and saw two men with burned faces laying there with blankets over them moaning. I climbed into the back of the small Datsun pickup truck with the two survivors and a young girl. I never attempted to talk to them. We were all badly burned and some suffered from multiple fractures. Our truck was the first to leave the crash site for Tegucigalpa.

I later found out that the couple in front of the truck was Carlos Pellas and his wife, Vivian, who had been traveling to their home in Miami. They had been in Nicaragua the previous week attending to business matters and visiting friends. The wealthy Nicaraguan couple sat in the fifth row behind the plane's bulkhead one row behind me. They lived in Miami but traveled regularly to Managua where most of the Pellas family business interests were managed. The Sandinista government made it difficult for Carlos and Vivian to live in Nicaragua, and they chose to raise their three children in the United States during the uncertain times.

Carlos came to after the crash and saw tall grass through a hole in the plane. He got out of his seat and escaped the aircraft, then re-membered his wife, Vivian, inside. Carlos returned to the plane, but couldn't find her. He finally recognized her by the blouse that she was wearing--her face was too disfigured. At this point, Carlos' shirt was on fire, and he was screaming his wife's name, "Vivian, Vivian!"

Vivian heard Carlos yelling in her subconscious. "It was enough to bring me back to life," she later told me. "I managed to open my eyes and saw my husband burning. When he tried to take my seat-belt off, he noticed he was missing two fingers from his hand. "Jump! At least one of us should get out for our children." He screamed at me. All this happened in a matter of seconds. He went out of the plane. I don't know how I was still standing, because I saw at my feet something like a bright window with light shining up. My eyes closed and I went into a dark tunnel, then I bounced out of the plane as if I had been pushed."

Vivian continued, "I came to and saw my feet again, in shreds, my toenails to the ground, the skin burned. I remembered my children back home and started running through a cornfield. It was just in time, as a huge explosion blew me through the air. I fell and hit the ground hard, and when I tried to get up, my clavicle bones had broken through my skin. I looked back and saw movement in the middle of the fire and smoke and thought it was my husband, so I pushed the bones back into my body and returned."

Vivian found Carlos, and they made their way to a schoolhouse where they encountered the owner of a small truck. The man was reluctant to drive down the mountain with a load of burned and bleeding people. He complained about the poor condition of the truck and the lack of fuel, but Carlos Pellas was not to be rebuffed. The owner finally agreed to drive the Pellas' to Tegucigalpa, after Carlos offered to buy him a new truck.

First Officer Reinero Canales, thirty-four years old, was at the controls of the aircraft from San José, Costa Rica, to Managua, Nicaragua. He joined SAHSA in 1986 after a career in the Honduran Air Force, where he was trained as a pilot. Captain Raul Argueta, forty-five years old, took over for the leg from Managua to Tegucigalpa. The Captain was well liked. He had an affable personality but a reputation with flight attendants for flying into turbulence with no warning. Both pilots had qualified to fly the Boeing 727 earlier in the year.

Canales told the press, "Upon leaving Managua, we were in contact with the control tower at Toncontin in Tegucigalpa. We were informed that it was partially cloudy around the capital and that the area of Cerro de Hula (which is on the flight path to Toncontin from the South) was dense with clouds and experiencing strong winds. We knew that these were typical atmospheric conditions for the southern approach at this time of the year."

As the aircraft reached 7,500 feet in altitude, flight #414 was authorized to begin its descent. Crewmembers were preparing for landing. The pilots saw only thick clouds, and Tegucigalpa in the valley below was not visible.

When the plane emerged from the clouds, the pilots were horrified to see how close they were to the mountainside. The aircraft was too low. They attempted to maneuver it away from the mountain. It was too late. Captain Argueta screamed, *"Vamos para arriba! Vamos para arriba! Vamos para arriba!"* ("Let's go up! Let's go up! Let's go up!")

There was no further communication as the Boeing 727 crashed into the mountainside. Canales told the press later, "I saw the sky, then the mountains, then the ground amid the confusion and blows to the plane and to my body. I sincerely thought I was going to die."

He did not lose consciousness, and within seconds he was aware of being surrounded by twisted metal, heavy smoke and fire. The windows of the cockpit were gone. He was able to unbuckle his seatbelt and move out of his seat. He was shocked to see the flight attendant trainee Guiomar Nuñez at his feet. "How did she get there," he asked himself. He looked up and saw that Captain Argueta was unconscious, partially boxed in by the smashed sides of the cockpit. He reached over and grabbed the Captain's shoulder and shook him. Argueta regained consciousness. The two pilots escaped through a small hole in the fuselage that Canales had ripped open through sheer force. They fled the aircraft, knowing it could blow any second.

Nivia Umanzor, the purser or chief flight attendant for flight #414, was sitting in the front of the plane by herself when, at the last minute, she decided to move Guiomar Nuñez, the flight attendant trainee, up from the rear galley to sit with her. She asked her to check passengers' seatbelts along the way.

When Guiomar reached the front galley and was belted into her seat, Nivia picked up the microphone to announce the impending arrival of flight #414 at Toncontin International Airport. She was standing up, and the trainee was seated in front of her. The trainee had less than six months' experience with the airline, while the purser was a twenty-nine year veteran. One was launching her career while the other was months away from retirement.

9

"I was standing when the first impact jolted us," Nivia told me in Tegucigalpa in October 1999. "It felt like a bomb had gone off in the plane." She embraced the trainee and then fell to the floor. My immediate thoughts were, 'I am going to die. This is the last day of my life. I'm going to heaven.' Everything was breaking, including the mirror in the bathroom, and I was hitting everything around me for eight to ten horrible seconds. It felt like I was in a blender, with luggage falling on top of me and bouncing against the walls around me. I blacked out momentarily, but was aware of the plane coming to a screeching stop. At that point I believed I was in heaven. But then I heard people screaming and thought I had to be in hell. I finally realized what had happened and became aware of heavy smoke in the air and explosions throughout the plane."

Nivia spotted an opening in the plane where it had broken apart. She crawled over luggage and bodies toward the light. She heard the flight engineer, Marco Esteban Figueroa, moaning and Nivia told him to hang on. She was able to crawl right out of a hole in the plane. The last thing she heard before exiting the craft was the flight attendant trainee crying for help.

The explosions continued. Even though the plane was wrapped in flames and the intensity of the heat was almost unbearable, Nivia reentered the plane to save Guiomar.

Guiomar Nuñez had finished checking the seatbelts of the passengers and was fixing her hair in preparation for landing. "I sat down and suddenly there was a ball of fire and everything was turning in circles. This continued for a short time and then there was silence, a total silence. Then the explosions and screams started."

Guiomar continued, "When I regained consciousness, my seatbelt was still fastened and I was surrounded by thick, black smoke and people were screaming. There was the strong odor of jet fuel in the air mixed with the stench of burning flesh and blood. I felt like I was going through a long, dark tunnel that had no end. I didn't want to move and couldn't move. The bathroom was on top of me, along with the pilot's control panel. I was trapped, but found that my feet were at the head of the flight engineer and I could touch his head with my toes."

"I saw this horrible scene of twisted metal, plastic objects, legs . . . I closed my eyes, and even though I was not religious at the time I said, 'Jesus, please, I don't want to die. Help me.' I wasn't sure if it was a dream, but when I opened my eyes again and saw the same thing and realized that I was bleeding from the head, then I knew it was real and said, 'Help me, God. Help me Jesus. I don't want to die! Please!"

"I was aware of fire, and there was no light to see clearly. I began crying and was resigned to dying in that spot. I could hear more explosions and people screaming hysterically. It was awful, ugly, with smoke everywhere. There was someone nearby trying to remove metal pieces from on top of me. It was the co-pilot, First Officer Reinero Canales. He was leaving the plane when he spotted me and began to take all this twisted metal off of me. Just then, Nivia Umanzor, the purser, appeared and helped me unfasten the seatbelt. She pulled me out and carried me from the plane, as my body was all beaten up."

The two flight attendants were walking away from the plane toward a schoolhouse when they spotted the pilot and copilot. Nivia started screaming at them, "What happened? What happened? Everyone is dead!" The captain responded to her by saying that he didn't remember anything, and the first officer was complaining that the plane had been too low.

Nivia told the pilots to go back into the plane to rescue the flight engineer, who was pinned down under his instrument panel. She told me later that the captain seemed to wake up and started back toward the plane, but it was too late. By this time, the aircraft was exploding, and the heat was too intense to attempt a rescue. A violent explosion knocked them all to the ground.

Ron and Helen Devereux were the only Australians on board flight #414. They had been looking at business prospects in Central and South America and planned to spend a month in Costa Rica. The week they were scheduled to leave San José coincided with a regional summit meeting of twenty presidents from the Americas, including George Herbert Bush from the United States and Brian Mulrooney from Canada. They chose to avoid the congestion in San José and other potential conflicts by leaving the country a week early. Their plane tickets were changed to TAN SAHSA flight #414 on October 21, 1989.

The Devereuxs sat just in front of the leftwing, with a young girl of about thirteen years seated on the aisle. Helen showed her how to buckle her seatbelt before departure. Across the aisle sat the girl's mother, nursing a baby alongside the father. The family was excited about making their first trip to the United States.

Both Ron and Helen described the early part of the flight as being beautiful with wonderful views of the mountains, and vapours trailing off their peaks. They wondered if these were volcanoes. As the plane descended to Tegucigalpa, Helen turned to hand her glass to the flight attendant and "then nothing."

Ron remained conscious through the initial impact. He thought, "It hit a bloody mountain. The guts have been torn out of it. I am going to die. I'm not ready yet."

The next impact hit and the luggage crashed through the cabin. My body thrashed around uncontrollably. It hit again. All the hull linings around me disappeared forward in a hail of broken shards."

Ron lost consciousness and was roused by the pain of melting plastic that was dripping from overhead. He looked around and realized that exposed electric wires were red hot around him.

He pushed a large cable off his arm and came to his senses. "That's it, then, I am alive. Helen was dead, bloody and motionless alongside. I can't walk. My feet and ankles are broken up. I will wait to be rescued."

Ron's memory of the crash is so vivid that he begins to relive it. "I hear crackling, smoke everywhere, and screams of terror. I know I am going to burn alive. The terror that engulfs me is such that if I can find the means to kill myself I will do it without hesitation."

A stream of light from outside the plane caught Ron's attention. He became focused on a hole five to eight inches in diameter in the roof of the plane above them. After rolling a large, heavy aluminum shaft out of the way, he was able to hoist himself up onto his seat.

He continues, "Forget the feet. I don't feel a thing. I can now reach the hole. It is cool to touch, perfectly round, punched neatly through the hull. It feels to be just over an inch thick, perhaps a little more. I am now almost completely detached from the scene around me. If I tear at the little fractures and roll it inwards, I can make the hole larger and get out. It tears readily, but is thicker than I thought. It's cutting into my hands. I stop. The screams of the passengers overpower me. I get my mind together and start again. The bigger I make the hole, the easier the work gets. I take another look at Helen, still and bloodied, then I heave myself out through the hole onto the top of the fuselage."

He smelled fuel and the crackling noise of fire seemed to be all around him. "Is Helen really dead? I can't go until I know," he thought to himself.

"In a back corner of my mind," Helen says, beginning her story, "I was in my bed at home and my feet were itching. I felt agitated. What was wrong? I rubbed my feet together, and felt I was rubbing off skin, like a sunburn."

In those few seconds Ron looked back down into the plane and saw Helen's head moving. He yelled at her to give him her hand.

Helen raised her left arm to Ron but felt a horrible wrenching and fell back into the seat. Ron shouted again, instructing her to open the seatbelt. With her left arm still extended toward Ron, she brushed the belt with her right hand and it opened.

Ron pulled Helen straight out through the opening "like a cork out of a bottle." She was barely conscious. The smoke was thick and Ron feared the plane was ready to blow up.

He yelled to Helen, "Go! Go! Jump! It's going to blow." He watched her disappear over the side of the aircraft.

The ground was twenty to twenty-five feet below. Helen jumped and tried to roll as she hit the ground. She found that one leg gave way when she stood up. As she attempted to move away from the plane, the effect of only using one leg moved her around in a circle.

Ron remained on the plane looking back in at the young girl who had been seated alongside them. She is now conscious and screaming. He continued, "I can't leave. I must help. I reach down. I have her hand. Her seat belt is buckled; I call for her to release it. She can't do it, or doesn't understand what I say. Fire suddenly takes hold of her clothing, her hair bursts alight, a halo of fire, heat and flames are now coming through the hole. I will always remember her eyes as I let go of her hand."

Ron rolled down the side of the plane and crawled away. He found Helen stumbling around and shouted at her, "Go! Go! Fuel is everywhere and it will blow!" He crawled for about twenty feet and found himself in a ditch with Helen, both their heads resting on a muddy ridge.

They heard horrifying wails and screams of agony coming from the plane. Ron and Helen looked back as the plane exploded in a fireball forming a mushroom cloud. Within seconds the worst was over and a quiet tranquility fell over the ruined aircraft. It was engulfed in flames and the faint crackling sound of a blaze emerged. All the passengers were gone.

Helen slid back down in the mud and asked, "Why, God? Why?" Ron lay alongside, a bloody and broken mess. Helen was struck by the look on his face. It was a mixture of pain and total exhaustion. He stretched out his arm and touched her, saying, 'Helen, we are alive.'

Their relief was followed by incredulity. Helen continued, "I could not believe it. Just in front of us, not twenty feet away, stood the pilots.

They were unscathed. Even their shoes were bright and shiny. Their shirts were white and clean, and there was only a small mark of blood on the forehead of one of them. I stared in disbelief, and hate poured out of me. Ron called to them, 'Help, Senor!' raising his arm. They did not. They turned and walked away."

Two campesinos ran up to the Devereuxs and half dragged them down the mountainside. Others joined them along the way and helped them get through wire fencing. They finally made it to a road where a local bus was stopped. The broken and battered Australians were helped on to the bus joining other survivors.

This group of survivors headed for town on a bus that was transporting school children and others from the surrounding area with business in Tegucigalpa. Ron thought, "This driver must himself be in shock. He was stopping at regular stops, and people getting onto the bus were recoiling in horror at our appearance."

Gene Van Dyk, a big American survivor, turned to Ron and asked, "How do I look?"

Ron looked him over and thought to himself, "He's not a pretty sight. His ear appeared to be melted into the side of his face. The flesh of his torso was hanging in tatters sloughed off in greasy blackened rolls. He was trying to push the bits of flesh back onto his body. Before responding he thought, 'he won't last long-a dead man walking.'"

Ron, nevertheless, gave him an encouraging answer, "One side of your face is okay but the other will need some work."

Ron surveyed the scene inside the bus. "The pretty young flight attendant was sitting in front of me staring glassy-eyed and still. The older flight attendant's face had been hideously cut through the brow, and the wound was hanging open and bleeding. Her arm hung loosely at her side, with a large chunk of flesh dangling from above her elbow. The blood was dripping like a tap. We all sat in sickening silence. I glanced around and saw the two pilots sitting in the back of the bus.

A Honduran man who had been sitting in front of us was also on the bus."

The driver continued to make his stops. Schoolchildren clambered on, took one look around, screamed and jumped off. One of the flight attendants yelled at the driver and the bus shot off down the twisting mountain road.

Ron thought, "This silly bastard will kill us yet."

"Choppers," said the American. He wanted to stop the bus. Helicopters were overhead and then suddenly gone toward the crash site.

They then heard sirens and the bus stopped. The entire group was loaded into one ambulance.

Once he was inside the ambulance, Ron briefly described the situation, "The big American cradled the hostess in his arms comforting her. Her blood and his mingled on the ambulance floor. Big man, big heart. Helen looked like she needed a cuddle. A morphine shot, and I was out like a light."

Helen explained that she was the only one of the group who could actually lie down in the ambulance. She was disoriented. "I could not see where Ron was, and found I could no longer move my head. I called out his name, but there was no answer. The American was placed on the side, sitting on the wheel well. He was bent over, and his arms were hanging. The older airhostess was placed on the floor alongside me, and the American lifted her head and cradled it on his knee. The blood from her arm and head was dripping down onto my face. I should not have felt revulsion and horror, but I did. Her life was dripping into my face, and I could not stop it. I can remember shaking uncontrollably, and the ambulance attendant who was crouched in the back corner took off his jacket and put it over me. I could hear sirens and helicopters and people shouting in Spanish. The ambulance took off at enormous speed towards the city and hospital."

Passenger Gene Van Dyk was less than a month away from transferring back to Washington, D.C. with his wife Toko. Gene was wrapping up his posting with the U.S. government's Office of Inspector General (OIG) responsible for audits and investigations. He had attempted to avoid going to Costa Rica that week for a meeting that he thought was unimportant. Gene hated to fly in and out of the Tegucigalpa airport. He called these trips, "white knuckle flights."

Gene arrived at the airport in San José early that morning with his colleague, Robert Hebb. They were the first to check in and among the first to board flight #414. As they entered the plane, they spotted the first-class type seating in the front section of the plane and staked claim to 3C and 3D. Gene said he thought to himself, "For the first time all week I feel like things are looking up. I will soon be cruising home at twenty thousand feet in the lap of luxury, enjoying a continental breakfast with a hot cup of coffee. Besides that, I am sitting in my lucky seat 3C." Gene was not superstitious, but had an accountant's fondness for numbers, particularly any number divisible by three. Sitting in the third row in seat 'C' (the third letter of the alphabet) gave him a sense of confidence about the trip and the day ahead.

He thought about how he might spend his Saturday and knew a driver would pick them up at the airport. More than anything, he hoped for a normal, relaxing day. Maybe a few light chores around the house and a little basketball with friends.

Gene was jostled and awakened from his thoughts. The plane hit a pocket of turbulence and he looked out the window into a thick cloud cover. He pulled his seatbelt tighter and saw a woman sitting near him cross herself. A hush came over the cabin, punctuated by occasional sighs and moans of anxiety and fear. The aircraft seemed to be descending. It looked like another hair-raising landing, like so many Gene had experienced flying into Tegucigalpa. Bad weather was not unusual. There always seemed to be low clouds and high winds to contend with.

Robert and Gene looked at one another and shook their heads in disbelief. "Here we go again," they muttered.

The plane descended and visibility continued to be poor. It seemed as if the cloud cover had no bottom. Finally the clouds started to thin, and as the plane began to break below the clouds, Gene and Robert were horrified by the sight of land. It was not 2,000 or 1,000 or 500 feet below them, as they expected to see, but only twenty!. In a flash, Gene knew by the terrain that they were not arriving at the airport.

"We're going to hit," yelled Robert, and it was over.

When he woke up, Gene realized that he had been in an accident, but did not know how much time had elapsed since impact. He was disoriented and wasn't sure whether to remain where he was or try to get up.

"It was a strange feeling. I realized I should get up, but felt like I would rather stay put for a while. I was alert enough to realize that if I wanted to live and see Toko and my family again, I had to get up and away from the airplane before it exploded," related Gene.

Gene made an effort to move but soon realized that he was still strapped into his seat. He found it difficult to unbuckle the seatbelt and kept trying, but it wouldn't release. Finally, he felt it open, but still couldn't move. Something was pinning him down.

"I couldn't move from my seat. I felt trapped and became concerned that I would not get out or be found. I don't know if my mind blacked out what I saw those initial minutes of the crash, or if I had my eyes closed, or if it was just too dark because of smoke and debris around me. However, I must have been in a horizontal position, because I remember that I was able to get my leg and foot in a position to push away whatever was pinning me down. This allowed me finally to get up."

Gene glanced around and saw light from what appeared to be an opening in the fuselage a short distance away. He felt extremely warm as he headed for the opening and may have been on fire without realizing it.

"When I reached the opening, I looked out and envisioned before me a sparkling clear swimming pool. I put my hands in front of me in the diving position and dove into that imaginary pool. I immediately felt my face come in contact with hard objects as I hit the ground and rolled."

From what he could see, the surroundings looked like a mountainous, sparsely-vegetated knoll in a rural area. Behind him, he heard frequent explosions and popping and crackling noises as he made his way down the hill. He was forced to stop frequently because of breathing difficulties. It was odd to Gene that it was so exhausting to walk a few feet, especially since he seemed to be going downhill.

"I had not gone far when I approached a crudely constructed wire fence, the kind used to mark farm boundaries and to restrict the movement of livestock. I bent over and squeezed between the two parallel wires. I realized for the first time that I had some injuries. I noticed skin hanging loose from my right hand and arm. I didn't think it was too serious, because I felt no pain. After getting through the fence I looked at my left hand and realized that it was broken. The hand was positioned several inches off center to the left side of my wrist. I noticed, too, that the face of my watch was precariously perched on my left wrist although the metal strap had been broken and was hanging loose.

Gene looked ahead and saw someone not far in front of him with outstretched hands and saying something. He could not make out the words at first, but soon recognized the person was one of the flight attendants. This was the first person he had seen since diving out of the plane and was thrilled that he had not been left behind.

For the first time since the crash, Gene felt a sense of relief that there was someone to help him. "As I got closer I realized that she was speaking Spanish, not English, and they were not words of comfort but rather a cry for help. *'Ayudame, ayudame, por favor ayudame!'* ('Help me, help me, please help me!')"

The flight attendant appeared to be badly injured. Blood was streaming from a deep gash in her forehead, and she seemed to be in a state of shock. Gene's initial feeling of euphoria quickly disappeared as he realized that she was expecting him to help her as much as he had expected her to help him. He didn't know what to do other than try to comfort her with words and to help them both get further away from the fiery crash site.

Gene noticed that they were standing next to a narrow dirt trail that led down the hill where a small structure stood. Together they made their way down the trail in the direction of the house. It was only a short distance, roughly the equivalent of a city block, but their injuries and shock made it a tiring and strenuous walk. As they approached the building, they saw that it was a small farmhouse.

A lady appeared from inside the dwelling. "She had a stunned expression, which is not hard to understand given that a commercial jet had just crashed in her backyard and injured passengers were wandering through her property. Just as we stopped in front of her, we were all startled by a large explosion from the mountainside above us."

Gene noticed there was a dirt road near the farmhouse. A small pickup truck had stopped, and several people were climbing into the back of it. He thought it looked like injured passengers. Gene wanted to join the people in the truck and started walking in that direction. The lady, however, held him back and told him that the pickup was full, a bus would be there shortly to pick everyone up.

"At that moment I realized there was a crewmember already waiting at the farmhouse. I looked around to see if my colleagues, Bob and Rolando, were there. I didn't see them and hoped they were among those getting into the pickup truck or waiting elsewhere.

The lady administered to Gene and the flight attendant. "She helped us sit down by the house. It felt good to sit and rest. Soon she came over and pulled my pants closed. I had not noticed. My clothes were torn and tattered. I was a little irritated that my shirt was torn. It was new, and I was wearing it for the first time. I realized I must have looked awful.

As the pickup truck pulled away, a bus was spotted coming down the dirt road. The lady motioned to the group to go down to the road to meet it. The trail was steep and rugged and Gene had to be careful not to stumble. He was winded when he got to the bus. Local residents assisted two other survivors, a man and a woman, to the bus. They were all helped onto the bus, and the driver was surprised by the condition of his new passengers.

The man and the woman appeared to be a couple with British accents. The husband had a broken leg and was in a great deal of pain. His wife sat across the aisle from him in front, but the cause of her pain was less apparent to Gene. The man with the British accent turned around and asked, "How do I look friend?" Gene responded, "I, uh don't see any noticeable injuries to your face." Now curious about his own appearance, Gene followed suit and asked the man how he looked. He said, "Your face is burned a little, but it looks like you'll be all right."

The bus finally started down the dirt road and Gene felt better about his prospects for getting medical help and being able to contact his wife and the American Embassy. "We had traveled about a quarter of a mile when the bus stopped and some people climbed aboard. At first I thought more crash victims were getting on, but as I looked closer I realized that these were local residents. The bus started down the road again, but soon stopped and picked up more local residents.

At that moment I realized that this was not a special bus arranged to transport crash victims to nearby hospitals but, in fact, was the local 'milk run' service to town. I thought at this pace, it would take us hours before we reached civilization."

"It seemed like the other crash victims on board simultaneously reached the same conclusion, as we all started to yell at the poor bus driver. This was the first real display of emotion that I can remember that day. It seemed like, until then, everyone was too dazed from the ordeal and their injuries to really think about what was going on around them or to grapple with cause and effect relationships."

It occurred to Gene that after surviving the impact of the crash and the subsequent fire that he might die because this driver was not going to deviate from his scheduled route. Poverty drives people to do strange things, and it was likely that the bus driver would feed his family that day with the money made on this run.

One of the flight attendants was successful in convincing the driver to make no more stops. Just as the bus reached the paved road, the driver saw an ambulance approaching from the opposite direction. He jumped out and flagged it down.

Gene and his companions were transferred to an old ambulance. "There wasn't enough space for all of us to lie down. There was only one stretcher. I selfishly thought to myself how nice it would be to lie down. The flight attendant laid on the floor and used my lap as a pillow.

"I remember little from the trip into town. I was physically and mentally exhausted. I had done everything I could, and now I was in the hands of others and was grateful for it. I don't know how long it took us to get to the medical clinic in Tegucigalpa. I vaguely remember being helped out of the ambulance and into the clinic, where I soon heard familiar voices."

Evenor Lopez and Hernan Madrid had traveled to Costa Rica together to attend a management seminar at the *Instiuto Centroamericano de Administracion* (Central American Institute of Management). They were good friends and lived in the second largest city of Honduras, San Pedro Sula. They boarded the plane together in San José but sat in different sections. Evenor took a seat in the fourth row, while Hernan drifted back to the middle of the plane.

The seminar had finished up late Friday afternoon, and the two friends went their opposite ways. Madrid, a deeply religious, family man, had dinner and turned in early. Lopez attended a party with other seminar participants until three in the morning.

He explained, "I was so tired that I slept the entire flight and woke up when they told us to put on our seatbelts for landing. Suddenly the plane began to shake. There was turbulence, and we were losing altitude. Everything happened so quickly."

After the initial impact, Lopez was sure he was going to die. "I found myself belted into the seat and on fire. I was able to get the seatbelt off and noticed an opening in the plane right next to me. I got up and walked out of the plane like everything was normal, even though I was on fire. I was concerned with putting it out and finally was able to by rolling on the ground. After leaving the plane I looked for help in the house of a humble campesino (subsistence farmer), who gave me a glass of water and a blanket."

Hernan Madrid was the second person to get on the plane and the flight attendant asked him to take one of the first-class seats. Instead he chose to sit farther back in the plane near the left wing. He normally said a prayer as his flight was taking off, but on this particular day he felt the need to pray as soon as he sat down.

Madrid related that it was a normal flight until the plane reached the mountain area above Tegucigalpa called Cerro de Hula. He had worked in this particular part of Honduras in previous years and was trying to spot some of the *aldeas* (villages) when the weather changed dramatically. The cloud coverage was so thick that he closed the window shade.

At that point he felt the plane moving in an unusual manner and the flight attendant asked that cigarettes be extinguished and seatbelts fastened. He could tell that the plane was descending, and he said to himself, "We are going to die."

Madrid told me, "Everything happened so quickly. If the pilot was aware that something was wrong, he didn't say anything and probably did not have time to advise us."

The father of five first felt the impact of the tail of the plane and leaned over and put his arms around his neck, dropping his head as if ordered to. "I felt like things were flying all around me, and I saw images of first my wife, then my parents and, finally, my children. I believed I was going to die." Just as quickly the plane stopped, and Madrid opened his eyes to see if he was alive. He found the seat next to him completely destroyed, as well as the seats in front and behind him. He was intact and could see an opening in the fuselage above him.

Madrid unbuckled his seat belt and then struggled to free one of his feet in order to get out of his seat and climb through the opening above him. He finally pulled the foot free, losing his shoe in the process. At this point he miraculously had no burns or fractures. Madrid saw no one else and found the air thick with smoke. He burned the palms of his hands as he climbed out of the plane onto what remained of the left wing. Without hesitation, he jumped through the smoke and flames that had engulfed the aircraft. Upon hitting the ground, he struck his head and passed out. When he woke up, the first thing he saw was his friend Evenor Lopez, who was badly burned and walking in circles.

Lopez was equally surprised to see Madrid and yelled, "You're alive! Let's get out of here before the plane explodes." Madrid was bleeding profusely from the head wound and could not see where he was going. In spite of his burns, Lopez led his friend down the mountainside to safety. They walked approximately one hundred feet to a small adobe house. Along the way, they ran into Captain Argueta, who at that moment wanted to go back into the plane to save the passengers.

They made their way to the adobe house below the wreckage. Madrid continued, "The old woman in the house gave Evenor a blanket because he was in terrible shape, and offered me a cup of coffee. The morning was very cold and we all wrapped up in blankets. One of the flight attendants was lying on a bed, and I went outside to put water on my head wound. The water from a tap was so cold that the wound stopped bleeding immediately."

Madrid escaped with burns on the palms of his hands and a head wound. He graciously chose not to go into Tegucigalpa in the small pickup so that those of us in worse condition could have more room in the bed of the truck. The three of us riding in back had sustained significant burns and needed to get medical attention as quickly as possible. Madrid subsequently boarded the local bus along with the surviving crewmembers, Gene Van Dyk and an Australian couple.

Ramon Sanchez Borba, an attorney, had been working in Managua for Teddy Norman, the Honduran owner of six fishing boats that had been plying the waters of Lake Nicaragua. The boats had been seized by the Nicaraguan authorities, and Sanchez Borba had been in Managua the week before, attempting to liberate them for his client. It was a grueling process of negotiation, and Sanchez Borba and Norman were flying to Tegucigalpa to spend the weekend with their families. Both attorney and client had to return to Managua on Monday but the short flight made it easy to go back and forth.

Ramon was sitting in the first row of the aircraft and commented to a young man sitting next to him that there were always clouds around Tegucigalpa when landing. At that point, the man screamed, "This plane is falling," because he could see how close they were to the ground. Then everything went black.

He regained consciousness after the crash and described his escape, "I unbuckled my seatbelt and walked a few feet toward the front of the plane because, I remembered that the exit doors were up there. Once I got up there, it was impossible to see anything, because the smoke was so thick--like coffee. I then went toward the back of the plane and saw that there was an opening. I passed where my friend Teddy Norman was sitting, but couldn't see him through the smoke. I yelled at him to save himself, but heard no answer. As I walked through the plane, I thought that I would have to break a window if there was no escape, but remembered that it is impossible to break airplane windows. I finally found a large opening and was able to jump out. I was not aware of having been burned. At that point I felt nothing."

When he finally was outside the plane, Ramon found that he could not breathe. "My lungs were full of smoke. It was windy on the mountain, and I kept taking deep breaths of air. Suddenly there was a major explosion, and I became aware that I was badly burned and bleeding. The explosion startled me, and I started walking towards a road. I came to a ditch and sat down to rest, trying to improve my breathing. Several men who apparently lived in the area came over and took me to a schoolhouse."

There was a road outside the schoolhouse and Ramon was helped down to a pickup truck. He climbed into the bed of the truck with other survivors and took off for Tegucigalpa.

Thirty-seven year old Nicaraguan Rosario Ubeda Gonzalez de Gean had boarded the plane in Managua and was on her way to New Orleans, where she lived with her husband Edgardo Gean. She had been in Matagalpa visiting her elderly mother. Rosario was seated in the back of the plane near the rear galley.

She explained that she ate the breakfast that was served and then fell asleep. She did not hear the instructions to fasten seat belts and woke up on the ground outside the aircraft to the sounds of other passengers screaming for help. By this time the plane was covered in flames.

Rosario sustained fractures of the pelvis, both legs and an arm. The Nicaraguan native said, "I had no idea what was happening. It all went so fast, and the next thing I knew I was outside the plane on the ground." She saw another survivor with a burned leg being taken away by campesinos, and then they returned to help her down the mountainside.

"The truth is that, if I had been awake and had been aware when the plane crashed, I would feel differently. But I didn't feel anything and am calm right now," she continued from her hospital bed.

Napoleon Rodriguez stood in the doorway of his house situated in a fold of Cerro de Hula, a mountainous area some forty-five minutes from the Honduran capital of Tegucigalpa. He peered out at the fog-enshrouded mountain that hovered above the small wooden structure. Rodriguez felt the earth start trembling. "*Dios Mio...es el fin del mundo!*"("My God, it's the end of the world!"), cried Napoleon.

He ran out of the house to see what was happening. Visibility was poor and he grabbed a tree, holding on as the quaking of the earth became so intense he was afraid of being knocked to the ground.

What he saw next, struck terror in his heart. A fireball of twisted metal was hurtling across the local soccer field located on a flat terrace above his house. It was heading toward him. Napoleon knew it was an airplane and he watched as the craft split apart and came to a screeching halt not more than twenty feet above where he was standing. There was no time to think. The wreckage was on fire, and he could hear voices from inside the aircraft. At the moment Napoleon emerged from his house, the control tower at Tegucigalpa's Toncontin International Airport in the valley below lost contact with TAN SAHSA flight #414.

Napoleon Rodriguez' home with wreckage above

In less than an hour after the crash of flight #414, fifteen survivors miraculously walked away or were carried away from the wreckage. I left the mountain in the back of a small pickup truck with four other survivors (Carlos and Vivian Pellas, Ramon Sanchez Borba, Evenor Lopez). Sanchez Borba and Lopez were lying down and I was seated next to them in the bed of the truck. Both had blankets pulled over them and appeared to be in worse condition than I was. The young teenage daughter of the truck owner sat with us and had a look of fear and revulsion on her face. The Pellas' sat in the front seat of the truck.

It took our little pickup a long and painful hour to reach Tegucigalpa. We drove out of the mist and gloom of the mountains and found sunshine as the rutted and bumpy dirt road straightened out. Each bounce left us moaning and as I was in much better shape than my fellow passengers. I screamed for the driver to slow down several times.

While descending the mountain road to Tegucigalpa, we drove past a family. Young parents and two freshly scrubbed children appeared to be out on a Saturday morning drive. It was another dreamlike moment. We were close enough to the family's car to reach out and touch them, yet no one in either vehicle said anything. We just stared at each other as our vehicles slowly moved past one another and then continued.

Mercifully we reached the paved road and descended into Tegucigalpa. Fire trucks passed us with sirens blaring. There were four fire trucks and one ambulance, and I thought to myself that it was an odd ratio.

Our driver did not know the capital, so we stopped numerous times to ask for directions to a medical facility. I became aware of how bad we all looked, as passing cars slowed or even braked to catch a glimpse of us and then looked away in horror. You could almost hear their questions. Who were these people and what sort of calamity had befallen them? Some cars began following us probably out of curiosity. Several remained behind our pickup all the way to the hospital.

After more than an hour of great discomfort while seated in the back of the pickup, we arrived at the Hospital Escuela, and were met by attendants and throngs of expectant faces. I found out later that family members waiting for the arrival of flight #414 at Toncontin Airport had been lied to by the TAN SAHSA personnel about the reason the flight had not arrived. Airline officials were reluctant to reveal the crash to the assembled in the airport and instead continued to state that the flight was delayed. Family and friends of passengers then began to hear second hand from the baggage handlers that the plane they were waiting for had, in fact, crashed. At that point, they dashed to hospitals and clinics in town, hoping to find loved ones among the survivors. Some went directly to the crash site to begin their search.

Upon entering the pandemonium of the hospital, my first impression was that there were numerous survivors. I reasoned that we had not seen them because we were the first group to leave the mountain. The mob outside the hospital wanted to believe the same thing and the hospital staff seemed to be gearing up for a large influx of injured passengers.

Those of us who survived were struggling with the shock of our own survival-second and third-degree burns, multiple fractures and the terror of what we had just experienced. We were quickly becoming aware of the fact that survival has both physical and emotional costs.

Engine of Boeing 727-200 belonging to
Continental Airlines at crash site

CHAPTER TWO

THE CRASH SITE

*"What we're seeing here is tremendous . . . a really
hellish scene. It's horrible, with bodies all over the place."*
— *Radio HRN broadcast describing the
scene on Cerro de Hula.*

When the Hospital Escuela opened its doors to receive us, there was an
increase in activity on the mountainside high above the city. Eyewitness
and newspaper accounts reported that locals, like Napoleon Rodriguez,
had helped many of the survivors off the mountain. Some of them were
starting to pick through the wreckage. They continued to be in awe
of and confused by the magnitude of what had occurred in their little
corner of the world.

Many family members of passengers who heard about the crash at the airport or while listening to the radio chose to go see first-hand what had occurred. Nothing like this had ever happened in Honduras and many people held out hope that they might find their loved ones alive. At that hour of the day, an experienced driver who knew the area could reach Cerro de Hula from Tegucigalpa in thirty minutes. Colonel Wilfredo Sanchez, the Honduran Minister of Defense later informed me that he was one of the first family members to arrive at the scene in search of his daughter Fanny who was a passenger on the flight. Newspaper accounts reported that helicopters from the Honduran Air Force landed near the crash site and began assessing the situation.

As family members of passengers arrived, a Honduran official informed an anxious woman that "the plane is completely burned, nothing is left."[1] The Boeing 727-200 had been filled with 17,500 pounds of fuel in Managua and had consumed less than 5,000 pounds in the flight to Tegucigalpa. Within seconds of slamming into the mountainside, the aircraft began to burn, and in a matter of minutes it became an inferno.

During the course of the day, hundreds of people moved into the area, and pillaging ensued. Security was lax, and people were permitted access to the mountainside, inviting theft. As word of the crash spread in Tegucigalpa, people who were simply curious about what had happened drove to the crash site. "It looked like a pilgrimage as a virtual caravan of cars stretched from the capital to Cerro de Hula," a local paper reported. The curious were allowed to walk through the area and pick up anything that caught their eye before returning to their cars and the capital. One onlooker was heard to say, "Poor people, this is a disaster. It is a miracle that there were survivors."[2]

Looters, souvenir hunters and curiosity seekers

One of the first outsiders to reach the downed plane was Ron Venezia, a veteran Foreign Service Officer who had been called that morning by the U.S. Embassy to fly to Cerro de Hula in one of his helicopters, look for survivors, and assess the situation. Venezia worked for the United States Agency of International Development (USAID) and had access to helicopters. He was the first person to be called by the quickly assembled Task Force at the U.S. Embassy in Tegucigalpa.

Within half an hour, he and his pilot, Bruce English, approached the crash site. The wind was extremely strong during the short flight up to the mountain, and Venezia reflected on how hard it had been blowing the night before. It felt to him like "gale force winds," and he remembered feeling his "apartment building quiver a few times."

As they approached Cerro de Hula, the mountain was visible to the two Americans, with the exception of the summit that was shrouded in clouds. After surveying the area, the chopper pilot found a place to land close to the tail of the wrecked plane, which appeared to be an "ashen shell," Venezia later reported to me. A quick review of the crash site revealed a scenario to Venezia that looked as if the pilots had tried to pull away from the mountainside at the last minute and the tail hit first, breaking off. It appeared that the plane then pancaked and skidded across an open field. He could see the skid marks, and the nose of the plane had broken off at some point.

Venezia arrived at the site less than an hour after the crash. By this time the fire had almost burned out and the plane was smoldering. The fuselage looked to him like an "open clamshell," with the top having been burned off. Venezia found the passengers and their seats intact, but as he walked down the aisle of the plane, he gazed upon charred bodies that looked to him like "Kentucky Fried Chicken" in the sense that all distinguishing features had been burned away. "They appeared to be deep-fried lumps-no ears, no fingers, no noses."

The only bodies he saw that were not badly burned were three or four people who had been sitting in the rear of the plane and apparently died upon impact when the tail of the craft broke off. "It was a horrible scene, and the air was thick with the stench of smoldering petroleum and burned plastic," Venezia later described to me.

There were no survivors to be found. He saw people picking through some of the smoldering remains, but then left as quickly as he came. There was nothing more that could be done.

Upon returning to Tegucigalpa, Venezia went to the U.S. Embassy and presented his findings to a team of people who were brought together to coordinate response efforts. He did not know any of the Americans on the plane, but was aware that there were several U.S. government employees among the passengers.

As the U.S. Government's Director of Field Operations for the Humanitarian Task Force for the Nicaraguan Resistance better known as the Contras, Venezia had two hundred fifty employees who were responsible for providing basic assistance and support to the thousands of Contra troops residing inside Honduras. This crash site was not the first field of horrors he had surveyed, but he was convinced that he would have nightmares from the experience.

News eventually reached me in the hospital, via a Honduran doctor, of how horrific the crash had been and the magnitude of human loss. Of the one hundred thirty-eight passengers, only eleven survived. Of the eight crewmembers, four survived-the captain, the first officer, the purser and the flight attendant trainee. The greater majority of passengers were Hondurans (thirty-five) and Nicaraguans (sixty-nine). There were thirteen Americans on board, and three of us survived. The remaining passengers represented thirteen different countries.

Rescue workers carry a body to an awaiting helicopter for transportation away from the crash site

CHAPTER THREE

ESCAPING HONDURAS

...the wheel is turning and it can't slow down, you can't hold on and you can't let go. You can't go back and you can't stand still, If the thunder don't get you the lightning will...

- Jerry Garcia, The Wheel

In spite of the fact that few survivors reached the Hospital Escuela, there was such chaos inside the facility that I felt more fearful lying there in relative safety than I had when I found myself belted into my seat on the mountainside. No one seemed to be in charge and it felt like the area where I was located was up for grabs. Confusion reigned, and the noise level made it difficult to hear anything being said. It seemed to me that there was no control over who entered and circulated through the facility.

I was put on a gurney and left in a large room with bright lights overhead. An attendant immediately put a catheter on me. I protested that it was not necessary, to no avail. Numerous people, none of whom identified themselves, were walking around and asking questions. I assumed they were reporters or hospital officials, but I never knew. At least six people asked me my name during the first hour and asked that I spell it out. I was happy to give this information to anyone who was interested and patiently spelled my first and last names in Spanish to each inquisitor. I repeatedly mentioned the name CARE Honduras to these same people, but no one was interested or concerned. They had their own responsibilities, and one of them was to get an accurate list of survivors.

October 21, 1989, was a Saturday and the date is a national holiday in Honduras-Armed Forces Day. Few people work, and typically there are parades and celebrations. As a result, doctors were not available, or it was difficult to locate them. Those of us who survived were largely attended to by students and interns, and it showed, as needles and catheters were being put into us with little regard for hygiene. No x-rays were taken. The stock of dressings and drugs for the hospital were locked up for the weekend, and the person with the key could not be located. It was a confused scene. The Hondurans were clearly not prepared to respond to a catastrophe of this proportion and even less so on a holiday.

After an hour, I was wheeled out of the large room and left against a wall in a hallway. It felt like a safer place simply because there was less confusion and movement of fewer people. I also had the security of a wall to press against and didn't feel so vulnerable.

While I was lying in this hallway, Cliff Moore, Assistant Country Director of CARE Honduras appeared at my side. I was thrilled and within minutes, Maureen Brand, wife of the CARE Country Director, and Patricia Gamero, Administrative Assistant for CARE Honduras, also appeared. It was a huge boost to my spirits to know that CARE was on the job.

Cliff had been at the airport to meet me and had a special security pass that allowed him onto the tarmac and into customs. A TAN SAHSA employee tipped him off about the crash long before the waiting family members were advised, and he immediately called the CARE Country Director, Ed Brand, with the news.

The two of them decided to begin checking the hospitals, and Cliff started at the Hospital Escuela. "There were already hundreds of people at the emergency entrance to the hospital," he told me years later. "They were not allowing anyone to enter, so I drove around to the other side of the building, climbed over a chain link fence and into an open window. I then started looking for you room by room, working my way back to the emergency entrance. I went into probably seven or eight different rooms, most of them filled with dead bodies, before I found you in the hallway."

Patricia Gamero, the Administrative Assistant to the CARE Honduras Director had heard the news of the crash on the radio in her home that morning and knew that a CARE employee from New York was on the flight. Her first thought was to find the cadaver and help make arrangements to have my body transported back to the United States. She later apologized to me for having had that thought, but frankly, what else would one think under the circumstances, particularly since the airline initially announced that there were no survivors. Cliff and Maureen had reached the same conclusion earlier.

Patricia decided to go to the CARE office to see how she might help. By chance she had to drive past the Hospital Escuela, a public facility. She noticed a tremendous commotion in front of the hospital, which she described to me. "There was a large crowd of people that included family and friends of passengers, along with the curious and soldiers from the Honduran Army trying to keep some order and maintain access in and out of the hospital for ambulances that were coming in. There were all types of vehicles-private cars, small buses, trucks and ambulances that were coming in with victims." The hospital was being converted into a makeshift morgue. There were few survivors. Friends and family were desperate for news, any information about their loved ones.

She explained to a guard at the front door of the hospital that she was looking for her boss, who had been on the plane, and gave him my name. The guard told her that I had just arrived and happened to be one of the survivors. She thanked God and was allowed inside the foyer, but not inside the hospital. Access to the interior of the hospital remained restricted. By chance, a nurse approached and told Patricia she couldn't go in because only medical staff was allowed to circulate in the facility. To her surprise, the nurse then gave her a white coat and told her to enter the hospital with an attitude of authority while masquerading as my physician.

Patricia walked through the front door and into the hospital. She approached a medical student, asking for a patient by the name of Curt Schaeffer. She ran into Cliff and Maureen and they proceeded to look for me together. A doctor pointed out the bed where I was lying. Patricia was shocked to see how big I was (barely staying on the gurney) and that I was black. She had never seen me before but assumed that I was Caucasian and was confused by my black, charred skin and curly hair. Maureen was also struck by how dark I looked and the fact that my hair came off in her hand when she touched me. She remembers my hands having a "grey, charred look" to them, and that I winced with pain when she took hold of one. Maureen was quite impressed that I was conscious and able to joke around. "You'll be okay Curt," she told me and I responded by saying, "Just as long as I can play basketball again."

What a relief it was to see familiar faces in this sea of madness. I repeated to Patricia a number of times, "I am alive, I am alive." Maureen Brand said to me in a loud voice so I was sure to hear her over the din of confusion in the room, "Curt, I am Maureen Brand, wife of Ed Brand, and I am a nurse. Rest assured that you will be taken care of." For the first time that day I felt some measure of security, like there might actually be an end to this nightmare.

Prior to receiving word that I had survived the crash, Mike Godfrey, the other Assistant Country Director for CARE Honduras, had been appointed by Ed Brand to handle the logistics of getting me out of the country, dead or alive. Either way, CARE was responsible for me. The response was classic CARE organization. All available staff were assigned specific tasks to carry out, which were to be followed the entire day until successfully completed.

Mike told me later that, he pulled every phone within reach into his office, and at times was working three phones at once. He had been informed early on by TAN SAHSA Airline "there are no survivors" and related the following story to me.

"The scariest moment was my decision to inform your family that you had died in the crash. This was based on the advice from TAN SAHSA that no one had survived. It took me awhile to track down the number, and then I got a recorded greeting at the Schaeffer residence requesting that I leave a message. I thought, 'Oh my God, I am not prepared to do that. Not now.' I hung up and tried to compose myself. I was hyperventilating, sweating and flustered beyond words. Ten minutes later I called again and spoke a quick, previously rehearsed message. 'This is Mike Godfrey calling from Honduras. I am a colleague of Curt's and we'd like to have you call back as soon as you can.' Miraculously, in the wait for the inevitable return call (about forty minutes) we received word in the office that you had survived and I was able to turn the call from one of tragic news to one of life saving help."

Mike was then faced with the difficult task of arranging for a medivac plane to fly to Tegucigalpa from the United States and to return me to a hospital in my country. All CARE employees who live or work overseas have a special insurance benefit for emergency situations like this one that calls for immediate medical evacuation from a foreign country to the United States or to another country with effective medical attention. The insurance company required a sign-off by CARE Headquarters in New York and by a recognized physician in Honduras. The dispatcher in Kentucky told Mike, "Don't plan on going anywhere, Mike, because I can't repeat information to others. You and I will be together all day." The process for sending a plane to Honduras on short notice was too complicated for the dispatcher to try to work with different CARE staff during the course of the day, so he insisted that Mike be his one and only contact person.

It was Saturday morning and CARE, at that time, had no established procedure for responding to this sort of emergency affecting an employee out of the country. As a result, Mike Godfrey had to call numerous phone numbers before finding a senior CARE official who could sign off on a medical evacuation.

It was equally difficult in Honduras to locate a physician who could confirm my condition and communicate the diagnosis in English. The U.S. Embassy physician, Dr. Steve Johnson, was attending to another survivor and was not available. It was obvious I was badly burned and needed medical attention as soon as possible. Ed and Maureen Brand took responsibility for certifying my physical condition.

At one point, a Honduran doctor came to talk with me. He was one of many people who passed by during the course of the day to check me out. He told me that it was truly my lucky day, because apparently there were few survivors. This was the first time that I fully understood the magnitude of the disaster and how fortunate I had been. Prior to this I believed that numerous survivors were being attended to throughout the hospital or elsewhere in the city. I had no reason to think otherwise.

At this moment, my primary concern was Magaly. She was due to arrive in Tegucigalpa that afternoon, and I wanted to make sure that someone was at the airport to meet her. Magaly later told me about her experience on the day of the crash.

She arrived in Miami at 9:30 A.M. from the Dominican Republic and was not scheduled to fly to Honduras until 2:00 P.M. While waiting to board a TAN SAHSA plane, a lady sat down beside her and was visibly upset. She told Magaly that she was nervous about flying to Honduras. Magaly asked why she was nervous, and the woman said that a TAN SAHSA plane had crashed that morning in Tegucigalpa. Magaly was astonished by the news and remembered that my flight had been scheduled to arrive in Tegucigalpa earlier in the day.

Unsure about what to do, Magaly walked over to the TAN SAHSA ticket counter and asked about the accident. They refused to divulge any information and were noticeably upset. She insisted on knowing that the flight that had crashed was the same one that had originated in Costa Rica. The man at the counter checked the flights on the computer and confirmed that it was the only TAN SAHSA flight from Costa Rica that day.

Magaly was dumbstruck. "I knew for sure now that Curt was on the plane that crashed. I did not react. I could not believe it. I did not move. I started to cry, but at the same time I tried to control myself and think what I could do. I was alone and my flight to Tegucigalpa was due to start boarding in ten minutes. I thought about calling Curt's parents, but decided it was not a good idea, since it was tragic news and I didn't know anything more. I was so nervous and afraid about the whole situation that I did not know where to go or what to do."

Magaly chose to board the plane and travel to Tegucigalpa to find out first hand. She thought that, if she stayed in the States, days might pass before she would know anything about my condition. She asked for permission to board the plane ahead of everybody else. Upon entering the plane, Magaly asked the pilot about the accident. He knew nothing. He was trying to get information about his colleagues, but names of survivors were not being released.

As later reported in a deposition, Magaly stated, "I sat and just looked through the window, thinking about the whole range of possibilities.

I even tried to be a little positive about the type of accident, but it was a pathetic attempt. I could not avoid thinking that my husband had died. I had a three-hour flight ahead of me, but in the first five minutes I had already considered all types of scenarios. I had a fax that he had sent me the day before, wishing me a happy birthday and telling me he loved me. I clutched that fax in my hands throughout the trip. It seemed to give me hope, and with that hope I gained new strength."

About midway through the trip, Magaly had a sudden rush of adrenaline. It was a special feeling, like an internal message telling her that I was all right. At the time, she dismissed it and considered it to be nothing more than wishful thinking.

It was Magaly's first trip to Honduras, and she had no idea where to go or how to seek help. Her employer was not expecting her until Monday. She decided that, upon arrival, she would contact the airline to see if I was dead or alive.

"I did not want to think about it," Magaly continued. "I pre-ferred to die. I felt I was going to collapse, but at the same time I felt guilty because I didn't want to think about myself, but about my husband. You were the one who was suffering and who had the accident. I felt selfish for even thinking about myself and my future without you."

"Fortunately, a lady sitting beside me offered to help me find you when we arrived in Tegucigalpa. She saw me crying and offered to go with me everywhere we had to go until we found you."

When the plane landed in Belize to pick up passengers, Magaly, again, asked the flight attendant about survivors. The flight attendant called over the radio, and found out that there were a few reported survivors. Magaly insisted that the flight attendant have the pilot call again, and she wrote my name down on a piece of paper. Five minutes before the plane landed in Tegucigalpa, the flight attendant appeared and told Magaly that she had heard over the radio that Curt Schaeffer was among the survivors.

"I could not believe it! After torturing myself for hours, now I was crying out of happiness!" Magaly later reported in a deposition.

CARE staff met Magaly at the airport and assured her that I was all right. "Curt is okay and worried about you. We found him in a hospital and he is coherent to the point that he remembered your flight number." Magaly later told me that she was relieved that I seemed to be stable and was told that I was even joking around.

She remained at Toncontin Airport as a passenger in transit. The plan was for Magaly and me to leave for Miami that night.

Prior to Magaly's arrival, Patricia Gamero was facing a difficult situation at the Hospital Escuela. The CARE staff had decided that I needed better care and made plans to move me to a smaller clinic, where I could get personal attention in preparation for returning to the United States. Ed Brand was at the Policlinica, a private clinic, making arrangements for my transfer. Patricia was responsible for getting me out of the hospital and transported to the clinic.

She was deciding what to do when the nurse who had helped her get into the hospital appeared and told her that the hospital would not allow CARE to move me until someone signed the necessary papers, freeing the institution from any responsibility. She also informed Patricia that no ambulance was available to transport me.

There was no question that I had to be moved. I needed medical attention, and I was not getting it at the hospital. The nurse, whom Patricia dubbed the "phantom nurse," appeared again and told Patricia about an available ambulance that belonged to the Psychiatric Hospital. With the confidence of a physician, Patricia stepped up and signed me out of the hospital.

I was loaded onto the floor of the old ambulance. It was not particularly comfortable, but I didn't care since it was supposed to be a short ride. We were ready to go when it dawned on the group that there was no one to drive the ambulance. After some discussion, I heard a familiar voice shout, "Yo voy a manejarla!" ("I will drive it!") It was Patricia once again. She jumped into the jeep, took the wheel and drove me in the commandeered ambulance to a private clinic. The phantom nurse remained with us.

Even though there were numerous people working on my behalf, improvisation was frequently necessary to move things ahead. Constant problem-solving and making the rules up as you go along are a way of life in many developing countries like Honduras. The important thing was that the objective of getting me out of the country was clear to everyone.

The day was one of chaos and pandemonium, but I felt a serenity throughout. In spite of all the confusion and the uncertainty of what would happen next, I knew I was in good hands and that the CARE staff would take care of me.

After a brief time in the clinic, the medical staff decided to wrap my burns from head to toe with cream and gauze. I was aware of having burns on my face, hands, arms, lower legs, ears and neck. My hands had taken on a claw-like quality, and it was painful to move the fingers. Burned skin loses its lanolin or self-moisturizing capacity as well as its elasticity. It becomes tant unless it is exercised regularly. My ears practically disappeared, as the little bit of skin and cartilage that makes them up had mostly disappeared.

The possibility of leaving for the States that same day seemed remote as the afternoon wore on. Standard closing time at Toncontin International Airport was 6 P.M. There were no landing lights on the runway nor an adequate radar system. The concern of those who were working feverishly to get me out of the country and into a hospital in Miami was whether or not the airport would allow us to leave after 6 P.M. It would be expensive to hold the plane overnight, and I needed medical attention for my burns that day.

Gloria Manzanares, a CARE employee from Honduras, had attended an unrelated funeral of a close friend's parent that morning outside of Tegucigalpa. She heard about the crash on the radio while returning to town from the cemetery and was concerned about her brother, a pilot with TAN SAHSA Airline. She wasn't aware that a CARE functionary from New York was expected on the flight, although she heard names of passengers repeatedly over the radio, including "Curtis Chafer." When she pulled up in front of her house, Gloria was met by a frantic housekeeper, who exclaimed, "Señora! Señora! The CARE office has called you repeatedly. There has been an accident."

By this time, Gloria knew her brother had not been involved in the crash, but realized that the poorly pronounced name she had heard over the radio was actually 'Curt Schaeffer' from the CARE New York office.

It was 2:30 in the afternoon when Gloria finally reached the CARE office. Mike Godfrey, who was in the midst of making the logistical arrangements to get me out of the country, quickly told Gloria that she had a key role to play. Her challenge was to go to the airport and convince the officials there to keep the facility open after 6 P.M. to allow the medivac plane to leave the country.

She headed directly to the airport, but had difficulty finding a working phone. There were no cell phones in 1989, and pay phones in the airport were routinely broken. She finally found a phone with a dial tone and called an old friend who was married to a high-ranking military official. She had not seen them in five years and was concerned about how they would react to her request.

Gloria got through to her friend and pleaded with the husband to help her keep the airport open that night. The military official told her, "You know we have strict rules about this sort of thing and keeping the airport open beyond the established hour is a long shot. We have rejected numerous requests to fly out of Toncontin after dark over the years." "Let me see what I can do." He instructed Gloria to go directly to the tower at the airport, and in the meantime, he promised to make a call. Confident in her mission, the CARE employee climbed to the airport tower and asked to meet with the people in charge. They listened to her explanation of the delicate physical condition of one of the survivors of the TAN SAHSA crash and how important it was to allow a CARE official, Curt Schaeffer, to leave for Miami that same day. Gloria Manzanares is articulate and aggressive, and on this day she used all of her powers of persuasion to convince the officials to remain open after 6 P.M.

Dr. Vernon Sichewski and flight nurse, Ann Baker, from an air ambulance service based in Ft. Lauderdale, landed in Tegucigalpa at approximately four in the afternoon. The physician and nurse emergency team had some familiarity with Honduras because they had been dispatched to the country several months previously to evacuate the wife of CARE's Assistant Country Director-Cliff Moore. She had complications with her pregnancy and required special attention in the U.S.

A CARE vehicle transported the medical team to the Policlinica to examine me. I was relieved to see them, as I did not feel particularly confident about any of the treatment I had received that day, either in the hospital or the clinic. I thought to myself that it was a minor miracle for the CARE staff to get these folks into the country that same day and still have a shot at helping me escape the country.

In the midst of giving me a thorough examination, Dr. Sichewski got an annoyed look on his face and excused himself. He took the Honduran doctor and Ann Baker away from me and the little group of people around me. I later learned of their conversation.

"Something is wrong here. I have an idea what it is, but I want to see the x-ray. Ann, could you get it for me?" Sichewski asked in his deep, raspy voice. Baker handed him the x-ray.

He quickly scanned the x-ray that had been taken earlier in the afternoon and Sichewski found what he was looking for. "That's it. I could tell he wasn't breathing normally. You can see that he has a collapsed lung on the right side," said Sichewski with an edge to his voice. "Okay, Ann. Get the trauma kit ready so we can re-inflate the lung." There was a long, uncomfortable silence, and the nurse finally blurted out, "I left the kit in Ft. Lauderdale, doctor." Sichewski was furious. "Ann, you knew this was a trauma case. What did you think we were going to treat, a cough?" Baker responded, "I am sorry, but I forgot!" Sichewski had about reached his boiling point. He turned to the Honduran doctor and said, "You should have seen this on the x-ray! I can't believe you missed it."

The trauma pack, among other things, contains a rigid chest tube that is designed to re-inflate a lung. It comes with a special container to drain fluids from the lung cavity. Most medical facilities have tubes available for these types of situations. Unfortunately, the staff at the clinic was only able to produce a rectal tube, made of rubber and more flexible than the preferred chest tube.

Dr. Sichewski was visibly irritated, although I didn't understand why. I hadn't heard the exchange between doctor and nurse, nor was I aware of the collapsed lung. He was a veteran of overseas emergencies and had faced far tougher problems than this. His cool demeanor under pressure was crucial to resolving the matter.

I was on my back, as I had been all day, and my gurney was surrounded by anxious faces. Most of these folks had been working since early morning to get me out of the country safely and the clock was ticking. Ed Brand told me later that he thought to himself at this point, "I just want to get rid of this guy," which was how the entire CARE group felt about me as the day wore on and one glitch after another presented itself.

Dr. Sichewski came over to me and said, "Curt, you have a collapsed lung, and I have to get it inflated again. I am going to push this tube between your ribs and into the lung cavity. The air and some fluid will drain out of the cavity, through the tube and into a container. As more air and fluid escape from the cavity, the lung will re-inflate."

I wanted to get on that plane and told him to go for it. As he shoved the tube between my ribs, Sichewski said, "This is going to hurt."

I had no idea how much it would hurt. The tube entering my body was a shock to the system. A knife would have been preferable to the round tube. I immediately vomited the only thing I had in my stomach, which was a pastry I had eaten that morning on the plane. I was then given an injection to guard against a stress ulcer from internal bleeding which felt like a little pinprick compared to the rectal tube in my side. The hospital produced an empty wine bottle for the tube to drain into. It was a crude arrangement, but it worked. The absurdity of it all gave us a brief chuckle, momentarily breaking the tension in the air.

Dr. Sichewski turned to me again and said, "You would not have lived another three to four hours with a collapsed lung, compounded by being in a state of shock with second and third- degree burns. You would have eventually gone into respiratory arrest and died." I responded with a "Thanks Doc" and Sichewski added that flying in a pressurized plane with only one lung could have killed me as well.

Once the lung re-inflated, the medical team gave me a thorough check and decided that I was stable enough to fly safely. It was close to 6P.M., and we were anxious to get to the airport. They loaded me into the ambulance again and off we went. This time a driver was ready to go.

The ambulance drove right out to the plane on the runway with the expectation of leaving immediately. As I was being unloaded, I saw Magaly for the first time, and we both burst into tears. Magaly later told me she was shocked by my appearance and immediately felt deceived by the CARE staff. She had been told that I was fine and expected to see me looking as I always appeared. It is hard to see an injured person you care about for the first time particularly when you have established a different image in your mind. The CARE staff had not misled her. I was alright but I did look like hell!

There was little time to talk and we got right on the plane. Gloria Manzanares had been successful in working with numerous airport officials to keep the facility open just long enough for us to depart. We left without further delay.

The Lear Jet 25 took off for Miami less than twelve hours after the crash of TAN SAHSA flight #414. I am convinced that Patricia Gamero, the "phantom nurse," Ed and Maureen Brand, Mike Godfrey, Cliff Moore, Gloria Manzanares, Dr. Vernon Sichewski and others who helped throughout the day had been sent by some higher authority to take care of me and see me safely out of the country. They accomplished the near impossible. The U.S. Embassy had not been able to move so quickly and actually requested space on my plane for another American survivor. The request was denied. My medivac plane was tiny with space for one bed only. Magaly had to sit on a small table at the foot of my bed where food for the crew was normally placed. No other space was available.

As the jet climbed out of the valley surrounding Tegucigalpa to a cruising altitude of 42,000 feet, I felt my body being overtaken by exhaustion. It had been a day of intense drama. The combination of pandemonium, shock and pain had kept me awake throughout but at this point I was numb and could not keep my eyes open. The impact of what had happened to me left me weak and tired. Magaly sat at my feet and I wiggled my toes to let her know I was all right. We were finally together again. The small plane was noisy and cramped. There was no point in trying to carry on a conversation. Sichewski and Baker were attentive, but there was little they could do other than to check on me once in awhile. Fortunately, my breathing was normal and all vital signs were stable.

I slept most of the trip and woke up as the plane was landing in Miami. There had been no fear of flying in my weakened condition. I had no choice.

Once on the ground, an ambulance backed up to the plane and my papers were carefully checked by an immigration official. My passport was in my briefcase somewhere at the crash site on Cero de Hula, so I relied instead on a letter that had been prepared by CARE, with the help of the U.S. Embassy in Honduras. Magaly and I were then whisked off to Jackson Memorial Hospital in downtown Miami, Florida.

I arrived at the hospital with the improvised rectal tube sticking out of my right side still draining into a wine bottle. The trauma intern on duty that night, Dr. Phil Wozman, looked in disbelief at the Rube Goldberg-like instrument that was attached to my side. He turned to his friend, Dr. Sichewski, and said, "What kind of a contraption do you have there, Vern?" Wozman immediately examined me and was surprised that I was awake, alert and able to answer all his questions. He had been forewarned about the gravity of the crash.

Jackson is a county facility with an excellent burn unit that is subsidized by local firefighters. I was admitted to the burn unit the day of the crash but before attending to me, I had to get x-rays. By this time it was close to midnight, and I was forced to wait for what seemed like hours on a cold, metal table before photographs were finally taken. I was exhausted and numb by the time I was wheeled into the burn unit and the night staff washed and wrapped me with gauze.

The nurses lectured to me about cleanliness, and the fact that infection was the leading cause of death from serious burns. I was told that the outer skin covering, the epidermis, acts as a natural barrier to infection. A burn damages this natural protection and leaves one vulnerable to infection.

Many hospitals, like Jackson Memorial, have established specialized units for the treatment of burn patients. A burn unit is usually a separate area of the hospital and is equipped with specialized technology and supplies used in monitoring and treating burn patients. The staff consists of specialists who devote most of their professional lives to the care of patients whose primary problem is serious burn injury. The patient in a burn unit will typically receive a high level of care not usually available to someone in a general medical ward of a hospital.[3]

Friends and family visiting me were required to wear a special gown and facemask to guard against the spread of infection. Packages were not allowed in and anything left from a previous patient was thrown away. Burn treatment is complicated and expensive, and it is often unsuccessful in developing countries, where strict sanitary conditions are difficult to establish and even more difficult to maintain.

The prescribed treatment for burns requires a high protein diet, daily physical therapy, timely removal of dead skin and plenty of rest. If followed consistently, the healing process accelerates and new skin generates surprisingly fast. In fact, the proliferative phase of healing extends from two days to three weeks with skin cells starting to make new skin at the hair follicle within days. The burn wound begins healing in the center first, with little "islands" of new skin developing in the middle. The islands start reaching toward the edges until they cover the burn wound.[4] Watching new skin generate on your body is an amazing experience.

For the first couple of days, I was confined to the intensive care unit and was on a respirator most of the time. I did not fully appreciate how badly I was burned nor how damned uncomfortable this whole process was going to be. Magaly and my brother Alan were with me, and it was reassuring to see them both frequently.

The press had been alerted to my presence in the hospital and wanted to interview me. At one point a nurse came to me and told me that there was a large contingent of reporters outside the building who wanted to talk about the crash. The hospital was concerned about letting all these folks and their cameras into the intensive care section of the Burn Unit where absolute sanitary conditions had to be maintained. Magaly was concerned about my psychological and physical strength in handling the situation and suggested that one reporter be allowed entry. I told her, "Honey, this is my one chance to be famous. Let them in!"

One local television station, Channel 10 WPLG, was permitted access for an exclusive interview, which was broadcast that night. An earthquake in the San Francisco Bay Area from the previous week had captured the headlines and there was little attention paid to the crash of flight #414 even though ten Americans had died. It was important news in Miami because of the large Nicaraguan community, and the fact that some of the deceased passengers resided in South Florida.

When I finally had a chance to talk to a doctor at the end of my first full day in the burn unit, he told me that I had burns on twenty-five percent of my body including my face, ears, hands, arms, part of my chest and lower legs. The burns were a combination of second and third-degree. While in critical condition, I was not in life-threatening danger.

Third-degree burns on more than fifty percent of the body is often considered to be life- threatening. A number of factors determine the level of risk including the age of the victim, the percentage of skin burned, the depth of the burn and past medical history. A seventy-year-old person with a bad cardiac history who suffers ten percent third-degree burns probably won't survive while a young adult with ninety percent second-degree burns could.

Second-degree burns affect the epidermis (outer layer of skin) and the dermis (the dense inner layer of skin underneath the epidermis), but do not pass through to underlying tissues. These burns are characterized by blistering and are pink-reddish in color. They may open and weep clear fluid. The burned area often swells and can be unusually painful. A second-degree burn typically heals in three to four weeks and some scarring may occur.

Third-degree burns destroy all layers of skin, as well as any underlying fat, muscle, bone and nerves. These burns look brown or black, charred, with the tissue underneath sometimes appearing white. The burns can be either extremely painful, or painless if the burn is so bad that it destroys nerve endings. Third-degree burns are life-threatening and are highly prone to infection. As the burns open, the body loses fluid, and shock is likely to occur. Scarring occurs and may be severe if not treated. Third-degree burns often require skin grafts.[5]

While my doctor reviewed the burns on my body, he deduced that I was saved by the cotton clothing I was wearing and may well have been burned by the intensity of the heat, not by flames. All exposed areas on my body were burned, with the exception of my lower legs where the synthetic socks melted into the skin. The value of cotton is that it burns quickly and dissipates into the air instead of sticking to the skin and causing further burning in the tissue. My lower legs would have been less damaged had I been wearing cotton socks.

Initially, my challenge was to take all necessary steps for new skin to generate, and to regain the full use of my arms, hands and legs. My burns were restricted to exposed areas, including my hands and lower arms right up to where the rolled up shirtsleeve stopped. I was left with a watchband of unburned skin on my left wrist where my wristwatch protected the skin. The other exception was my right arm, where it appeared that the heat went right up my sleeve and across my chest.

Much to our surprise, my older brother, Alan, was waiting when Magaly and I arrived at the hospital. Alan had been fishing with friends in the Florida Everglades over this particular weekend. After reaching their limit of sea bass on Saturday afternoon, he and his friends returned to their lodgings. The following is his description of what happened from a letter he wrote the next week to the extended family.

"As soon as we arrived back at John's house, the phone rang and it was my wife, Beth. She advised me that Curt had been involved in an airplane crash in Honduras, that it was a 727, that had crashed and in excess of a hundred people had died. The information otherwise was very sketchy. Curt was being medivaced out of Honduras to Miami and should be there sometime around 9:00 P.M. I put a call through to the CARE office in Honduras that was coordinating everything. Their information was not much more complete than what Beth had told me, but they confirmed that Curt would be in Miami around 9 P.M. I cleaned up, excused myself and headed for Miami.

"I arrived at Jackson Memorial Hospital at about 8:30 P.M. This hospital is a county facility that services a low income and indigent clientele. One of the nurses told me that they recover about forty percent of their patient costs. I couldn't find anyone to help me until I spotted a Catholic priest. I explained my situation to him, and after he gave me a theology quiz, he agreed to help me. It took about two hours, going to fifteen different offices within the hospital to get a pass to allow me into the Emergency Room area and, more important, into the Burn Unit. The priest excused himself and left me outside the ER, where I watched a steady stream of people entering with gunshot wounds, knifings, drug overdoses and more.

"Curt finally arrived around 11:00 P.M. by ambulance from the airport. His face and hands were wrapped in gauze, but he was coherent, logical, lucid and even had his sense of humor. They immediately took him into one of the trauma rooms in the emergency area. After about an hour he came out, and we were able to speak to him for a few minutes. He then went into x-ray for another hour-and-a-half.

"When he came out, most of his bandages had been removed. He looked terrible, but still did not seem to be in any great pain. He finally went to the burn unit for medication and gauze wrapping. Magaly and I left the hospital at about 5:00 A.M. on Sunday morning. We went to bed knowing Curt was going to be all right."

CHAPTER FOUR

REGAINING MY HEALTH: THE HORROR OF BURN TREATMENT

Make your own recovery the first priority in your life.
–Robin Norwood

During those few seconds after the plane crashed, I was somehow soaked in fuel oil. It remains a mystery to me that I did not turn into a human fireball. A week after the crash, my pants and shirt, that were recovered from the Hospital Escuela, still reeked of gasoline. The cotton clothing was flammable, yet none of it burned. My synthetic socks were the only clothing on me that burned. The only way I can understand what occurred before I was ejected from the plane is that I somehow avoided flames and was burned by the oven-like heat.

Immediately after the crash, whatever negative feelings I harbored for the pilots or the airline were secondary to my own physical and psychological recovery. There was no time or energy for hatred or revenge, even though both lingered in the back of my mind. I was a burned and broken individual, and my future was unclear. I had come face-to-face with my mortality and somehow survived in the face of enormous odds against me. What did this mean? How was I to deal with survival when so many had perished? What was I supposed to do with my survival? These and other questions plagued me and would continue to plague me for years. The immediate concern, though, was my physical recovery.

The most serious result of the crash was that I lost my good health. I was thirty-nine years old and had been in solid physical condition. For the first time in my life, I felt miserable and wasn't sure when, or if, I would ever be pain free again. Nevertheless, I was determined to return to a state of physical well-being. I had no idea what this would involve.

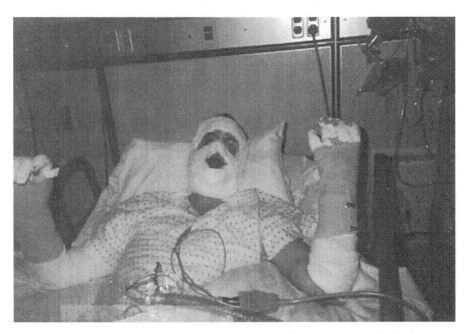

Author in intensive care

The generation of new skin requires significantly more nutritional intake per day than is normally consumed--up to six thousand calories. Healing can be delayed if there is inadequate intake of carbohydrates, proteins, fats and vitamins. I was encouraged by the hospital staff to eat all the food offered to me and virtually anything else that I liked, including beer. The high protein diet was one of the few things I enjoyed in the hospital, and Magaly surprised me with treats on a daily basis. Much to my own disappointment, beer did not appeal to me, nor did I have a taste for tobacco again for months after the crash.

After three days, I was moved from the intensive care wing to the regular burn unit just down the hall. I fell into a routine that started each day with a visit to the debriding room. I immediately dubbed this place the "Chamber of Horrors." Debride means "to cut away," or "the surgical removal of eschar (dead tissue) from a wound."[6] It is the first but probably the most important step in treating burns after a victim has been stabilized. The procedure is based on the well-established fact that all burned tissue must be removed in order to allow new, healthy tissue to grow. The burn unit was full of people who chose not to cooperate with the recommended program and who resisted the removal of the burned skin. It was too painful a process. They were often alone and fearful of treatment they had no control over. The result was that they languished in their beds for months on end, depressed and non-communicative.

It became a daily ritual to go to the Chamber of Horrors with my nurse and join the other burn victims, each with a nurse going through the morning routine. I hated to enter that room. The mere thought of it conjured up images of jumping out of the window or running into a busy street instead. Anything would have been better than this torture which I was forced to submit to.

The ritual was simple. My nurse removed the dressings from the previous night and then gave me a light bath. I always had a hospital gown on, which means I was semi-exposed particularly after the dressings disappeared. A hospital is no place for modesty. Sitting around the debriding room with little covering me did not bother me in the least. There were too many other things on my mind, like screaming patients and the sight of the clean scalpel that would soon be knifing through my skin.

The bath was followed by a shot of morphine. It was just enough of a dosage to give me an immediate high, but not enough to anesthetize me from what was to follow. As the euphoria of the morphine began to wear off, the nurse pulled out her scalpel and began hacking dead skin from the burned areas. I writhed in pain and could barely remain in my seat. Each slash jarred my entire system. The nurse talked non-stop, trying to distract me from the cruel but necessary task she was performing. I always asked for more morphine and never got it. The nurse told me that they wanted the patient to be aware and engaged, not nodding off from the drugs. The dosages were limited to avoid addicting the patients as well.

There was a dynamic tension between nurse and patient over the removal of dead skin. The process was designed to push the patient to the threshold of pain. Without a doubt, I remained engaged as long as a scalpel was cutting into my body. When the agony was too much to bear, the nurse backed off until the next session. Her objective was to remove as much skin at each session as humanly possible. I set the limits on what was humanly possible. The nurses, however, were my heroes, and I had confidence in them in spite of the pain.[7]

After the assault on my body, the nurse lathered me up with soothing silver sulphadiazine, commonly known as silvadene cream. This anti-microbial ointment kept the wounds moist and protected them from contamination. After the cream was applied, I was swathed in gauze and wraps. The open wounds screamed for relief when exposed to the air, and I urged the nurse to load me up with the pain-reducing cream as quickly as possible. I actually loved the feeling of having my burns covered with fresh ointment and wrapped up with new dressings.

Afterwards, I retreated to my bed, a haven, where I felt safe until the next scheduled attack on my body.

The process was repeated each night in my room before going to bed. I cooperated most of the time and waited for the evening session to complain the loudest behind the closed doors of my private room. In the mornings, I attempted to maintain my composure during the public debriding session and serve as a good example for the other patients. Many of them were younger than me and had a harder time with the painful experience. The result was a roomful of unhappy, loudly complaining burn victims. For some reason, I seemed to have a higher tolerance for pain than many of the other patients.

Some nurses were tougher than others, but one in particular, Ana from Jamaica, pushed me to my absolute limit for enduring pain. When I complained loudest she would ask me in no uncertain terms, "Do you want to get out of here, or do you want to sit around like some of the other people here?"

Initially I responded, "Yes, I want to get out of here but couldn't I have more morphine to help me get through this?" Excruciating pain reduced me to beggar status. The standard retort from the nurses was, "No, I have given you the maximum allowable dosage and that's all you get!" My begging only lasted a couple of days, until I realized the futility of it and ceased. Ana's tough, effective style was instrumental in helping me heal and getting me out of the hospital because she pushed, cajoled and finally insisted that I allow her to remove the dead skin.

Physical therapy was done without the benefit of morphine. It forced me out of bed. Abandoning the comfort and safety of my room were more important to my recovery than I knew at the time. I was emotionally distraught and suffering physically. It was natural for me to feel sorry for myself and want to withdraw from everything and everybody. I regularly sat and waited for the physical therapist hoping she was sick or had a conflict, but she always appeared.

Among other things, burned skin loses its elasticity, and physical therapy is crucial to getting arms, wrists, hands and fingers working again so that they don't freeze up and become inflexible. I found myself crying from the anguish of moving body parts that had been rendered temporarily non-functional, particularly my swollen right arm which suffered third degree burns. Without physical therapy I could have lost a great deal of my flexibility on the right side of my body. There was no question that the daily sessions were essential. I knew I had to do it if I wanted to progress and get out of there.

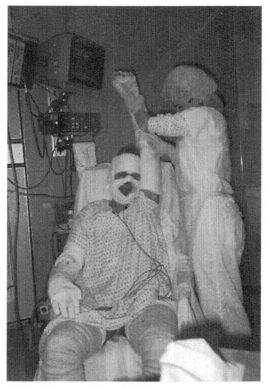

Physical therapy

I surprised myself by how emotional I was about the crash and the many lost lives. My emotions came to the fore during the debriding

and physical therapy sessions, when physical pain forced me to confront my emotional agony. The nurses were skilled at treating my burns,
but not trained to deal with my emotional needs. They were excellent
listeners, but could do little else through no fault of their own. Still, I
used the opportunity to talk to them and begin to unload the emotional heaviness that I was carrying around. Previous to the crash, it had
always been difficult for me to cry, yet I found myself openly weeping
in front of nurses I did not know.

On other occasions, I cried without consolation with my wife and
mother. I felt a burden of sadness that would not go away. I could not
get the dead passengers out of my mind. I screamed at Magaly one
day, "Why me? This is not fair!" A combination of emotions that I did
not understand were at work in my mind starting with guilt over the
incredible loss of lives, anger at the airline and vulnerability over my
physical situation. I was used to being in control of most everything I
did, but this was unchartered territory. I not only didn't like it, but I was
scared.

One nurse gave me a copy of the book *Many Lives Many Masters*
by Dr. Bryan Weiss. Weiss, a conservative Jewish psychiatrist, found
that all of his conventional treatments were useless in getting through
to a particular patient. Out of desperation, he put her under hypnosis.
The woman proceeded to recount in great detail numerous former in-
carnations she had lived over the previous centuries. In most of these
lives, the patient was poor and destitute, and died at a young age,
often in a violent manner. Revealing her previous travails helped the
patient improve and made Dr. Weiss a believer in reincarnation.

I wasn't sure why the nurse gave me the book, but Magaly and I
both devoured it and talked about its meaning with regard to what was
going on in our lives. Surviving the crash helped us be more open to
other possibilities in life, and the book gave some perspective on the
unknown. It also helped me deal with survival which I continued to feel
guilty about. The notion that each person who died in the crash might

go on to another life, that each spirit could continue in the body of another person was comforting.

Magaly and I discussed the value of accepting things over which we had no control including surviving a plane crash and life after death. The book gave us relief at a time when relief was in high demand.

As the weeks progressed, my burns slowly healed while my emotions remained raw. I was intensively treating the former while pretty much ignoring the latter. Unlike most of the patients in the burn unit, I was surrounded by family and friends on a daily basis, and there was always a buzz of activity in my room until visiting hours stopped at 8 P.M.

Magaly was my constant companion for the first two weeks. She was mostly on her own taking care of a burned husband. One night she was awakened by a phone call from her father in Venezuela. Through tears and sobs he told her he had been trying to get through for days but no one understood his Spanish. He had purchased a ticket to fly to Miami and give her support but decided that it was better to stay home. It was the first time he had expressed feelings openly to Magaly. She felt like her father truly cared for her. Her father revealed a vulnerability and tenderness that she had not experienced with him in the past.

My parents flew to Miami from Oregon and stayed for three days followed by my brother Mike. Having family around gave me a big lift and something to look forward to each morning when I had to face debriding and physical therapy. Cousins and old friends from the area and colleagues from CARE and USAID also visited.

I was blessed to have so much support. Phone calls and cards inundated the hospital. This was the only time in my life when I did not want to be the center of attention. At times, it was more than I wanted to deal with. Visitors and phone communications required an additional expenditure of energy that I did not have and usually did not want to give. Repeating the story of the crash and describing my wounds to numerous callers and visitors wore me out. The important thing was that someone, who loved me, was in the room throughout the day, everyday.

All the attention was stimulating and flattering. Mail call each day was something I looked forward to. I couldn't help but feel motivated to dive into the stack of cards and letters. All these people truly supported my recovery! The many messages I received said things like:

"Curt couldn't die yet."

"I knew you had nine lives after all those drinking bouts over the years."

"I know you like attention but this is going overboard."

"And I thought I was having a rough year."

"Shit happens."

"We miss you but God loves you."

"All of us at 660 (CARE New York Headquarters) are happy, relieved and thankful that you somehow survived the crash in Tegucigalpa. We all feel very lucky."

"There are easier ways to make national news."

I could not have asked for a more supportive, nurturing environment to recover in. CARE paid for all of my treatment expenses, and I really had nothing to worry about except my recovery. Instead of reaching out to the people closest to me, though, I chose to deal with my physical recovery on my own. I knew what I had to do, and I did it without sharing the experience with Magaly or with others who were in my midst. It seemed natural to just deal with the pain without revealing to anyone how I really felt. I had been doing this my entire life and didn't consider anything else. I was unaware and simply fell into the same old behavior pattern.

One morning I had just returned from physical therapy and answered the phone as I walked into my room. I was hurting, and my father asked how I felt. In a rare moment of candor, I told him I was in pain from the physical therapy. Instead of pursuing it with me, he said,

"Okay then, I'll get off. Bye." Neither of us wanted to talk about it. We were birds of a feather.

I did not lose my sense of humor during the recovery period, and it played an important role in my healing. I had always relied on humor to get me through difficult times and, frankly, to hide behind when I was uncomfortable with other people. In many ways, humor had served as a convenient crutch for me over the years, and it was invaluable in the depressing, drab corridors of the Jackson Memorial burn unit.

Those hallways took on new life when a friend gave me an audio cassette tape that was an hour of non-stop laughter. Listening to this tape gave me a lift every time it was on. It seemed to affect everyone else in the burn unit, as well. I would sneak into the nurses' lounge and leave the tape playing at high volume, so it could be heard throughout the ward. Patients and staff alike started smiling and would go to the door of their rooms or out into the hall looking for the origin of the laughter. A nurse would eventually locate it and then bring it to my room with a lukewarm rebuke.

My best attempt at humor while in the hospital was on Halloween. My habitual hospital outfit of being wrapped in ace bandages and cotton gauze was complemented by an eye patch. I had the one-eyed mummy look, and it was my best Halloween outfit ever. I attempted some trick or treating, but there wasn't much action in the burn unit. We all looked like freaks.

Approximately two weeks into my hospitalization, Ana scraped a large piece of dead skin off the lower palm of my right hand and matter of factly said, "That's it! That was the last dead skin on your body. We no longer have to use the scalpel on you, and all you have left to do is to grow new skin."

Ana was already my hero, and it was only fitting that she be the nurse to finish this ugly process. I could now put all my energy into trying to look normal again. The only down side was that no more dead skin meant no more morphine. For a couple of days I missed the rush of the drug entering my system but was thrilled not to have to return to the Chamber of Horrors.

Once the dead skin was removed, the speed of my physical improvement was dramatic. While not yet fully recovered, I had experienced the miracle of a body rebounding and healing from serious trauma. Watching it happens so quickly and appreciating what was involved motivated me to continue to push ahead.

Recovering physical health may be one of the most satisfying accomplishments a person can experience. Without a sound body, I felt like I was nothing. I knew that there was still a long road ahead, but successfully completing the intense regimen for burn treatment left me elated. It was the first step toward restoring balance to my life and allowing me to regain what I had lost physically.

There are few mirrors in a hospital burn unit for obvious reasons. I avoided the small mirror in my room at Jackson Memorial. My face was only briefly exposed in the morning and at night during dressing changes so there was little opportunity to examine the damage, and I didn't want to look at it anyway. I had no idea what would emerge.

Several days before leaving the hospital, the burns on my face had healed sufficiently to leave it exposed. The moment of reckoning had arrived. I approached the small mirror and found a face covered with scabs and a lower lip that looked as if it had been through a meat grinder. I could tell, though, that I was going to emerge from this with my looks intact.

Basically, I had had the equivalent of a face job and had healthy new skin with no scars. The new face didn't look bad at all! Most importantly, it didn't look different from before the crash.

As I gazed into the mirror, I couldn't help but flash back to those few seconds in the plane before losing consciousness and being thrown from the aircraft. I remember covering my face with my hands because the heat was so intense. This reaction probably saved my face which suffered second-degree burns while the back of my hands experienced the wrenching pain of third-degree burns.

I had progressed quickly and was feeling so good that my doctor decided it was time for me to leave the hospital. I was more than willing to oblige. It was time to move on to another phase of recovery. One in which I would have more control over what happened to me.

CHAPTER FIVE

STRUGGLING WITH SURVIVAL

I spent close to a month in Jackson Memorial Hospital. Walking out of there with my brother Doug at my side was truly liberating. I thought it must have been similar to the way people feel when they leave prison-the heightened excitement of freedom coupled with the fear of starting anew. I looked and felt different, but I was alive and had plenty to look forward to.

Doug flew out from California to drive me to Ohio, where I planned to convalesce at my parents' home. As much as I wanted to put up a brave front, the thought of getting on a plane terrified me.

After weeks of watching numerous nurses take care of me, it was time to take responsibility for removing the gauze from my body, washing the wounds and applying cream and fresh wraps back over the wounds. I had new skin on my face and hands, but open wounds on my arms and legs. These wounds looked like raw hamburger and would until the miracle of regeneration took over and covered me with a new wrapping.

I fell into a treatment routine similar to the hospital. I followed it twice a day until my entire body was healed. The first session was initiated around 5 A.M. each day. I was not sleeping through the night and was happy to get out of bed and do something productive. Treating my burns was a welcome relief from the recurring nightmares and sleeplessness. Night terrors usually took the form of dreams about fire. I woke up smelling fire in the air or the stench of fuel oil on the sheets. It was real to me at that time and I had to get out of bed and look for the source of the fire until I realized there was none or in some cases ask Magaly to change the sheets and blankets to "rid" the room of the smell.

My month in Dayton was focused on closing the physical wounds and beginning to address my psychological state. I was safely ensconced in the familiar surroundings of the home where I had been raised and was supported by my loving family. It was the ideal place to rehabilitate except for Magaly who continued to work in New York and flew to Ohio each weekend to be with me.

I had six counseling sessions with a Jungian therapist in Dayton. Carl Jung did not specialize in brief therapy, but I was having such vivid dreams that this approach worked well. Mostly I talked about the horrific day in Honduras and the feelings it engendered in me. I continued to weep openly and my vulnerabilities started coming out in the dreams. I had a repetitive dream that had bothered me for years, a dream about my parents' death and attending their funerals. This dream was clearly about losing people who were important to me, and no doubt was sparked by the loss of life I had experienced through the crash. In one dream I had a violent reaction to a person who was close to me in which I threw a chair across the room at her. This may well have represented my anger over having been thrust into this nightmarish experience. In another, I dreamed I was walking on a beach late at night and was accosted and raped by two men. This dream was the most upsetting. I believe it spoke to my feelings of vulnerability over being out of control and not being able to do much about it. The darkness of my near death experience in Honduras crept into all of these dreams and reflected the grieving process I was going through. These dreams gave me some insight into my feelings of anger, inescapable pain, enormous loss and being the victim of an airplane crash.

This was a temporary but extremely helpful psychological interlude. At the very least, I was able to begin to air out my pent-up emotions. I felt a sense of release and relief in talking to a professional. I was well-aware, too, that my delicate psyche would require extensive counseling in the future.

After a month in Ohio, it was recommended that I return to New York and begin intensive physical therapy to correct the damage done to my body by the burns. At this time most of my wounds were beginning to close up and show off new skin. The possibility of skin grafts on my arms was being considered. The swelling on my right arm had not subsided, and I needed physical therapy. I initiated a demanding physical therapy program and there wasn't any time to lose in the rehabilitation process. The regeneration of skin had been easy compared to this final step-regaining full use of my appendages.

I was put on a strict outpatient physical therapy program through the Cornel Medical Center in Manhattan. An essential part of the program was to follow a twice-daily routine of exercises utilizing machines designed to help me regain full use of my hands, fingers and wrists. The exercises were time consuming, demanding and expensive like everything else involved in my recovery.

It was a relief finally to be covered with new skin, but the process had been so painful, and I was so sensitive to any contact, that it affected my relations with Magaly. So many parts of my body were sensitive to the lightest touch that I was afraid of intimate contact. My situation, in turn, made Magaly uncomfortable. Whenever she got close to me,

I tensed up. Avoiding pain was constantly on my mind and being in proximity to others, even my wife, sparked a reaction, often an overreaction. Sexual relations between Magaly and me were difficult, and for months after the crash we just did not engage in any. I refused to shake hands with people because it hurt my hand, and I stayed away from close embraces. At a time when I most needed intimacy and physical contact, I was forced to shun it. I struggled with my emotions every day, but could not be lovingly embraced.

Magaly was well aware of my sensitivity to intimacy but wanted to be close to me and felt rejected. She told me later that she wanted to show how much she cared for me but did not know how to express her feelings for me. It hurt her to see me in so much pain, but she was at a loss as to how to be close. This physical withdrawal only reinforced my emotional retreat. Again, this was the opportunity to let it all out and develop some measure of emotional maturity. Instead, I pulled back, even from my wife.

I didn't realize that the development of skin was such a long and involved process. It wasn't enough to simply ensure that skin regenerated. I was told that an essential element to the normal development of new skin was the use of pressure garments. These tightly fitting elastic clothes were custom made and designed to keep the healing skin smooth by flattening out scars; to help stop itching common to newly generated skin; and to restore normal color to the beet red or, at times, purple skin. The garments had to be equally distributed over the body. This required me to wear a full body suit from neck to ankles, even though my burns only covered twenty-five percent of my body skin. The only respite was that I did not have to wear a facemask. I also was allowed to clip the tips off the fingers of the gloves to be able to eventually use a computer at work. Much to my chagrin, the body suit had to be worn twenty-four hours a day to have its intended effect.

The act of dressing each day with what felt like extremely tight long underwear was involved, time consuming and painful. I had always marveled at how young and not so young women were able to wear skin tight jeans, and now I understood. Not easily, and often with help!

The garments were expensive, and I had only two outfits. This meant that, while I wore one tight fitting suit, the other had to be washed by hand each night and hung to dry for use the next morning. I had to wear these uncomfortable underclothes for almost two years. While most of the pressure garments were skin tone in color, my first outfit was black. It gave me a truly freakish look, something akin to Darth Vader without the mask.

Shortly after starting outpatient treatment, the doctor recommended skin grafts on the inside of my forearms where I had third-degree burns. This skin was taking longer to heal than new skin on the rest of my body therefore surgery was recommended. I resisted because I was loath to return to a hospital as an in-patient. My stay at Jackson Memorial in Miami had been enough, and I was willing to put up with the complications of not having the skin grafts.

The skin on my arms simply took longer to heal and blistered constantly. For months I went through a ritual every night of taking a hot, sterilized needle and using it to pop the blisters on my arms and then drain the fluid out of them. At the end of each day I had a new set of blisters to contend with. Like a lot of things that I was forced to do, I never looked forward to this nightly home surgery procedure, but it was just one of those things I did without thinking twice about it or feeling sorry for myself.

A longer-term consequence of having had burns on different parts of the body was that my skin continued to be sensitive to the sun and needed to be protected whenever I was outside. This prohibited me from going to the beach and from playing golf or tennis for several years after the crash. These were activities that I had regularly enjoyed prior to the crash. My new skin was so sensitive that something as simple as resting my left arm on the door of the car with the window open while driving was painful when the sun was out.

It had always been important for me to spend time outside, so I began to look for solutions to dealing with the sun. I started wearing special shirts made of a lightweight, synthetic fabric that effectively blocked out the rays of the sun. In this case, the synthetic material (95% nylon, 5% synthetic) was a more effective screen than cotton. Hats and sun block were also welcome relief, and I took a large umbrella whenever I went to the beach.

Perhaps most upsetting was that I lost my appearance and had to work very hard to return to what I looked like before the crash. Getting my looks back meant more to me than I realized. Most of us want to maintain our God given looks for as long as we can, and a great deal of our self-image is wrapped up in our physical appearance. No one chooses to look disfigured.

My greatest fear was that my appearance would change permanently, possibly to some disfigured form. Psychologically, this was tough to face. I knew from the reaction of the few people who saw me that I had an odd appearance. I was also haunted by this image in my head of a former president of Bolivia (Jaime Paz Zamora) who I had met in a small, rural village in that country years previously. He had been badly burned in a helicopter crash and had grotesque scarring on his face. This did not stop him from becoming President of the republic, but it did leave a lasting impression on me.

I stood out in public because my new covering was bright red. Sometimes the skin took on a purple hue due to poor circulation, particularly in my arms. It looked like I had fallen asleep in the sun without applying lotion, or that I had a serious alcoholism problem.

We lived in New York at the time of the crash and rode the subways regularly. Practically anytime I looked up from my seat or the strap I was hanging onto, I found most everyone on the opposite side of the car staring at me. Who was this guy with the bright red face and the funny gloves on? I always thought it took a lot to attract attention in

New York, but I was wrong. My burn treatment appearance made me more conspicuous than I thought possible in the Big Apple.

Rarely did anyone stop and ask what had happened to me or why I looked like a lobster wearing hobo gloves. When someone did ask, I was relieved, because it gave me an opportunity to talk about the experience, and it broke the monotony of the endless stares. People are so conditioned to maintain distance from those who are different in appearance or somehow look odd. I always preferred that a stranger satisfy his or her curiosity by asking me what happened, instead of skirting the issue or fearing that somehow I would break down if I had to retell the story one more time. I never lost my composure while recounting the experience hundreds of times, but I often felt emotional-a tear in the eye, a tightness in the throat. I still do.

Another issue that plagued me was employment. CARE tempted me with the offer of full disability for a year. Yet I was intent on not losing any professional momentum and chose to return to work two and a half months after the crash. By coincidence, my boss resigned just as I returned to the office, and within days I was promoted to Acting Regional Manager for Latin America.

What I lost by going back to work so quickly was an opportunity to engage in my own form of grieving over a trauma that I did not understand and that left me feeling guilty for having survived. I was horrified when a friend living in Honduras sent me the official list of deceased passengers. It seemed to go on endlessly. None of the names were familiar to me, but upon leaving Managua we were all together on that plane. Thirty minutes later a handful us had survived.

The quick return to work also gave me a detachment from the event and its impact for a number of years. Returning to work and burying myself in a busy, professional daily routine served to minimize the experience in my own mind. Yes, I did engage in physical and psychological therapy for several years after the crash, but it was of secondary importance to maintaining a demanding job on a daily basis. Work remained my priority.

At that time, I had no interest in communicating with other survivors, nor was I attracted to any type of post trauma stress support group. This was my own form of avoidance. I talked openly about the crash and made a pilgrimage to the crash site, as well as to Jackson Memorial Hospital as part of my therapy. The bulletin board in front of my desk sported photos of me in the hospital, and I had an exercise machine on my desk for the still swollen right arm. My psychologist wrote in September 1990, close to a year after the crash, "On the surface CS has made a remarkable adjustment—almost too good to be true, and that is in part what concerns me. C's ability to get it and keep it 'together' has enabled him to go back to work quite quickly and show little evidence to the world at large of the trauma he has been through. He still cannot assimilate what he went through and uses denial to cope with the extent of the trauma."

I was careful not to internalize the experience, nor to try to block it from my memory, but I did avoid dealing with it in any deep or profound manner. I eventually quit counseling, and the crash experience became something akin to a trophy in my life. I was glad to talk about it and receive sympathy and attention from people, but that was as far as it ever went.

More than anything, my rush to return to work several months after the crash was about restoring my self-confidence, proving to myself and to others that I could perform again. I was weak physically and emotionally when I returned and had trouble making it through an eight-hour day. Our apartment was in the neighborhood, so I frequently left the office in mid-afternoon to nap at home. Taking on the responsibility of Acting Regional Manager for Latin America was an opportunity I neither sought nor welcomed. I had the additional burden of no deputy to support me.

My new job put me in charge of eleven country office operations in Latin America and the Caribbean. The CARE country directors reported directly to me. I was responsible for reviewing and approving all new projects, as well as providing day-to-day management support, input on fundraising initiatives and coordination of responses to natural disasters in the region. The workload was overwhelming and clearly more than I could handle, but I chose to do it. I decided I had to work and made up my mind that I would do as much as possible and not worry about the rest. My self-image and the image others had of me demanded that I work as if nothing had happened in my life.

I knew my physical ailments would correct themselves over time. The burns were already healing, and physical therapy was making a difference. Psychologically, I was less confident about the future. I was aware of post-traumatic stress disorder (PTSD) and knew that everyone who had been through an experience like mine suffered from it to some extent. I couldn't help but question my mortality and felt humbled by having survived something that killed so many. It had always been important for me to be in control of my life, and now I felt as if I had no control at all. I was just hanging on, trying to make it to the next day. I was a survivor, yet I was already learning one of life's fundamental lessons: Nothing is guaranteed. I still had to make my way and take responsibility for each day. I couldn't use the experience as a crutch to prop me up in the future.

The crash was on my mind constantly, and different images from that day popped into my head like recurring bad dreams. They were, in fact, flashbacks. These images at times were so real, so graphic, that I would go into a trance-like state and block out everything that was going on around me and focus on the moment. It was uncanny to suddenly find myself reliving the impact of the crash, feeling out of control and hearing the screams of the other passengers or to feel a scalpel cutting through my skin as I writhed in my chair in the hospital debriding room.

Flashbacks occurred more often than not during a meeting. It seemed that CARE headquarters staff spent much of their time in meetings. As I lost touch with what was going on around me, I had to fight back tears and occasionally left the room to compose myself. These symptoms of post-traumatic stress disorder were caused by re-experiencing the trauma. The American Psychiatric Association describes it thus, "These flashbacks come as a sudden, painful onslaught of emotions that seem to have no cause. The emotions are often of grief that brings tears, fear or anger. These emotional experiences occur repeatedly, much like memories or dreams about the traumatic event."[8]

I knew that if I allowed myself to break down and cry in front of colleagues in the office that I would quickly develop a reputation within the organization. I imagined them saying, "Yeah, Schaeffer seems to have recovered pretty well from that plane crash, but he just can't keep it together in the office." No one ever said this or even hinted at it, but that is the way office culture operates. One tearful experience would have been enough to cast my professional image in bronze as a weak-kneed survivor.

I discussed this with my psychologist, and she encouraged me just to let the tears fly whenever my emotions rose to the surface, to "feel safe crying." I argued against it, and in fact, never allowed myself to cry in public during this period, even though I felt like it many times. This was truly unfortunate. After a lifetime of suppressing my emotions, here I was consciously doing it again at a time when I could have truly benefited from allowing myself to weep openly. I was committed to confronting the anguish of the crash and keeping it in front of me, but crying in public was not part of the plan.

The psychologist asked me, "At what point can you take up your space on this earth and feel free to allow your emotions to pour out?" It was a good question. It was a missed opportunity.

Losing what I had taken for granted for years made me question my future. One of my biggest fears was not being able to travel by air. My job with CARE required considerable travel. This was one of the benefits of working for an international organization. I also enjoyed traveling on my own time and could not fathom a life without that freedom.

I was not yet ready for frequent air travel when I returned to New York two months after the crash, but I knew that I had to conquer my fear of flying, the sooner the better. My baptism occurred on a flight to New York from Dayton.

On a bitterly cold December morning, I was scheduled to fly out of Dayton. I had been visiting the airport to watch jets take off and land. Hearing the powerful sound of jet engines and watching normal air traffic helped me prepare for getting back on a plane. It was almost as if I had to re-familiarize myself with the notion of flying.

Magaly was at my side. Flying conditions were downright ugly. The low ceiling and cold blustery weather made the wind and light rain on the day of the crash look mild by comparison. No sooner had we boarded the plane than the pilot announced that the sound we heard on the roof was the de-icing machine. The sub-zero temperatures forced a second treatment before we took off.

Once I was seated on the plane and de-icing commenced, there was no exit. The sound of a machine operating on the roof of the plane was disturbing. The plane was still on the ground. I was belted into my seat and there was nothing I could do about it. Fortunately, I had a warm hand to hang onto.

Magaly did not know what to expect from me and was concerned about my reaction to the awful weather conditions. She told me later that my eyes were closed as the plane took off, but she was relieved to see that I was breathing normally and taking it in stride.

The two-hour flight was like a roller coaster ride, with constant jerks up and down. The FASTEN SEAT BELT sign was never turned off and no drinks were served to the passengers. We all hung on, and I hung on the hardest. I felt like screaming out of fear and repeatedly thought that there had to be a reason for this experience.

It was the most turbulent, heart-in-your-mouth flight I had ever taken. When we landed at LaGuardia in Queens, my shirt was wet. My resolve to fly again had been truly challenged. I was shaken and scared, but not defeated. I knew then that if I could endure a flight like that, I could fly anytime, anywhere in the future.

In reflecting on the flight, I believe I was being tested that day, almost as if God was telling me to just get over it and here's how I will help you do it. I do not look forward to flying, but do not shy away from it either. The possibility of dying crosses my mind every time I step onto a plane, but I also believe that the odds favor me.

CHAPTER SIX

GAINING FROM THE EXPERIENCE

The tragedy of life is not death, but what we let die while we live.

Norman Cousins —

As one of the few survivors, I believed for years that it was my destiny to do something influential for the betterment of mankind. After all, I had survived and it must have been for a reason. I labored with this notion of grandeur or distinction, and it was reinforced by others telling me that I had been "chosen by God" or that I was destined to be a religious leader, a motivational speaker or even a fortuneteller. After leaving Jackson Memorial Hospital, Doug and I stopped in a South Florida pharmacy to buy silvadene cream. The pharmacist asked what had happened to me and I briefly described the crash. He got a tortured look on his face and started exclaiming, "You should be a rabbi! You should be a rabbi!" Doug and I exited quickly.

Entertaining notions of grandeur left me confused. My feeling was that surviving the crash in the first place was enough, I had already accomplished something pretty amazing. Why did I have to "be somebody" for others and in the eyes of others? I felt as if I was already somebody, and I was happy with that person.

Questioning my survival and what it meant was further exacerbated by my feelings of survivor's guilt. Why did I survive when so many lost their lives, particularly children and young adults? What did my survival mean?

I believed in synchronicity or synchronistic events, which are meaningful coincidences in life that sometimes, occur in groups. The idea is that nothing happens by chance. There is a reason for every occurrence, and it is connected to a larger whole or a broader context.

I was not aware of the numerous synchronistic events that occurred on October 21, 1989, until my good friend, Tony Gerlicz, started quizzing me at my bedside in Miami. He had flown in from Oregon to pay a surprise visit and wasted no time asking about what happened. A pattern of events emerged that surprised us both.

Was it by chance that I was traveling alone and knew no one on the plane? Was it by chance that the flight attendant trainee I encountered as I stepped onto the plane encouraged me to sit in the large overstuffed first-class seats? I was headed for the back of the aircraft and she pushed me to sit in the front. Was it by chance that the plane broke open where I was seated, and my seat was ejected? Was it by chance that I was covered with fuel oil but did not burn up? Was it by chance that the seat I was belted into landed upright in a field? It could just as easily have landed on one side or the other or face down, and I would surely have had multiple fractures. It could have killed me. I often think that my back could have been broken from the impact. Not only did the seat land upright but the overstuffed, first-class seat provided a much needed cushion to the impact. Was it by chance that the seat was thrown far enough away from the plane to protect me from the numerous explosions, the intense heat from the fire and the flames themselves? In this sequence of occurrences, I was spared the screams of the passengers on board who were burning up. I lost consciousness as I was being ejected from the plane, and when I came to, I heard nothing more than an occasional small explosion coming from the fuselage. While I was unconscious, a large number of passengers were incinerated. Was it by chance that I was spared this orgy of suffering?

There were other examples during the day which, in retrospect, make me wonder why all this happened to me at a time when so many people met their ultimate fate. Not only did I survive, but I survived in a manner that was little short of miraculous. My good fortune extended to the support I received on the day of the crash which still makes me feel as if someone was watching over me.

It is unusual in any CARE country operation for the entire senior management group to be in town at the same time. But on this day they were at home and available and collectively worked to help get me out of the country. From finding me in the hospital to keeping the airport open so the plane could take off after sunset, a large number of people worked tirelessly and successfully on my behalf. It is interesting, too, that this same group had recently gone through the exercise of sending a dependent out of the country by medi-vac plane and knew the complicated routine well. If Dr. Vernon Sichewski had not arrived that day and diagnosed my collapsed lung, I would have died from respiratory arrest.

It was synchronicity that Magaly's birthday was October 20, and we had planned to meet in Tegucigalpa for the weekend to celebrate. I was blessed to have her next to me on the medi-vac plane that flew me to Miami.

Finally, my brother Alan happened to be fishing in the Florida Everglades for the first time in his life. He was able to get to Jackson

Memorial Hospital in Miami to meet me as I was wheeled out of the ambulance and into the burn unit. His presence and humor were a big support to me and to Magaly.

There is no answer to the question, "Why did I survive?" I believed there was a reason. I just didn't know what it was or what I needed to do to justify my good fortune.

I had already dedicated my professional life to working for others. I was a sociology major in college and worked in a number of human service jobs. During college I was a VISTA Volunteer (domestic version of the Peace Corps) and was involved with different issues affecting low-income neighborhoods like voter registration, improved housing and health services. After finishing my undergraduate work at Pitzer College in Southern California, I moved to Portland, Oregon, and worked briefly for Aid to Families with Dependent Children before finding a job with the Multnomah County Public Defender's Office. There I worked as a member of a defense team to find alternatives to the county jail for young offenders entering the criminal justice system for the first time. Subsequent jobs included stints as a teacher in Bolivia and in the United States. While in Portland, I was offered a job with Nike Shoes that was just starting its meteoric rise to success. Nike offered to put me through a one-year training program and then send me overseas to manage the construction of shoe manufacturing plants. It was a tempting offer but in the end I turned it down. I decided that my real interest was in serving people not making shoes.

I went to work for CARE in 1988 in New York after spending the previous five years in Bolivia working for the U.S. government and several international non-profit organizations. My work in Bolivia involved managing rural health programs and a disaster relief response to a severe drought throughout the Andean Region. I had been at CARE exactly a year as a Deputy Regional Manager for Latin America when the crash occurred.

I continued to hear from friends, acquaintances and people on the streets that I was "chosen" and "destined to do great things." It was still not clear to me what this meant nor how it would actually play out in my life. One day the light finally went on. I realized that what I had been doing all my life had been sufficient. I had always believed that the best I could do, and the most anyone could ask of me, was to be kind and respectful with those people I came in contact with every day. People I knew as well as those I didn't know. I had tried to live my life according to this principle, although I had stumbled at times. I believed we are all capable of making the world a better place by being effective in our own small environment. Respecting myself and those around me was enough. It was a relief to come to this conclusion and no longer feel like I had to prove something to others as a means of justifying my survival.

Learning to live with a tragic experience can be traumatic. The trauma does not go away, and attempting to block the experience in your psyche or to pretend that it did not happen only serves to strengthen its potential impact upon you. As one survivor, Helen Devereux said, "The slightest sound or movement can trigger a flood of memories and emotions that can be overwhelming, even after all these years." What I learned is that I had to manage the trauma and its impact on my life instead of trying to erase the experience.

More than five million Americans suffer from post-traumatic stress disorder (PTSD). It is not unusual for them to relive the experience through nightmares and flashbacks, have difficulty sleeping, experience panic attacks and feel detached or estranged. These symptoms can be severe enough and last long enough to significantly impair the person's daily life.

PTSD can make or break an interpersonal relationship. According to the American Psychiatric Association, "It is often the phobic avoidance of situations that resemble or symbolize the original trauma that can lead to conflict, divorce or loss of job." Fortunately this did not occur in my situation.

While I had some of the symptoms of PTSD, I forced myself to fly again and essentially confront and become comfortable with the symbol of the trauma. Instead of threatening our marriage, this experience created a stronger bond between us. I was overwhelmed by Magaly's love, and we both felt incredibly thankful for each day together.

Anyone who says that they do not require counseling after experiencing a trauma is only fooling herself or himself. We all have extraordinary coping skills. Some of us manage to move ahead with our lives with greater ease than others, but the fact remains that everyone suffers to one extent or another from having experienced a life-threatening trauma like an air crash. Not every trauma victim suffers from PTSD, but every trauma victim can benefit from counseling.

I was fortunate to have strong support from family and friends from day one. In fact, this experience confirmed the goodness of people who did not hesitate to help me and lend support to my family. When I went to Dayton to recover, one of those welcoming me home was my Uncle Bob who had experienced extensive third-degree burns as a Marine pilot in World War II. He was shot down by a Japanese Zero in the Pacific and subsequently experienced months of painful burn treatment. He knew better than anyone what I had been through and was continuing to go through and was particularly kind and tender with me.

At my father's behest, I had been consulting with a team of attorneys to explore my legal options. They arranged for me to be thoroughly checked out by a psychologist in New York, specializing in brain damage. Everything inside my cranium seemed to be functioning well, but you never know how the brute force of a large jet crashing into a mountainside can affect you.

About this same time I decided I needed counseling and began seeing a psychologist of my own choosing, Dr. Susan Shapiro, twice a week. Both professionals diagnosed me with post-traumatic stress disorder. Dr. Richard Schuster, the psychologist appointed by the attorneys, ran me through a battery of tests for six hours and concluded the following:

Mr. Schaeffer is an individual of high average cognitive potential who luckily has avoided traumatic brain dysfunction. However, there are indications of psychological ramifications from his injury. His lifestyle has been drastically altered. From an energetic individual who enjoyed an adventuresome, free spirited life, his life is now restricted and focused on his rehabilitation concerns. Psychologically, he is plagued by repercussions from his injury. Intrusive thoughts, nightmares, fears, and anxieties are noted, all indicative of post-traumatic stress disorder. Given the near brush with death, the catastrophic circumstances he experienced, the death of almost everyone about him, and the aftermath of his initial medical care, such a reaction could be anticipated. In fact, given the circumstances he experienced, the fact that he has returned to work and is attempting to live a more normal life highlights his internal strengths and motivations.[9]

According to the American Psychiatric Association, "Post-traumatic stress disorder can occur at any age and symptoms usually begin within the first three months after the trauma. The severity, duration and proximity of an individual's exposure to the traumatic event are the most important factors affecting the likelihood of developing this disorder. There is some evidence that social supports, family history, childhood experiences personality variables and preexisting mental disorders may influence the development of post-traumatic stress disorder." Four months later, Dr. Shapiro wrote:

Mr. S is suffering from post-traumatic stress disorder secondary to his survival of an October, 1989 crash in Honduras. Although the acute symptoms have to some extent abated-nightmares are less frequent, the psychological numbing is beginning to lessen, and there are still numerous signs of continued distress. In addition to continued difficulty sleeping through the night, often awakening to the smell of burning gasoline, Mr. S finds himself questioning the meaning of his life and the value he places on his activities as he struggles to come to terms with his survival. He avoids fully realizing the extent of the changes in his life. Mr. S has adapted surprisingly well over the short term and takes pleasure and pride in this. Such adaptation is made possible in part y post-traumatic numbing and by a premorbid defensive structure which kept feelings locked inside.[10]

Both psychologists recognized my rapid rehabilitation and recovery from the trauma and correctly recommended that I continue in therapy to avoid the potential recurring symptoms of PTSD. After returning from a business trip to Washington in March, 1990, I questioned my own positive recovery. My journal entry included the following:

Wonder if something is wrong with me-have been relaxed, sleeping well and act almost as if nothing ever happened. Handle work well and have surprised my colleagues--now walking and exercising more than ever and feeling good. Burns continue to bother me, but it's now more discomfort than anything else. It's as if I feel too good.

In June, 1990 I traveled to Guatemala and wrote the following in my journal:

Do feel comfortable flying-probably more so than many people who have never had an accident. Is that so bad?

In July I went to a New York Mets baseball game with a group of high school buddies who lived in the New York area. We had a raucous, beer-soaked afternoon followed by more drinks and adolescent behavior in a bar throughout the evening. On the bus home from the Port Authority to West New York, New Jersey, where we lived at the time, I fell asleep and was awakened by the driver at the end of the line some twenty miles north of my destination. Dr. Shapiro described this incident in the following manner:

C had one disturbing incident of self-endangering behavior in which he fell asleep on a bus, missed his stop, was unable to get a taxi that late at night to take him home, took some poor advice and ended up trying to hitchhike on the turnpike. The man who picked him up made a pass at him and after he got out of the car he wandered down the turnpike in a state not unlike his immediate post-accident state as he wandered down the road waiting for someone to help.

Magaly and I were both upset and concerned by this occurrence. It was explained to me that survivors of major accidents sometimes see themselves as being "chosen" and, as such carry around an odd sense of invulnerability. The attitude becomes irrational at times. "Of course I can cross the street walking through traffic and nothing will happen to me," or in this case, "of course I can hitchhike down the turnpike at 3 A.M. and expect to get a safe ride home."

This sense of "nothing can happen to me" is portrayed effectively in the Peter Weir movie *Fearless*. Jeff Bridges, the protagonist and a plane crash survivor, truly believes he is invincible, almost as if he had taken on angel status as a result of surviving a crash and leading other passengers off the plane. He risks his life repeatedly, but in the end comes to grips with the fact that he is a mere mortal trying to make it through each day like the rest of us.

I do think that, unconsciously, I suffered from a larger-than-life complex that I believed protected me from virtually anything that might plague other people. Dr. Shapiro described it this way:

I see it as a possible dissociative reenactment of as yet unassimilated aspects of the trauma. On one hand Mr. S's premorbid personality style using humor and a certain lack of introspection has helped in his initial recovery, but this makes it more difficult to determine the true extent of his recovery and working through difficult material. It also makes him more vulnerable to dissociative intrusions.

I was feeling better about myself, because the physical recovery was proceeding well and I was not only back to work but also had been promoted. As the turnpike incident points out, though, I was still struggling with the effects of the crash experience. I noticed that

I was uncomfortable riding a New York City subway, because it often felt to me as if it was out of control as it barreled into the next stop. At the same time, I realized that I had no fear of fire and even engaged in careless, risky behavior in the kitchen while cooking, picking up hot pots without a pad or passing my hand too close to a flame. More than anything, I now believe that the overriding desire to prove to myself and to others that I was okay guided my actions. I wanted to appear normal and to show that I could do whatever anyone else did. Mostly I succeeded. My will to get on with my life was an essential piece of the puzzle, although just as important was the counseling I engaged in and my relationship with Magaly.

My counselor challenged me to confront the crash in a number of different ways. In so doing she was helping me work through the scars left by the trauma while keeping the experience in front of me, ever present in my mind. The first and most difficult challenge was returning to the crash site. One year after the crash Magaly and I went to Honduras. We flew into San Pedro Sula and drove to Tegucigalpa, as I was not yet prepared to land at Toncontin International Airport. Simply returning to the country, let alone the scene of the crime, was enormously difficult.

A CARE driver took us to Cerro de Hula on a beautiful Sunday afternoon. It was a warm day with a soft breeze. The bright sun and clear sky over the mountain contrasted with my image of the area on the morning of the crash. We stopped along the way to buy flowers. I had been told about HERMAFAME-the association of family members of deceased passengers that had purchased the land where the crash occurred and planned to establish a memorial park. As we climbed up to the site from the road, I could see the burned-out hulk of the fuselage on the mountainside. Each step felt heavier and heavier. I hesitated and thought of turning around, but decided to continue.

It was shocking to see the remains of the plane. Anything that had not burned up or been picked over by looters remained on the mountainside. A barbed wire fence surrounded the property, and a caretaker was living in a portion of the plane. I was upset by the presence of this man on what I felt was sacred ground. In my opinion, no one had the right to live on the property, let alone inside the burned-out fuselage. The caretaker started complaining to us that some of the local people had not gotten their blankets back from the survivors after the crash. I could feel my anger level rising, since I had never received the blanket I so desperately wanted on the cold, damp morning of the crash. I finally walked away from him so as not to lash out and say something stupid. I already had a sour taste in my mouth from the failure of the campesinos to come to my assistance after the crash. Finding this guy living in the plane and telling me that I owed the local people blankets was upsetting.

Remains of the plane on the mountainside

Walking around the remains of the 727-200 conjured strong feelings about my own trauma. I found myself kneeling down next to the charred fuselage and crying uncontrollably. I walked to the spot where my seat had landed after being thrown from the plane and marveled at my fate that day. There was a purging of emotions as sadness yielded to an increasing anger over what happened. Viewing the wreckage a year later reinforced the senselessness of it all and the enormous pain and suffering inflicted on so many people.

The caretakers home forged from the remains of the plane

I retraced my original steps off the mountainside down to the small house on the road below, but did not enter the adobe dwelling.

Instead, I walked out on the road to the spot where the small pickup had been parked before taking five of us survivors into Tegucigalpa. Magaly held me while I cried one more time and looked back up the mountainside at the spot where people had lost their lives just a year before. I vowed to myself that I would never return to the site. One visit was enough.

Later that day and during the following week, I met with CARE staff who had been so instrumental in finding me and getting me out of the country in a timely manner. It felt good to be able to thank them personally for their many kindnesses.

On the same trip, we stopped in Miami on the way home and returned to the burn unit at Jackson Memorial Hospital. Many of the nursing staff that had cared for me were still working there, including Ana, the nurse who pushed me the hardest and who had facilitated my recovery. What surprised us was the reaction of the staff. When Magaly and I walked off the elevator they immediately recognized her. They did not know my face. They had never seen me as a whole human being, without burns, scabs, gauze and cream, but were able to figure out who I was through Magaly. They were thrilled that we had returned to thank them and one nurse stated, "It is rare that a former patient takes the time to come by and thank us and it is even rarer that we get to see one of our success stories."

Once again I was able to personally thank people who had meant so much to my recuperation. We did not stay long but it was worthwhile to confront the scene of so much suffering and torment in my life. The sounds and smells of the burn unit were all too familiar and made me shudder. As we left, I mentioned to Magaly how thankful I was to have survived this place intact.

While I exhibited some of the symptoms of PTSD, I did not fall into a PTSD funk that is often characterized by snapping at people and avoiding others, places or things associated with the trauma. For years after the crash, I started smoking as soon as I approached an airport and usually quit again upon returning home. I traveled so frequently that I was constantly stopping and starting the nicotine habit. Friends suggested that I drink or take drugs before a flight, but I chose to smoke cigarettes.

Magaly and I began arguing with some frequency during this period. At one point I told her, "You will never understand what I have been through." She responded by saying, "You will never understand what I have been through either." We were both right but the exchange was indicative of our poor communication.

We decided to individually pursue counseling in New York. We had been through our own traumas and were still struggling with what had happened to us. It became apparent to us both that counseling, with a particular focus, quickly leads one into other issues and other periods of your life. It is all connected. Your psyche does not conveniently arrange events in your life for therapeutic benefit.

The emotions that had bubbled to the surface as a result of this tragedy also led us to a number of individual and collective issues that had been dormant within us for years preceding the crash. Magaly saw a therapist to help her deal with her own trauma over her husband's survival of a major plane crash. She dealt with our experience and unresolved issues with her mother. I spent many sessions talking about my survival but digressed into numerous pre-crash issues including several near death experiences while living in Bolivia and a long-standing pattern of sleeplessness. After each counseling session we compared notes and this helped improve our mutual understanding and communication.

The crash and its effects on me and our relationship had been particularly tough on Magaly from the moment she heard the news in the Miami Airport. Magaly was expected to be the good wife and to provide emotional support and companionship that you can only get from your partner. She did this and much more, but I was the center of attention and everyone wanted to talk with me. Everyone wanted to hear about my experience, while Magaly was often left in the background.

Magaly experienced a jumble of emotions that left her confused. She couldn't help but feel saddened by what had occurred and at the same time scared about the future and our relationship. Thinking about herself and her own welfare while I was suffering left her guilt ridden. Friends kept telling her to "be strong" instead of inviting her to share her feelings and explain what she was going through.

I was so focused on my own needs that I was not even aware that she was having a tough time. Magaly's incredible support throughout this long period of rehabilitation and recovery was a big reason for my returning to a normal life. Her most valuable help came in just being present with me. This means that she consistently made herself available to me. Whether I needed her or not, I knew that she was always by my side—assisting, guiding and loving.

CHAPTER SEVEN

MR. MOM

Maybe I was a little confused, maybe I was a little frustrated but I knew what I was doing was important because it means something to raise human beings. What saw me through was pride.
– The Movie Mr. Mom (1983)

One of the big issues for us after the crash was having a child. We felt as if I had survived the air crash for some reason, and maybe it was for us to be parents. I had dreamed about being a father even before getting married.

Alexa was born March 24, 1992. The birth of my daughter was truly the greatest gift I have received in my new life, after my own survival. Survivor's guilt, grandiose ideas of who I was supposed to be and do for mankind continued to plague me, but the birth of our child effectively minimized the importance of these illusions. Childbirth also served to truly form a family, to create a different type of closeness. We became focused on Alexa and blocked out extraneous distractions that previously seemed to matter.

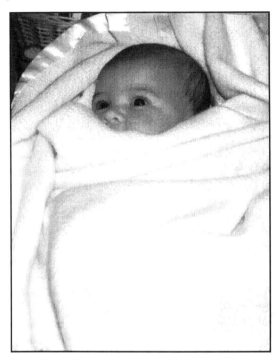

Alexa Paula Schaeffer, 1 day old

Magaly stayed home for the first three months with Alexa. During this time, my father and Magaly's father both died, leaving us feeling shell shocked but also thankful that in death there is new life to celebrate.

We were thrilled to have this beautiful, easygoing daughter and spent the first couple of months of her life wrestling with one of the great modern-day dilemmas. What does a working couple do with a newborn child? It sounded callous, as if this were another material possession that could be stored in a closet or a dog to be put in the back yard until we were ready to use it or play with it. In fact, we were talking about a human being, our own flesh and blood, and we took our new responsibility seriously.

After many discussions, we always came back to why we chose to have this child in the first place. We came to the conclusion that it was to experience parenthood while helping our child grow and develop and eventually make it on her own in the world. The thought of handing our daughter over to a stranger and giving that person primary responsibility for raising her was unacceptable to both of us. Magaly and I made a pact that one of us would stay home with Alexa for the first five years of her life, and we would be flexible in coordinating our work to make this happen.

The next step was to figure out who would stay home initially. I had never really taken a break from the daily grind of a demanding job in a busy New York office. I also realized that I had not taken enough time off after the plane crash to sort through my own trauma. Staying home with my daughter was attractive to me for all these reasons. Two and a half years after the crash I had proven myself professionally. I was thrilled by the idea of leaving my job for a new challenge, to reorder priorities from career to family.

This was a workable plan since Magaly had a good job with International Planned Parenthood Federation. We had our finances in order. So it was officially decided that I would take a leave of absence from my job, and Magaly would return to work after three months at home with the baby. I gave CARE notice and left the job several weeks after Magaly had returned to work.

The decision shocked a lot of people. It was reassuring to hear supportive comments from family members and close friends. I was particularly pleased when my conservative father gave me his blessing one night over the phone shortly before he died. "I think this sounds like a good idea," he said. There were a few subtle jabs thrown my way like, "What will you do for intellectual stimulation?" or "How can you possibly afford it?" I received some nice notes from mothers, in particular, which reaffirmed the decision.

I had already spent a great deal of time with my daughter during her first three months of life. In fact, staying home and nesting with Magaly and Alexa during the two weeks after the birth turned out to be one of the most exciting and stimulating experiences in my life.

The difficulties I soon encountered as a stay-at-home dad had little to do with the daily tasks of changing diapers, feeding the child or getting out of the house for a walk. They had everything to do with my own ego.

Within a week of staying home, I found myself terribly uncomfortable with the sudden loss of job, job status, salary and the postponement of a career. I went from managing operations in eleven countries to managing the life of an infant. I was clear about which endeavor was more important, but had a hard time adjusting to the new responsibilities. I was reluctant to tell others exactly what I was doing and why. It was easier to say that I still worked at CARE.

I had a strong work record and had always given it my best, but never put much stock in a career. I was more interested in taking on different challenges and became bored with jobs that I stuck with for too long. Within days of staying home with Alexa, it became painfully apparent to me that my work was more important to my persona than I realized. After my marriage, my work represented my primary commitment in life. Like most humans, I identified myself to others through my work and often forged relationships with like-minded people from the same or similar line of work. I spent more time at work than I spent with my family. The commitment I had made to leaving a job in order to raise my daughter was truly a radical change, and one that I was not prepared to deal with. It took me several months to work through my own insecurities over leaving the job and assuming my new role as a stay-at-home father.

Raising a child was just as challenging and difficult as starting a new job, maybe more so since I had no formal training to fall back on. As I quickly found out, caring for a child and managing a household is hard work and makes most office jobs look easy. As a male, the experience bordered on being a hardship because there are no men at home during the day. I loved being with my daughter but found it terribly solitary.

After eleven months as a dedicated Mr. Mom, I returned to a different job at CARE. I had become proficient at changing diapers, cleaning baby bottles, vacuuming, cooking, doing the laundry and, most important, hanging out with the kid.

The experience was another defining moment in my life. Year after year working in an office job tend to blur together, but this time with my daughter will always stand out as being special for both of us. My survival made it possible.

When I returned to CARE, the organization was in the midst of planning a major move from New York to Atlanta. We looked forward to getting to know a new part of the country and threw in our hats to make the change. It wasn't difficult to leave the New York area after five years.

My philosophy had always been a "be here now" approach toward work and living life to the fullest. This was well-established long before flight #414 crashed in Honduras. I was considered to be a bit off-beat and kind of "crazy" from an early age. I loved to have a good time as often as possible, and had little regard for what others thought of me, sometimes to a fault. I was never cowed by individuals in higher positions and relished questioning authority. I liked to shock people and do strange things that sometimes got me in trouble. I had always been outspoken, opinionated and, at times, obnoxious. My mother used to tell me after I had crossed the line, "Curtis, you never learned your limits!" The plane crash did not change my philosophy toward life. It did help me slow down and set priorities, with family and myself.

The issue of work continued to be a source of concern for me. As the years progressed, I found it increasingly more difficult to work in an office setting. CARE provided me with plenty of opportunities, an excellent salary and compelling work. Yet I was not content working there. What was wrong? I couldn't just walk out the door, and financially it was important to continue working. Magaly enrolled in a master's program in psychology after our move to Atlanta, and I was the sole breadwinner. Nevertheless, something was eating away at me, and I had to pay attention to it.

In 1996, my position at CARE was eliminated in a major reorganization, and I decided to take the severance money and move on. This was the opportunity I had been looking for, but I had no idea what else I might do. I went to a career counselor, who put me through some tests and helped me look at different options that I could pursue. At this time, Magaly graduated with a master's degree in psychology. She was ready to launch a new career as a counselor, just as I was looking for a change in my life. It wasn't clear to me what I was looking for, but I felt unsettled. In retrospect, the unfinished business of surviving the plane crash was still bothering me, still at work in my unconscious.

Moving to California loomed as an option because we were looking for a change and found the West Coast attractive. CARE had no sooner eliminated my position than Magaly and I decided to sell our home of three years and move into an apartment to save money. We thought this would be a temporary situation until we were ready to move West. We put the house on the market just as the Olympics started in Atlanta, with no great expectations. One of the first people to walk through the door made an offer. Within two months we had sold the house and were living in a gated apartment community.

CARE offered me a temporary position for six months, and Magaly secured a counseling job with a county mental health program. Our plans to leave Atlanta were put on hold. I stayed at CARE for two more years, but continued to look for the source of what was bothering me. During this period I took several night classes (Recovering Your Creative Self; How to Be a Standup Comedian), went to a palm reader, participated in an intensive weekend self-actualization group, started seeing a Jungian analyst and attended an eight-week dream interpretation group. I was searching for something.

Over time I became more aware of my dreams. It was apparent that there was a disturbing pattern in my unconscious. I frequently found myself lost no matter where I was, in a store, in a restaurant or on a road. I not only was lost, but I was unable to find my way out. The other recurring dream was being naked in front of other people. This was repeated in different settings but the feeling was always one of discomfort. I wasn't taking my clothes off to amuse people (as I had done many times in my youth) but instead found myself naked in front of people who I didn't know or in formal settings where I stood to lose face by being naked, by being exposed. Both dreams made me uncomfortable and were so vivid that sometimes I woke up in the dark of night wondering if the dream had actually accoured.

The dream of being lost potentially represented confusion and a lack of satisfaction in my life, which was further exacerbated by my feelings of vulnerability, the nakedness. I eventually became Chief of Staff at CARE working closely with the President, but took the job on the condition that I would leave after sixteen months. I had ascended to an executive position in one of the world's largest non-profit organizations, yet I was putting limits on how long I would be willing to do it even before starting the job. I had never had a better job-salary, benefits, responsibility, authority and status all exceeded anything I had done previously, but something was missing.

Each of these experiences gave me insights into myself and my own strengths and weaknesses. I felt inadequate in the class on creativity, because I found myself surrounded by accomplished, albeit frustrated, artists who had allowed an event in their lives to stymie their creative capacity. The comedy class was an attempt to be creative and wound up being one of the most nerve-wracking experiences of my life. The last class required a standup routine at a comedy club. I was glad to get through it without forgetting my lines and fortunately got a few laughs but not enough to return to the stage. The palm reader told me that I was on this earth to witness history, whatever that means, and the dream group helped me understand what I was dissatisfied about. The self-actualization group helped me decide to leave CARE. The standard line of the group leader to a reluctant participant was, "What are you waiting for, you're going to die anyway."

We continued to move during this period (which may have represented my conscious actualization of being lost) going from the apartment to a condominium and within a year back to a house. We were experts at packing, moving and unpacking, but were never quite clear about why we were moving and what we were looking for. The job dissatisfaction and the wanderlust of constantly looking for a new place to live were reflected in my dreams. These dreams were not nightmares, but they made me uncomfortable and were more vivid than most dreams.

Magaly did not object to the moves. In part, she was experiencing her own emotional instability by going through a radical career transition. A lifelong dream was realized when she successfully completed a masters program in psychology and launched a career in psycho-therapy. This was quite a departure from her MBA background in finance and management. She told me years later that she felt she had to be supportive of my desire to move, "How could I say no to you after all that you had been through?"

Like it or not, I was a different person after the crash and it manifested itself in unusual or odd behavior. We lived in a lovely home that the entire family enjoyed, but I insisted on selling it and moving into an apartment. I had an excellent job, but I chose to limit how long I would do it and then resigned at a time when my career had reached a pinnacle of success. Dissatisfaction, discomfort and confusion over what I wanted and where I wanted to live may have been symptoms of post-traumatic stress syndrome. I had put so much energy into working and succeeding as if that was the answer to what was bothering me or to what made me feel inadequate. It clearly was not.

I finally left CARE in May 1998. My departure had little to do with CARE and everything to do with confronting my inner conflicts. This was the end of one phase of my life and the beginning of another. I wasn't sure what would come next, but I knew I had to deal with the experience of the crash in some manner.

I was still struggling with survivor's guilt and a whole host of issues from the crash that left me angry, frustrated and unhappy. It was as if I had been living a double identity. My outer persona was calm and collected. I rarely showed emotion related to the crash either as a manager in a high-pressure setting or as a father and husband in a busy family. I was always under control. Underneath all of that control, though, was a person who still felt burned and battered, who needed to grieve and heal from the crash experience. A new journey in my life was just beginning. My plan was to do consulting work and start documenting the crash experience. For the first time since I survived, I wanted to find and talk to the other survivors.

CHAPTER EIGHT

THE OTHER SURVIVORS

Do not fear death. Fear the unlived life.
-Angus Tuck, Tuck Everlasting

Nine years after the crash, I was home in Atlanta on a Saturday night and heard my wife, Magaly, call out, "Curt, come in here and watch this!" On television, an attractive woman was being interviewed in Spanish. She was talking about her experiences with burns, and as I listened I felt a tingling sensation throughout my body. I did not recognize her, but she was describing her survival of the crash of flight #414.

The woman was Vivian Pellas, a Nicaraguan, who had escaped the aircraft along with her husband. They subsequently built a burn unit in Managua for children. I felt an immediate bond with her as a fellow survivor and was inspired by her humanitarian commitment.

For years I had chosen to have nothing to do with anyone else who had suffered as a result of this tragedy. My focus was on my own recovery and nothing more. This chance viewing of another survivor was a clear indication to me that I needed to open myself up to the full effect of the plane crash, something I had avoided doing up to that point.

The quest to better understand this event in my life motivated me to begin talking to other survivors and people associated with the crash with the intent of documenting the experience. My research took me to different parts of the United States and Central America. I believed that everyone who had been associated with the tragedy had a story to tell. I was particularly interested in the other survivors and what had happened to them since the crash, but was haunted, too, by a passenger list that I had kept on my desk for years. Who were all these people whose lives were extinguished in such a cruel manner? Didn't they deserve more than simply being relegated to a list of the deceased?

I initiated my journey of research and documentation by writing my own account. Confronting this experience after nine years brought me face-to-face with my long dormant fears, frustration and anger over what had happened and how it had affected me. My journey became a personal pursuit that forced me to examine my own healing along with others who had experienced painful survival or catastrophic loss. Thornton Wilder was right, either life is orchestrated for us or it's just one big experiment.

Surviving a plane crash that killed most of the passengers and crewmembers was a defining event for all fifteen of us who walked or were carried away from the raging fuselage on October 21, 1989. Survival was just the first step in returning to some semblance of a normal life. With the exception of the Captain and the First Officer, the survivors suffered varying degrees of burns, fractures and wounds. For some, physical recovery became a never-ending pursuit. Others found that, struggling with the memories of their trauma made life arduous. A few survivors experienced long, anguishing physical rehabilitation and then resumed their lives more fully than before the crash.

All of the survivors have lived with the terror and trauma of having been in an airplane that crashed. No matter how our lives have evolved, all of us will carry this experience around in our psyche until we go to our graves.

Each survival experience was unique and personal. How each person dealt with that experience was also unique and personal. What worked for one survivor may have been impossible for another. Something as basic as flying again was relatively easy for some of the survivors, even to the point of traveling more frequently after the crash. Others got on a plane only if they had to, and some not at all. Only a handful of the survivors sought psychological counseling. Instead they relied on the strength of their character, the support of their partners and families and, in some cases, their strong religious faith to get them through the worst moments and to help them forge ahead with their lives.

Ten of the fifteen survivors emerged from the wreckage with their spouses or traveling companions. There is no explanation for this except that four of the five pairs remained conscious throughout the impact period and remained aware enough to help the other person get out of the plane. Tegucigalpa Fire Department spokesman Francisco Medina said at the crash site, "Most of the people died from the searing heat inside the fuselage. Only the few who could escape before the jet burst into flames survived. There were maybe five or ten minutes before the plane exploded and was consumed by fire, which gave some people the opportunity to get out."

TAN SAHSA Flight 414 – Seating locations of survivors

Captain
Raul Argueta

First Officer
Reinero Canales

Flight Attendant
Guiomar Nuñez

Flight Attendant
Nivia Umanzor

Gene Van Dyk

Ramon Sanchez Borba

Curt Schaeffer and Evenor Lopez

Vivian Pellas and Carlos Pellas

Lea Browning (seated in the
middle of the fuselage but
unable to pinpoint location)

Hernan Madrid

Ron Devereux and Helen Devereux

Rosario Ubeda Gonzalez

As detailed in Chapter One, Ron Devereux pulled his wife Helen from her seat. Carlos Pellas urged his wife Vivian to unfasten her seatbelt and escape. First Officer Reinero Canales gave Captain Argueta a hand in climbing out, and Purser Nivia Umanzor reentered the burning plane and carried Flight Attendant Trainee Guiomar Nuñez to safety. Evenor Lopez, who was sitting next to me, escaped on his own, but then ran into his good friend and traveling companion Hernan Madrid on the mountainside as they were fleeing the wreckage. These people survived because they were conscious after the impact, acted quickly, and were able to move about to save themselves and their traveling companions. We know from various accounts that additional passengers survived the impact but were semi-conscious and/or unable to move from their seats and escape the plane.

It is a miracle that there were any survivors at all. The plane flew out of a cloud right into the mountainside. One possible mitigating factor was that the pilots did have a few seconds to try to pull the plane back up into the air and, in so doing, caused the nose to break off. Most of the survivors were sitting in the front of the plane. It was propitious, too, that the aircraft made impact on a small but relatively flat soccer field and not on the rougher terrain of the surrounding mountainside.

The healing processes of the survivors followed no formula. It was clear from talking to most of them that there were no easy answers or pat approaches to the conundrum of how to rebuild their lives after surviving the trauma of a plane crash. I was struck by the fact that the survivors I met and talked with did not waste time blaming the pilots or the airline for what happened. They recognized their good fortune and appeared to be a collectively positive group, intent on looking ahead and not back.

VIVIAN AND CARLOS PELLAS

Prior to October 21, 1989, Vivian and Carlos Pellas lived a comfortable life befitting one of the wealthiest families in Nicaragua. They maintained residences in Managua and Miami and wanted for nothing materially. Everything changed when they survived TAN SAHSA flight #414. From their hospital beds, the couple concluded that they had been saved for a reason. They decided that it was their destiny to do something more in life than they had been doing previously.

I contacted the couple through a friend and met with them at an upscale restaurant in Managua in October 2000 on my first trip to

Nicaragua. It was the first time we had seen each other since we had traveled together in the small pickup truck from the crash site to the hospital in Tegucigalpa. The Pellas had commandeered the truck that took five of us into Tegucigalpa and safety.

Vivian Pellas, who was thirty-one at the time of the crash, is a small woman with tremendous energy and enthusiasm for life. She is a native of Cuba and was raised in Honduras. Vivian is stunningly beautiful, with long flowing hair, and has an ability to get right to the heart of a matter without being pushy. She was forced to endure a lengthy and painful recovery period owing to a combination of third degree burns and multiple fractures. Vivian is my inspiration for writing this book and is a beacon of hope for numerous Nicaraguans who benefit from her efforts to help others, particularly children with burns.

Carlos Pellas is a short, stocky man in his late forties who is relaxed and prefers not to talk about the crash. He shows no outward signs of having been through such a horrible experience, except for having three rubber fingers on his right hand. A successful businessman in Nicaragua and Chairman of Miami-based Popular Bank, Carlos comes from the Chamorro family, one of Nicaragua's best-known families.

When she arrived in Miami after the crash, Vivian was unable to speak because her jaw was broken. While laying in her hospital bed recovering, Vivian kept muttering through clenched teeth that she was going to build a hospital for children with burns in Nicaragua. She was barely intelligible, but her family understood her desire. Vivian had long been involved in charitable fundraising in Nicaragua, but now she was determined to do much more.

From their hospital beds, Vivian and Carlos started sending money to Nicaragua to establish a burn unit for children. They eventually set up a nonprofit association, and the burn unit was built as a wing of a public facility, Hospital Fernando Paiz.

Vivian and Carlos were living in Miami at the time of the crash, but had been in Managua the previous week to participate in a charity fundraiser put on by the *Damas Diplomaticas de Nicaragua.* (Female Diplomats of Nicaragua). The night before taking flight #414, Vivian Pellas danced in a fundraising performance at the Embassy of Spain in Managua to support programs for poor children. She remembers feeling sad. Something was wrong, almost as if she knew that her life was about to change irrevocably.

Since the crash and her recovery, dancing has become even more of a passion for Vivian. She organizes three shows a year in Managua to bring artists and the public together and focus attention on the efforts of her foundation. These shows, presented at the *Teatro Ruben Dario*, represent Vivian's celebration of life and symbolize her commitment to helping others live with dignity.

Vivian stated with conviction, "With these performances we show the kids that through dance one can help others. In Nicaragua, eight thousand people are burned every year and seventy percent are children. Only a fourth of them are treated in hospitals. The rest are crippled for life and worst of all, they are unable to be a part of society. Part of our job is to integrate them back into society. Otherwise, they sit in a corner or stay inside their house for years because of shame. It is not only about healing the burns but also about bringing the victims back to life."

In 1993, Vivian and Carlos established *Asociacion Pro-Ninos Quemados De Nicaragua* (The Association for the Burnt Children of Nicaragua). Vivian explained their commitment, "I had to do something for children because of the pain I felt, the pain of burns. It is terrible. I had to wear a mask for two-and-a-half years. I recovered because I have been in good hands, but not everyone has the same good fortune. At the hospital where they attended burn victims, there really was no burn unit. The rooms where they kept the children had windows to the streets, and often they died from contamination."

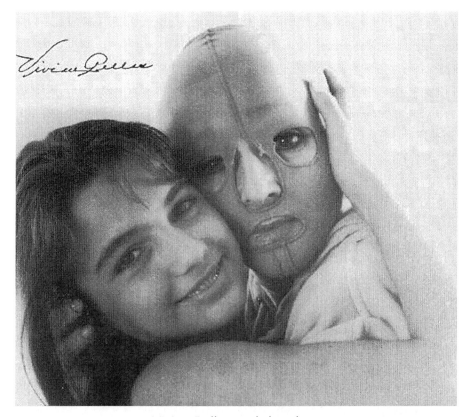

Vivian Pellas and daughter

Vivian and Carlos built the burn unit that has operating rooms for pediatric reconstructive surgery operations. Along with the staff of the Association, they go throughout the country with national and international medical brigades like Human Relief Organization, Doctors for Peace from Virginia, Interplast from California and doctors from Switzerland and Italy. The burn unit service helps children from all over Nicaragua safely and effectively recover from burns.

In addition to the burn unit, the Pellas' subsequently built a first-class private hospital in Managua-the Hospital Metropolitano Vivian Pellas. One of the services it offers is to treat burned children from all over Central America. As Vivian explains, "We are thinking of Central America because we are poor countries and we have the same needs." The hospital has been designed to give specialized attention to all burn victims, patients with congenital deformities and patients who require reconstructive plastic surgery. It offers a full range of quality medical services. Ground was broken in April 2002 and the much-anticipated hospital facility opened on May 31, 2004.

In reflecting on the horrifying experience of surviving flight #414, Vivian stated, "Never, never did I think I could be burned. I always have liked to help others, but I believe that the feeling was dormant, because one grows up with many inhibitions and prejudices, which stunt personal development. When I had the accident, I found out that there are more important things in life and that inhibitions should just go to hell. I believe I died and came back to life."

The Pellases credit their motivation to survive and thrive to their strong faith and their three children, who were all under ten years of age at the time of the crash. Vivian and Carlos suffered significant burns and fractures and remained hospitalized for months in Miami. Vivian had sixty-two bone fractures in her face, a broken jaw and broken collarbones along with a number of third degree burns. Carlos had third-degree burns, lost three fingers and suffered a serious head injury. The Pellas' were treated in a hospital just blocks away from Jackson Memorial where I was being attended to.

Vivian explains her survival in the following manner, "I am convinced that I am not here by chance. I can only attribute my survival to the will of God. A will with a clear purpose –to carry out a mission in our poor country of Nicaragua. A mission I have interpreted as changing tears into smiles."

In 1999, Vivian Pellas was recognized for her dedication to Nicaraguan children. She was presented with the award "Servitor Pacis," by the Catholic Church through the Path to Peace Foundation under the Holy Office of the Vatican's Seat to the United Nations. Upon receiving the award, Vivian said, "I want those who have money and power to know that the greatest satisfaction in life comes from helping others, not from the accumulation of riches and power."

Working in service to others, sharing who you are and sharing what you are may be one of the most noble and healing experiences in life.

The Pellas' have used the crash of flight #414 as a springboard for helping others. They do not dwell on the crash and its impact upon them, but instead look ahead to plan and determine how they can best use their time and resources to benefit others.

On the wall behind the desk in Vivian Pellas' office is the following quote:

> *Little One: I shall shade you with my tresses*
> *And in the wind, I shall search*
> *For the coolness to relieve your pain.*
> *And if the fire still burns,*
> *I shall extinguish it with my tears...*

Vivian and Carlos Pellas middle – flanked by the Schaeffers

RAUL ARGUETA

Captain Raul Argueta walked away from the crash of flight #414 unscathed. *La Tribuna* in Tegucigalpa reported that the forty-seven-year-old pilot had a small cut on his right arm, but that was the extent of his injuries. Another miraculous survival story.

From the time that he was found wandering around on the mountainside, Captain Argueta said that he did not remember what occurred. His wife told the press three days after the crash that he was suffering from "nervous shock" and could not speak to the press, because he had no memory of the crash. The pilot was also ordered by the airline not to talk to the press for legal protection. A brother-in-law admitted that Captain Argueta had talked with the NTSB investigators and with officials from TAN SAHSA Airlines within days of the crash "but only about technical questions."

It is possible that Captain Argueta did not remember those final moments on the mountainside, and it is possible that he claimed loss of memory as a means of avoiding the horror of what happened. I don't remember, so therefore I am not responsible. This could well have been his own way of protecting himself through real or imagined amnesia caused by shock.

Known as the *tiburon* (shark) by his friends, Argueta was considered to be one of Honduras' more experienced pilots. He was licensed to fly in 1976 and was promoted to captain in 1983. He had logged more than 20,000 hours on different types of aircraft and had passed a complete physical less than a month before the crash.

I was told by several sources close to TAN SAHSA Airlines at the time of the crash that Argueta called the offices of the carrier on the day of the crash from his hospital bed and asked when he would be flying again. It was reported, too, that he kept asking for the other crew members and was told that they all survived.

Life has not been easy for the Captain of flight #414. Shunned by society, he lives in isolation, a virtual recluse in the middle of a forest. He is not able to practice his profession, and there remains the possibility that someone might hold him responsible for the crash and attempt to harm him.

REINERO CANALES

Unlike Captain Argueta, Canales spoke with members of the press on numerous occasions from his hospital bed. He openly theorized about what had caused the tragedy, and may well have been using the press as a forum for soothing his own guilty conscience.

On October 24, 1989 only days after the crash, he made a statement to the press that he planned to continue flying. In the statement he said that his survival was not luck, but a miracle of God. He told the press that he had always been a good Catholic, but now would be even closer to God and to his wife who was pregnant at the time. Canales has three children and stated that the first thing he thought of after surviving the crash was his children.

Reinero Canales speaking with the press days after the crash

According to Canales, he returned to the plane to save four passengers. Nivia Umanzor confirmed that the first officer helped free Guiomar Nuñez before the Purser carried her out of the plane. There is no other report of survivors being saved or helped by either Canales or Argueta. The Devereuxes reported that they saw both Canales and Argueta after fleeing the wreckage, and called to them for help but were ignored.

Reinero Canales had worked for TAN SAHSA for three years and had fifteen years experience (eight of those in the Honduran Air Force) as a pilot, logging a total of 6,653 hours. He was divorced after the crash and has since remarried and lives in San Pedro Sula. Like Captain Argueta, Canales has not worked again as a pilot.

Canales' second wife is Patricia Rosenthal, the daughter of Jaime Rosenthal who is among the wealthiest men in Honduras.

GUIOMAR NUÑEZ

Guiomar Nuñez had a full day planned for herself the day the plane went down. After the scheduled arrival in Tegucigalpa, she had an appointment to do some photography work and then was going to meet friends in the afternoon. She was twenty years old, beautiful and seemingly in control of her life. Launching a new career with the Honduran airline was just one of her many pursuits. Life was full and she was happy.

Guiomar related to me in a 1999 conversation that this all changed on October 21, 1989. The experience of struggling to survive over the next year forced her to grow up more quickly than she had planned. The crash had a profound impact on Guiomar. She has suffered from bouts of depression over the years while forging ahead with marriage, childrearing, studying for a university degree and embarking on a new career. She has done all of these things successfully, with the support and love of her husband.

Guiomar Nuñez, now the attractive mother of two young children, is in her thirties. She has managed to get on with her life both professionally and personally, but there is a sadness in her face and in the way she carries herself. It is apparent from talking with her that she continues to feel the effects of the enormous trauma of surviving a plane crash. She wept through much of our conversation when we met and talked at a Tegucigalpa McDonalds. Guiomar had to excuse herself several times to go to the restroom. Life continues to be a struggle for her, and reliving the horror of the crash was just too much at times.

The trainee flew to Houston just after the crash. She stayed there for a year and a half, because her recovery was complicated by respiratory problems, broken ribs, a punctured lung and the loss of blood not to mention two broken collarbones and numerous skin grafts for burns. She was close to dying three different times and experienced a heart attack during her convalescence. As she struggled to deal with her physical and psychological woes, Guiomar was further devastated by the news that TAN SAHSA, her employer, wanted to have nothing to do with her.

While she was in the hospital in Houston, she was introduced to a group of family members of deceased passengers who were in Texas to file a class action lawsuit against the airline and the owner of the plane-Continental Airlines. Among the group members was a woman who greeted her and kept catching her eye during numerous meetings over the period of a week. The day before the group was scheduled to return to Honduras the woman approached her and said, "Guiomar, I can't wait any longer. I want to know if you remember my daughter." The woman gave her the name of her daughter, but Guiomar told her that she couldn't remember names or faces of passengers from the crash. Then, like a good mother, she pulled out a photo of her daughter and showed it to Guiomar. There was immediate recognition. Yes, she remembered serving drinks to this young girl and joking around with her.

Guiomar told the mother, "I remember serving her three coffees and we laughed a lot. She rested with her head on the window of the plane and I remember that she wore a pink sport shirt."

"I told the mother all that I remembered. It was so vivid in my mind. She had an incredible look on her face and hugged and kissed me as if she were finally at peace. I felt like I had been privileged to be able to serve her daughter."

In spite of this experience, Guiomar has not been able to look up family members of deceased passengers to whom she attended that day on the plane. In some cases she knows who the passengers were and who their families are in Tegucigalpa. Guiomar told me that reliving the experience and talking about it with anyone is too terribly painful for her. "My heart aches."

One of her greatest obstacles has been overcoming her own fear of flying. She said in our meeting, that approach and landing have been particularly difficult for her to deal with. She related the story of a mother who boarded flight #414 in San José with two young girls. She remembers taking care of the girls, who were terrified of flying and crying from fear. The flight attendant trainee took the girls up to the cockpit to meet the pilots and hopefully begin to overcome their fears. They did not survive the crash, and thinking about these girls and other passengers she took care of that day is almost more than she can bear.

Like others who were affected by the crash, Guiomar finds the anniversary each year to be a time of sadness and depression. She has attended a few anniversary masses in Tegucigalpa but has never been able to return to the site of the crash on Cerro de Hula.

At the same time, she told me how fortunate we were to have survived this tragedy and the fact that she gives thanks every day for being alive. I thanked her for encouraging me to sit in the front of the plane when we boarded in San José. I am convinced that she saved my life, and it was gratifying to finally have a chance to tell her. I know that was not her only generous act that day, but Guiomar was truly touched to be thanked for her kindness to me.

We talked about survivor's guilt and how it has plagued us over the years, knowing that we were somehow chosen to survive when so many lost their lives. Guiomar stated that she thinks God has a special plan for us and that there is something more for us to do in this life.

Before leaving the restaurant, Guiomar said to me, "I have been thinking about this meeting since last night, and when I saw you I felt something in my heart, my blood flowed faster and the heart beat stronger. I didn't know you before and we were together just a brief time, but we were united forever, and now I give thanks to God for seeing you again."

NIVIA UMANZOR

I met Nivia Umanzor in Tegucigalpa the day after interviewing Guiomar Nuñez. The Purser for flight #414 is a self-confident, strong-willed woman. Her life changed radically after the crash. In spite of suffering numerous setbacks, Nivia was upbeat and maintained a positive attitude-the kind of attitude you would expect from a person who was always in charge, always responsible for the crew and the passengers.

Four days after the crash, Nivia traveled to Houston for medical attention. She went through months of physical and psychological therapy. Nivia had two operations to remove glass from her head and suffered from burns all over her body, including her feet. Her back and coccyx were fractured. During her stay in Houston, Nivia was required to see a psychologist as a part of her treatment. She talked with the counselor about the possibility of working again as a flight attendant. The recommendation was to look for different work. Working again as a flight attendant could potentially trigger anxiety and create problems for her, such as landing in Tegucigalpa or flying through fog.

While the pilots were taken care of by the airline, Nivia was treated like a pariah. She was refused employment or any compensation for her service to the airline or for the trauma experienced from the crash. Her plans before the crash were to retire in ten months, but she wasn't given that opportunity. Twenty-nine years of dedicated work were lost. Nivia felt she was deceived and defrauded by an airline that she gave her professional life to. It was only after she and Guiomar Nuñez joined with a group of family members of deceased passengers in a legal action that they were able to wrestle some compensation from TAN SAHSA's insurer. Nivia went twenty-two months without any income while incurring medical costs and struggled to keep her family and home together until a settlement was finally reached.

Nivia told me, "You can never forget. It seems like it happened yesterday. The pain is always there, trapped among my memories. It still makes me nervous, and I would like to forget about it. Carrying this experience around is hard for me and sometimes I feel like I just can't deal with it."

Not flying on a regular basis was the biggest adjustment for her. For close to thirty years she had lived an unusual life, with demands on her time that made it impossible to lead a normal life or to develop close friendships. Over the years, Nivia missed numerous family gatherings and special events. She felt even more isolated after the crash, and being shunned by the airline only made it worse. Trying to make do with no income forced her to sell her home and put enormous strain on her family.

During our conversation, Nivia was open and candid with me and said she had dealt with the trauma by talking about it with others. "I was ready to die, but I have been reborn. This experience has brought me closer to God. He was merciful with me because I was never fearful about dying and to this day have no trouble flying. I am not sure what God wants me to do or expects of me since he chose me to live," Nivia told me in a soft but confident voice.

Nivia is proud of her career and looks back with fondness over the many years of air travel with the Honduran airline. She is grateful for the many opportunities to travel all over the world. Nivia was a hero on that October morning. Years of experience and training gave her the wherewithal to return to the burning, exploding aircraft in a weakened condition, find Guiomar and then carry her to safety. She continues to live her life with the same vigor and conviction that she demonstrated throughout her career.

HELEN AND RON DEVEREUX

"When it's a choice of burning alive, you could squeeze your way out of a tin can," Ron Devereux told a group of reporters huddled around his hospital bed the night of the crash. Helen Devereux was in bed in the same room, listening to her husband's description of the crash and later told me, "I learned the true horror of the crash as I listened to Ron talk to the reporters. The chilling truth seeped into my mind. I could only ask, what if! I was devastated. I could not touch him. We were ten feet apart in beds on each side of the room. What do you say to your husband who has rescued you from a hideous and agonizing death? There are no words. If I could have cuddled and held him, words would not have been needed, but he was in so much pain a cuddle was the last thing he needed from me."

Ron Devereux was fifty years old and his wife Helen forty-seven at the time of the crash. The handsome couple spent twenty-one days in Honduras (much of it in the hospital), until they were cleared to return home.

Ron's heroic efforts after the crash are even more impressive given the extent of his injuries. His left ear was practically torn off and left dangling. Three ribs were broken. His left arm where the hot wires draped over him suffered third degree burns, and his right ankle was broken with little more than a bit of flesh and muscle keeping it connected.

The left ankle was broken as well and he had numerous cuts, gashes and burns all over his arms and legs.

Helen was more fortunate suffering burns to her feet and left leg. Falling luggage struck her head and opened a scalp wound and left her with severe neck muscle damage. She also had burns and cuts up and down her legs and arms.

The Devereuxes were treated well by numerous Hondurans, medical staff, new friends, well wishers and the curious. At night, though, they were alone and lonely. Their primary interest was to go home, and the long wait felt like an eternity. After numerous delays and frustrations, they were given tranquilizers, pain killers and sleeping pills and left for Australia on a long, circuitous route that took them from Tegucigalpa to Houston to Amsterdam to London to Singapore to Perth. It was a cruel but necessary means of getting home, leaving Honduras on Wednesday at 6 A.M. and arriving in Australia on Friday at 7 P.M. This may have been a test for the couple when they least wanted to be tested. It is amazing what people will do if they want something badly enough, in this case simply to go home.

Magaly and I met the Devereuxes for dinner in New York several years after the crash. We spent the evening recounting our experiences the day of the crash and since. The painful memories were still fresh in our minds.

Recovery was challenging not only because of the physical and psychological pain that they suffered every day, but also because of battles with insurance companies. Worry over their financial situation left them tired and stressed out. Like other survivors, they continued to be incredulous about their fate. As Helen Devereux told me, "We survived. Too many men, women and children did not. It is a nightmare that will not go away. A word, a gesture, a sound-and it all tumbles back into your mind again. Whenever I see little girls, it cuts me up."

Ron Devereux still wrestles with the question that people want to ask him but are afraid to; "Do you feel any guilt at not saving the girl who was sitting next to you and your wife?" Ron explains, "At the time I wondered if I could have done more. Helen was off the fuselage and alive. I suppose if she was at that moment still inside, I would have gone in again. If that had been the case you wouldn't be reading this today. There simply wasn't enough time."

Over the years, the Devereuxes have struggled with their strong feelings towards the pilots. They believe that the pilots were "truly evil, macho men" who were "playing with our lives." In their worse moments they have thought it "a pity they didn't die."

The couple employed a number of coping skills to help them get on with their lives. The first thing they did was to change their lifestyle by simplifying it. The business, the large home and most of the material possessions had to go. Their home was sold with most of the furniture in it.

They made a pilgrimage to England and Ireland on a Russian freighter to get away and to look for records of Helen's ancestors. She felt a need to document her Irish ancestry, to obtain her Irish Nationality and, in the process, make a connection with her past. Helen would always be Australian, but as she said, "The need to establish my Irishness was great." They also spent time tracking down records of her mother's family in England. She was proud of the fact that her mother's family could be traced back to 1690.

The final and most important change in their lives was purchasing a ship that would serve as a "moveable home." They found a mid-water trawler used in the North Sea and converted it into a three-masted, gaff-rigged sailing schooner. After years of continuous work, the couple enjoys their simple life on the work.

Ron has found the ship an important diversion. He feels as if the constant demands of converting and refurbishing their new home have served to keep his mind off the past. As he says, "I had a glimpse of hell, so I try to live every day the best I can. It doesn't always work, but still I try."

Similarly, Helen explains, "The lifestyle we set for ourselves has been rewarding and we have made many new friends along the way. Our next goal to achieve is the management and running of a sailing ship. However, these extra years are a bonus. We should have died in that plane crash on the mountainside on that day in October 1989 in Honduras. Each day is precious."

Ron and Helen feel fortunate to be alive and to be able to enjoy their devoted daughter Marion and grandson, Mason. Ron has chronic pain in his ankle, and Helen still has restricted head movement as a result of the muscle damage. They are the best of friends and celebrated their 45th wedding anniversary in December 2005.

The Devereuxes avoided flying for years and traveled instead by rail and by ship. In recent years, they have made an annual trek to Perth (twenty-two hour trip by air) to escape the English winter and to visit friends and family.

GENE VAN DYK

A gravely wounded and burned Gene Van Dyk was so comforting to Nivia Umanzor that fateful day, from the time they met on the mountainside and throughout the ride into Tegucigalpa, that she subsequently wrote a letter of thanks to the United States Embassy. Based on that letter and another letter from the Australians, Gene Van Dyk received the State Department Award for Valor. This award is presented to U.S. government employees overseas "who have demonstrated outstanding performance under unusually difficult or dangerous circumstances that require exceptional personal bravery and perseverance to complete any assignment." The award was presented to Gene at a ceremony at the State Department in September 1991.

When Dr. Steve Johnson, the US Embassy physician, found Gene Van Dyk in the hospital, he had an intravenous solution attached to his foot dripping one drop at a time. Gene looked up at the doctor and said, "I am going to die. Get me out of here."

Johnson knew that Gene's extensive burns required attention, and he decided to move him immediately. Van Dyk was taken out of the hospital and loaded into an ambulance. Word had been relayed to the U.S. Airbase in Palmerola to send a helicopter to Tegucigalpa to pick up Gene. Johnson drove the ambulance at high speed to the airport with a colleague, Shelly Schwartz, hanging out the window screaming, *"Emergencia! Emergencia! Emergencia!"* They drove right out to the tarmac, and by the time they arrived, Shelly was almost naked. During the trip he had shed most of his clothes to cover Gene to help him stay warm.

Dr. Johnson and a nurse climbed into the helicopter with Van Dyk and his wife, and they took off for Palmerola. Upon arrival, they were met by a trauma team. The diagnosis was not good. Gene had multiple fractures and third-degree burns, including respiratory burns. He had to have a tube inserted into his larynx to prevent respiratory failure.

From Palmerola, Gene and his wife, Toko, flew on a C-140 military transport to Brooke Army Medical Center (BAMC) in San Antonio, Texas. The trip took five hours. He had low blood pressure, was in a severe state of shock, and nearly died en route.

Gene remained at Brooke for six months. This was followed by two months of additional surgeries and the beginning of an aggressive and lengthy rehabilitation program at the Washington Hospital Center in the nation's capital. He then went through ten months of outpatient rehabilitation therapy.

Gene Van Dyk was one survivor who stared death in the face the day of the crash and was forced to do it again and again throughout his recovery period. At one point, his military doctor in Texas gave Gene a forty percent chance of living. Sixty percent of his body was burned and most of the burns were third degree. Skin grafts were so common that they reached a point where there was no more skin on his body that could be found for grafts.

After close to a year of proving that he could survive, Gene did not exercise his option to retire from the U.S. government. Instead, he returned to work in Washington and subsequently was assigned to a U.S. government accounting operation in Bonn, Germany. He retired in 1996.

His wife, Toko, supported Gene throughout his recovery period, and just as he was released from the hospital, she was diagnosed with breast cancer. They bravely worked through their setbacks and recovered.

Gene reflected on his experience in a 1999 conversation near San Francisco, California. "I spent six months at Brooke Army Medical. I went into surgery eleven times for multiple skin graft procedures and to repair my broken bones. My treatment was complicated by recurring skin and lung infections. Midway through my treatment, I developed a pulmonary embolism, which set me back several weeks. The daily multiple dressing changes were always painful. I was mostly bed-ridden and unable to move my extremities because of splints and dressings for much of my initial hospitalization. My joints became extremely stiff. I had to relearn how to walk. I could not move and bend my arms to feed myself. Having to depend on others for basically all my needs was very difficult for me. Also, being in a military hospital was more regimented than I was used to."

"The only bright moments I looked forward to every day were visits from Toko and others who came to see me. Toko stayed in military housing adjacent to the hospital and played host to many relatives and friends. She came twice a day to help feed me and keep me company. One thing she did to help me put my stay in perspective was to create a large wall calendar, which she used to record all kinds of information, including my various surgeries. My physicians came to rely on the wall calendar in the preparation of their daily reports. The only ones who did not appear to look favorably at the calendar were the chief military officials who made daily rounds and who were concerned about their patient stay averages. As the calendar continued to take more and more wall space, the top brass became more nervous. I actually believe the calendar resulted in the officials bending their discharge criteria. I was transferred to a civilian hospital earlier than was anticipated for my condition."

"After six months at BAMC, I was flown by commercial jet to Washington, D.C. I had mixed feelings about this trip, but was comforted by Toko and my former boss and good friend Shelly Schwartz. It took some work and effort, but Took was able to get the government to allow us to go first class. As I was still weak and very fragile, it was obvious I would have trouble negotiating the narrow economy passenger seats. Even getting into the first class seat was a little difficult and resulted in some additional skin damage. I am just grateful for the support and the tenacity that Toko demonstrated throughout this ordeal. I saw many burn patients in the hospital that had very few visitors or outside support. I don't know how they managed."

Gene was transferred to the Washington Hospital Center, which is an older hospital known for its regional burn unit. He spent two months at this hospital and underwent additional surgeries as well as beginning an aggressive rehabilitation program. Just prior to his release, Toko returned to Honduras to pack up their belongings. She thanked people for their help and made a visit to the crash site. She went to the farmhouse on the road below the crash site and visited with the lady who provided comfort to her husband. Toko expressed her gratitude to the woman and presented her with gifts and money.

"I required approximately ten months of outpatient rehabilitation therapy, on a daily basis seven of those months. I gradually was able to return to work, first on a part-time basis and then full-time. Some encouraged me to apply for a disability retirement, but to me anything short of going back to work would have meant failure. Going back to work was an affirmation of my well-being and something that I worked very hard to do. It was a good feeling to be back in a work environment. I knew that when I decided to stop working it would be my decision and on my terms, and not until I had proved to myself that I could perform as well, if not better, than before the crash."

Gene was informed in the summer of 1991 that he would be given an award for valor for assisting some of the survivors of the crash. He told me, "I still don't feel I did anything special to deserve this recognition. In fact, what bothers me most days when I think about the crash is that I didn't have the presence of mind to search for Bob and Rolando. I know I was extremely lucky just to have gotten myself out of the airplane, but I can only think they must have been close by and could possibly be alive today if I had only done more. The day of the award presentation I was overwhelmed by the kind words and standing ovation. It is a day I will not forget, but a day I wished I could have shared with both Bob and Rolando."

"What has helped us get through this difficult period in our lives? The strong love and support that we have for each other. We both enjoy life and each other very much. This has been the motivation that has helped us through these difficult times. Toko was there for me during my accident, and I have been there for her during her two bouts of breast cancer."

"Each person deals with these matters based on collective experiences and personal outlook toward life. Reading about other peoples' experiences can help. I know I was motivated by a television story about a dog that lost a back leg to an accident and later a front leg to a disease. This dog loves life and was able to get around and play on his two legs by using his tail to keep his balance. I found this amazing, and whenever I start to feel sorry for myself I think of this dog."

Gene and Toko experienced a role reversal after Gene's accident. She was forced to take the lead role in the relationship and run their lives fully after Gene was incapacitated. She became such a strong person that the military medical staff consulted with her on everything they did associated with Gene's treatment and care. Today, Gene and Toko live in retirement and split their time between California and Japan.

EVENOR LOPEZ

He has never looked back at his life before the crash. Evenor Lopez suffered second- and third-degree burns on forty-five percent of his body and underwent painful burn treatment in Houston. When he finally recovered and was able to return to Honduras, he became an advocate for others who survived plane crashes.

Numerous people connected with the air crash had mentioned Evenor Lopez to me, and I was finally successful in tracking him down through his restaurant in Tegucigalpa. After talking with Evenor by phone, I flew to San Pedro Sula and had lunch with him and another survivor, Hernan Madrid. Lopez and Madrid were good friends and had traveled to San José, Costa Rica, together to attend a management seminar at the Instituto Centroamericano de Administracion de Empresas (Central American Business Management Institute). They boarded the plane at the same time, but chose to sit in different parts of the aircraft. We determined later that Evenor sat next to me in the window seat of the fourth row and Hernan farther back in row seventeen, in front of the Devereuxes.

Six months after the crash, Evenor Lopez returned to Cerro de Hula and picked through the wreckage. He found some personal belongings of passengers, including the watch and wallet of his good friend Hernan Madrid. He has attended different anniversary masses.

Evenor Lopez subsequently married Gladys Aguilar de Portillo, a Honduran woman widowed by the crash. Her husband was Luis

Alfredo Portillo Flores, a twenty-nine year-old engineer and professor in the Industrial Engineering Department at the Centro Universitario Regional del Norte, Curn. Portillo Flores was returning from San José, where he attended the same seminar with Evenor and Hernan.

He credits the psychological counseling he received in a Houston hospital as being instrumental in helping him recover. He is comfortable traveling and flys approximately fifty times a year.

Lopez is best described as a resourceful man, who was involved in a number of businesses ventures, including a small restaurant in Tegucigalpa and rental property in San Pedro Sula. In addition, he worked for U.S. law firms by contacting survivors of plane crashes to secure their written commitment for legal representation.

In 1999, Evenor appeared on a special Univision television program called, *Sobreviventes de Tragedias* (Survivors of Tragedies) along with Nivia Umanzor and Napoleon Rodriguez. He was interviewed at the crash site on a beautiful, sunny day and said, "I was born again on this mountainside." He maintains a positive attitude about life and stays in contact with other survivors and family members of deceased passengers.

HERNAN MADRID

"I'm alive because God saved me," the Honduran university lecturer told me. "All the other people around me were crushed beneath steel, couldn't get out, and burned to death." Hernan Madrid was sitting in the central part of the plane. The hole that he spotted in the roof of the fuselage and then escaped through what may have been the hole that Ron Devereux had fashioned to save himself and his wife, Helen. Hernan survived the impact with few injuries, had the wherewithal to move around in search of an exit, and was close enough to an opening to escape the plane. Madrid and the

Devereuxes were the only passengers in the central part of the plane who survived.

Madrid escaped the plane with burns on the palms of his hands and a minor head injury from his tumble from the wing of the plane. His rehabilitation was short and he had the luxury of having his wife, an economist, temporarily take over his classes at the National Autónomous University. Madrid was thirty-nine years old at the time of the crash. He had five daughters and lived and taught in San Pedro Sula.

He credits his strong faith in God for helping him to recover from the crash and to readjust to life as a father and university professor. He told me, "God has always chosen people to live and yes, we were chosen." He said that he talks with his wife regularly about the air crash and the miracle of his survival. He was raised in the Presbyterian Church but converted to Catholicism as an adult.

The priest who assisted in his conversion told Hernan before the crash that he had been chosen by God. After surviving the crash, he reminded Hernan of what he had said and told him that God had a plan for his life.

Other than the pilots, Hernan was in the best shape to return to the plane and try to save other passengers. I asked him about this and he said that it was impossible to go back in because the plane was exploding and there was no way to reach the other passengers who were engulfed in flames.

Madrid has had other brushes with death during his life, and he said that trying to figure out why we survived is no different from trying to understand why we aren't on the street begging. There is no explanation.

Madrid's wife had a forewarning of the crash and had asked him not to travel to Costa Rica. She was sure that something would happen on the trip and cried over his leaving. Madrid told me that the crash had a greater impact on his wife than on him. He has been able to live normally and has never suffered from nightmares or any other common symptoms of post-traumatic stress disorder. For a long period of time after the crash, Madrid's wife woke up frequently during the night dreaming that he had died.

While he was in San José the week before the crash, Hernan was aware that he was praying more than ever before in his life. He woke up in the morning and immediately started reciting the prayer "Our Father." He said it over and over again throughout the day. He has no explanation for praying so much but wondered if he didn't unconsciously know that misfortune was stalking him.

Madrid believes that you can live normally after experiencing a trauma of great proportions, but readily admits that it has been easier for him to get his life back on track than it was for the other survivors who had serious physical problems. He carries no resentment toward the pilots and believes that is one reason he has been able to live normally since the crash.

His life since the crash has not been without setbacks. He invested some of the money he received from his settlement with the airline in a small coffee plantation. Unfortunately, it was ravaged by Hurricane Mitch in November 1998 and then closed down altogether in 2001 due to a poor market. It cost him more to harvest the coffee than it was worth.

Madrid remains optimistic and continues to hold down two jobs at different universities. He is carrying out his life plan which focuses on his family, Christianity and being successful. In the fall of 2001, he proudly told me that his oldest daughter was the number one student in the university. The other daughters have achieved academic excellence at their levels, and the family has truly distinguished itself as a group of scholars.

Author with Evenor Lopez (l) and Hernan Madrid (r)

SANCHEZ BORBA

I met with Ramon Sanchez Borba in his office at the Technological University of Central America (UNITEC) on the outskirts of Tegucigalpa in October, 2000. Ramon and his wife both work at the private, technical university serving 4,000 students. They were among a handful of people who helped found the school in 1987. The university is well regarded for academic excellence in Honduras and throughout Central America.

Sanchez Borba seemed surprised to find out that I was a fellow survivor, and even more surprised to know that we left the crash site together in the little pickup truck. I showed him my name on the survivor list and recounted my own experience, and then he shared his account with me. It has been interesting to discover how quickly I have bonded with fellow survivors after some initial discomfort. It is only natural when two people meet for the first time to take some time to warm up regardless of the circumstances.

Ramon and I met out of a genuine interest to know each other, tinged with curiosity over what the other looked like and how each of our lives had evolved since the crash. We became fast friends.

Ramon is convinced that God exists and was looking out for him the day of the crash and afterwards. He has had no fear of flying again and, in fact, he and his wife have traveled extensively since the crash to far-flung places like China, Egypt and Argentina. He continues to work at the university and clearly has a zest for life.

Like many of the other survivors, Sanchez Borba was not out of danger once he fled the mountainside. After spending several hours at the Hospital Escuela, Ramon was transferred to a private facility. As in my case, there was no one to drive the ambulance and his brother-in-law, a neuro-psychiatrist, had to take the wheel.

After a week at the Hospital Viera in Tegucigalpa, it was apparent that Sanchez Borba was not improving. His wife, Norma Ponce de Sanchez, told the press four days after the crash that he was on oxygen constantly and was unrecognizable. Before the crash Sanchez Borba had white skin, but with burns on much of his body he was described by his wife as looking like *"un San Benito de negrito"* (a little black saint).

Norma Ponce de Sanchez became so alarmed over her husband's worsening condition that she went to the TAN SAHSA offices and insisted on having him moved to a hospital in the United States. She wound up making the arrangements to transfer him to a hospital in Oklahoma City, Oklahoma. A cousin in Dallas helped her get a small plane into the country to take Ramon to Oklahoma and probably saved his life in the process.

For many years, Sanchez Borba functioned as the Paraguayan consul in Honduras and was a successful attorney, specializing in maritime law. In recent years he phased out of his law practice and dedicates full time to his job as rector at the university. He is currently organizing interested people to support the construction of a hospital in Tegucigalpa for burn victims.

FRANCISCA ROSARIO UBEDA GONZALEZ

Rosario Ubeda was transported to the Hospital Escuela in Tegucigalpa from the crash site. She initially was in serious condition with fractures of the pelvis, both legs and an arm but escaped the misery of burns. For a number of years after the crash, the Nicaraguan native helped her husband run a Mexican restaurant in Shreveport, Louisiana. I was unable to locate her.

DEBORAH LEA BROWNING

Ms. Browning lived in the Washington, D.C. area. I communicated with her by email on a number of occasions, but it never worked out for us to meet and talk about the crash and her life since that time. According to newspaper accounts, she was found unconscious at the crash site and taken to Hospital Escuela and then was flown to the University of Alabama Medical Center in Birmingham where she was treated for burns over 25 per cent of her body, a fractured vertebra and cranial trauma. Ms. Browning was returning to Washington, D.C. with Charles Anthony Friedrich-both human rights attorneys who had been working in Nicaragua as part of a pro bono project established to monitor presidential elections in Nicaragua sponsored by the International Human Rights Law Group (IHRLG).

***

I am proud to be a member of this group of fortunate few who survived the crash of flight #414. Some survivors risked their lives to save someone else, others like me were just lucky and still others defied all physical odds against them to survive. The one characteristic that stands out as a common thread through the lives of all the survivors with the possible exception of the pilots is that they do not want to dwell on the crash and what it has meant to their lives. As a group, all of us have all worked very hard to piece our lives back together and start anew. It has been easier for some than for others. We were given the rarest gift of all, a second chance in life.

CHAPTER NINE

THOSE LEFT BEHIND

*Only people who are capable of loving strongly can
also suffer great sorrow, but this same necessity of
loving serves to counteract their grief and heals them.*
Tolstoy

A tragedy of this magnitude leaves countless family members and
friends in its wake. I have talked to many of them in recent years in
Nicaragua, Honduras and the United States about their loss(es) and
the impact it has had on their lives. Those who lost family members in
the crash of flight #414 were survivors too. They had to repeatedly call
upon survival skills by first confronting the tragedy and then learning
to find fulfilling lives again. All of the surviving family members have
been marked by the experience. Life continued for some survivors

without parents; for others, without a spouse; and what may have been the cruelest loss of all, for those who carried on without children or grandchildren.

Forewarnings of a tragic event, either consciously or through dreams, were common among the passengers and their families prior to the crash of flight #414. There was no explanation for these premonitions, but there were enough of them to make one wonder.

A husband who lost his wife told me that she had been an extrovert-always smiling and outgoing with other people. After the crash, a friend gave the man a photo of his deceased wife that had been taken a day before she boarded #414. It struck him that, in the photo, his wife was looking down at the ground in a pensive pose. This was unlike her. That same day, she had also asked a friend in San José to take her to church to pray. This, too, was unusual, as his wife rarely went to church other than for Sunday worship.

A young man who was very religious told his family repeatedly over the years that he would die at thirty-three, the same age as Jesus Christ. On September 29, 1989 he turned thirty-three years and the crash occurred less than a month later. When his body was recovered by the family, he was one of the few that had not been burned.

A woman who lost her sister in the crash had a dream the week before the flight. In the dream, a pearl was suspended by a thread hanging over a vast, open expanse. The thread broke and the pearl fell to the ground. The woman believed the pearl to be her sister and in the dream she never saw her sister again. She shared the dream with her sister at the airport before she took off. This was not the first time that the sister had shared dreams and it had almost become a joke between them. On this particular day, the traveling sister, upon hearing about the dream, said, "uh, oh, here comes the witch again." She was intent on flying and ignored her sibling's dream. She was given one of the last available seats on the plane.

A young attorney, who was fourteen at the time of the crash, told me that he went to the airport to bid farewell to his departing uncle. He loved airplanes and being at the airport. That morning he was looking at the TAN SAHSA plane and immediately had a premonition that the plane would fall from the sky. He felt as if something was going to happen to his uncle and begged him not to take flight #414. The adults in the group found this amusing, and made jokes about his life insurance not being paid up. The teenager began praying for his uncle, but when he saw the plane take off, he admonished himself for believing something bad would happen. When he and his mother walked in the door of their house, there was a phone call informing them that the plane had indeed fallen from the sky.

Another man went to a small, rural church near the crash site to say confession the week before the plane went down. He had never been to this church and it was almost as if he were readying himself for death. The same man had visited his daughter in the United States months before the crash, and she felt that he was saying goodbye to her.

A mother was upset because her son left for Houston without saying goodbye to her. The son had always taken the time to bid her farewell, and she felt it was a bad omen. She told her daughter, after the plane took off, that "Something did not feel right about this trip." Minutes later the call came through that her son was among the dead from the crash of flight #414.

THERE BUT FOR THE GRACE OF GOD GO I

A number of people were fortunate enough to miss the flight or were refused a seat. By chance or by design, this group did not fly on flight #414 as scheduled or as they had hoped to.

Retired Colonel Manuel Maldonado, the Honduran Ambassador to Nicaragua, was denied a seat in spite of his status and repeated demands to board the flight. He was scheduled to attend an official Armed Forces Day ceremony in Tegucigalpa. An indignant Colonel Maldonado drove to Honduras instead.

Engineer Luis Andres Gradiz was one of nine Hondurans who attended a seminar put on by the Instituto Centroamericano de Administracion de Empresas (INCAE). He remained in the Costa Rican capital with a friend, who also tried to convince another classmate of Gradiz' to stay overnight.

"I decided to stay," said Luis Gradiz, "because Thursday night I had a dream about an accident and told Luis Portillo who I was sharing a room with. He talked about staying in Costa Rica until Sunday but at the last minute decided to return as scheduled on flight #414. I think Luis had a premonition, too, because the night before the flight he was sleepwalking in the room. He walked toward the door and then returned to his bed."

Four of six Hondurans who were attending a seminar at the Centro Agronómico Tropical de Investigación y Ensenanza (Center for Tropical Agronomical Research and Training) in San José decided not to return to their country on October 21 but at a later date. Two of their colleagues from the seminar, José Fasquelle and José de la Cruz Caceres, both boarded flight #414 and perished.

Two employees from the *Superintendencia de Bancos, del Banco Central de Honduras* (Office of Bank Management, Central Bank of

Honduras) changed their plans to return to Tegucigalpa on flight #414 at the last minute. The office director of the bank, decided to remain in San José for the weekend to see the city and enjoy some time off. He was not even aware that other Honduran economists and colleagues from the Central Bank were in Costa Rica. The news of the crash surprised and saddened him. He was fortunate to have missed the flight but lost good friends.

Another employee of the Central Bank of Honduras, Marco Tulio Funez, received a phone call from his fiancé, Suyapa Antonia Cruz, the day before he was to return to Tegucigalpa. She suggested they spend the weekend in San José and return to Honduras on Monday. "It was a spontaneous decision that was made at the eleventh hour," the young woman related. The two planned to marry shortly after the crash.

A Nicaraguan man had plans to fly to Honduras on October 21, but at the last minute opted to drive. He was the Director of the *Agencia de Noticias Nuevas Nicaragua* (Nicaraguan Agency for New News). Among the fortunate was a group of Cubans who boarded flight #414 in San José but got off the plane in Managua, their final destination.

SURVIVING HUMAN LOSS

Family members of passengers first heard the startling news of the crash and then had to go through the anguishing limbo period of not knowing what had happened to their loved ones. Were they still alive?

They were forced to deal with an airline that was ill-equipped to handle a disaster, in a capital city that was unprepared to respond to a tragedy of this magnitude. The news and pain associated with it only worsened during the course of the day and the following weeks.

It is natural for people to deny the reported death of a family member, particularly when it happens so unexpectedly. Nicaraguans were just returning to their homes from the airport after bidding farewell to their loved ones, when they heard on the radio or received a phone call that the plane had crashed. The news was that most, if not all, of the passengers were dead. Hondurans were at the airport waiting for their loved ones when TAN SAHSA personnel chose not to inform them of the crash. They then heard the news of the crash informally from baggage handlers. Nicaraguans returned to the airport to search for information or tried in vain to reach the airline by phone. Hondurans made a mad dash to Cerro de Hula or went to local hospitals. They were driven by a desire to see firsthand what had occurred and, hopefully, to find the traveler they had been waiting for.

My experience from living and working in Latin America since the 1970s is that the people of the region are accustomed to being lied to by officials at all levels. Public officials say one thing but do another and never does one admit error. Broken promises are commonplace and it is difficult to trust officials and their institutions.[11]

There was no reason to believe anything that TAN SAHSA Airline personnel said about the status of flight #414. At first they refused to inform the waiting family members at the airport that the plane had crashed. Then the airline announced over the radio that everyone on board had died. Going to the crash site to verify what had happened was a logical thing for family members of the passengers to do. At this point there was no denial, simply the sinking fear of knowing that something bad had happened, and an attempt to get at the truth by seeing the situation first hand.

It was thirty-six hours before officials cordoned off the area. When the National Transportation Safety Board investigating team arrived several days later, they found everything "trampled down," according to the team leader.

NTSB investigators searching for clues to the crash

Toward the end of the first day it was apparent to rescue workers and onlookers that no more survivors would be found. By the end of the second day, all efforts to recover bodies were suspended. By contrast, the earthquake that hit Northern California two days before the crash of flight #414 was still producing miracles. Rescue workers found a man in Oakland who had been trapped in his crushed automobile for more than eighty hours. Days after the crash of flight #414, the wreckage still smoldered but no miracles were expected.

Once family members of the deceased passengers accepted the fate of their loved ones, they had to appoint someone to undertake the horrible task of identifying a charred body or body parts, or to identify personal possessions that were randomly stuffed into plastic bags and taken to the morgue. Identification proved to be an almost impossible task. Many of the passengers had been burned beyond recognition or bodies were not intact. Looters at the crash site stole rings and watches, making identification even more difficult. Families were forced to get dental and medical records and, in some cases, had to call in their dentist or the family physician to help make the identification.

Family members of deceased passengers who were forced to go to the Tegucigalpa morgue to identify loved ones were appalled by the conditions as the facility was small and poorly ventilated. A limited number of people were allowed in, and family members had to wait in line until a space was freed up. The close quarters, the stench of rotting bodies, the callous attitudes of some of the workers and the deteriorating cadavers made the entire experience nightmarish. Those who were spared additional anguish were fortunate. Those who were forced to undergo painstaking identification were further traumatized.

While many Hondurans worked to help the families, others attempted to exploit the situation for personal gain. The local funeral homes were charging the airline exorbitant amounts of money for caskets and for the use of salons for wakes and funeral services. It was reported that cab drivers were charging unusually high fares to transport the hundreds of grieving family members (mostly Nicaraguans) to and from the airport and around town.[12]

In spite of their fundamental ideological differences, the presidents of Honduras and Nicaragua cooperated in responding to the impact of the crash. The Sandinista Air Force committed four planes to transport family members to Honduras to identify corpses and return them to their native land. The government of Nicaragua sent metal caskets in the planes for the deceased. Customs officials in Honduras worked long hours to expedite paper work so the Nicaraguan families could go home without further delay.

Both presidents maintained high profiles during the week after the crash. They attended funerals and burials, while speaking out in the press. President Ortega met planes in Managua that returned the caskets of dead Nicaraguans and their family members. He also took advantage on the first speaking occasion to denounce the United States government-supported Contra rebels for having killed eighteen Nicaraguan military reservists on the same day as the TAN SAHSA crash.

The Nicaraguan public exerted tremendous pressure for the cadavers to be returned to the country quickly but identification in Tegucigalpa was slow. Some frustrated family members waited for days at the airport in Managua.

When bodies began to arrive in Managua, officials called for calm and prepared family members for the worst. Rogelio Ramirez Mercado, a member of the Nicaraguan Legislative Assembly, flew to Tegucigalpa to identify the body of his relative Humberto Lopez. Upon his return he said, "We have to be patient, because many of these bodies are burned beyond recognition. This is a difficult situation, and our countries are not prepared to deal with a tragedy of this dimension." The government of Nicaragua sent physicians to the airport to give grieving family members drug injections to help them calm their rage and emotional outpouring.

HEALING BEGINS

A Catholic mass was held at the crash site on Cerro de Hula nine days after flight #414 went down. This was an act of healing for a shell-shocked populace. More than two thousand people attended the service that was officiated by Padre Aureliano Santaolaya from the nearby parish of Santa Ana. His consoling words reached out to the assembled as they stood amidst the wreckage and debris of flight #414, "Don't cry brothers. You have cried. You have suffered enough..."

Colonel Wilfredo Sanchez helped organize the mass. He lost his daughter, Fanny, in the crash. The 23-year-old professional had attended a technical course on economic research put on by the *Instituto Centroamericano de Administracion de Empresas* (Central American Institute of Business Administration) and wanted to return to Tegucigalpa to be with her father on Honduran Armed Forces Day. Colonel Sanchez was the Minister of Defense and had just been promoted by the Honduran Legislature to the position of Brigadier General. Fanny wanted to congratulate her father and celebrate his success.

Tragically, her brother, Wilfredo Sanchez Bulnes, died in an air collision during Armed Forces Day maneuvers in San Pedro Sula two years to the day prior to the crash of flight #414. Colonel Sanchez was one of the first family members to arrive at the crash site and spent days looking for the remains of his daughter and her belongings. He subsequently was one of the founders of HERMAFAME and served as the first president of the organization made up of family members of deceased passengers. Sanchez led the HERMAFAME initiative to purchase the land where the crash occurred and create a park for the deceased. This included erecting a monument in their honor.

During the ceremony he read the names of the deceased and announced that he had commissioned an artist to begin work on a monument to be erected on the same site to commemorate those who were lost but not forgotten. Padre Santaolaya declared the crash site a place of prayer and reflection that would henceforth be considered sacred ground.

THE INTERVIEW EXPERIENCE

For years an official list of the deceased passengers sat on my desk. We made move after move to different cities, from apartments to houses and back to apartments, yet the list remained on my desk. Occasionally I would pick it up and read the seemingly endless string of mostly Spanish surnames. I did not know any of the people who died in the crash of flight #414, but it always bothered me that this group of people had been relegated to the obscurity of a faceless list. Who were they? What was behind those names? What were their histories, their stories? Was all of this human capital eliminated in a matter of minutes in October 1989? I couldn't escape the list. I was not only motivated to meet the other survivors, but I realized it was important to talk to the family members of the deceased passengers as well.

The people I spoke with all had different stories to tell about their losses and how their lives had changed since the crash. Each person had taken a different approach to coping with their trauma and trying to build a new life. In most cases, it did not include mental health counseling. In Honduras and Nicaragua, counseling is not readily accessible nor culturally acceptable. There are few counselors and even fewer support groups of the kind that are so common in the United States. The social stigma of being *loco* (crazy) is very strong. It was only natural, then, for many people affected by the crash to block their traumatic experiences as a defense mechanism for avoiding pain.

When I started documenting the experience of the crash and life thereafter by interviewing people affected by the experience, my first concern was whether or not people would be willing to talk with me. What would I find years later? Time helps heal the worst experiences in life, but had enough time gone by? My background was limited to field surveys in rural villages on community development issues. I was uncomfortable with what I might encounter. Organizing and launching the project left me feeling excited by what I might encounter and learn but at the same time apprehensive over doing something I had no familiarity with. I was a gringo with a difficult name to pronounce intruding into the lives of people I did not know to query them in my second language.

With fellow survivors the connection was an easy one. With family members of the deceased passengers, I was treading on unfamiliar territory. I had been fortunate enough to survive, while they had lost a loved one. I was living a full life, and they were left with memories.

All of the conversations were emotional for me and for those kind enough to meet with me. As it turned out, they were so emotionally draining that I could not carry them out for more than four or five consecutive days. Hearing about the painful experiences of others along with recounting my own experience over and over again often proved to be more than I could stand. While there was tremendous therapeutic value for all of us involved, I found myself avoiding or postponing them for a future visit.

I received a broad range of positive and negative responses to my idea of launching a project to document the crash and to recognize those involved. It was noteworthy, too, that so many people I met and spoke with had endured other hardships before and after the crash of flight #414.

I typically initiated an interview by explaining my own experiences on the day of the crash. My account was followed by several questions that, with few exceptions, opened up a floodgate of emotions. Years of pent up pain, anger and frustration rolled out. It was wrenching for all of us, but in the end a tremendous relief. The interviews proved to be an essential portion of my journey to understand and make peace with my own inner conflicts.

The question that was most frequently asked of me was to explain what actually happened. Most of the people I talked with had heard the rumors about the pilots, but knew no details about the crash itself. There has never been an official statement beyond the Honduran government report written by the Honduran Civil Aeronautics Commission, and most people did not receive a copy of the report.

One of the primary concerns was whether or not their loved one(s) had suffered during the crash and its aftermath. This was impossible to say, it all happened so quickly. I answered that I was convinced that many of the passengers died instantly from the impact of the plane hitting the mountainside, particularly those in the rear of the craft. It was probable, too, from everything I had been told by other survivors, that some of the deceased passengers survived the impact, but died when the plane exploded and burned up. This was difficult for me to say, and even more difficult to hear if you had lost a loved one in this manner.

Among effected families there was universal frustration with and anger toward the airline that apparently did very little to help them through the often long and agonizing process of identifying the remains of their loved ones. One Nicaraguan family member told me, "Yes, they paid for my hotel, but made me feel as if I was a beggar asking for a handout. They did little else for us."

The crash had a profound impact on everyone affected by it, because of the enormous suffering and loss of life that resulted from it. Not only were individual families staggered by the event, but a pall was cast upon the collective populations of Nicaragua and Honduras.

My healing journey brought an unexpected benefit--the opportunity to become friends with the survivors and family members and friends of the deceased. My journey opened up another realm of understanding and connection with other people that has been enormously satisfying. My initial motivation was purely selfish. I wanted to collect information about the crash to better understand what happened in order to help myself. It has evolved into a mutually beneficial activity that has helped all of us confront our pain.

During my first research trip to Honduras in 1999, I visited a man who lost his daughter in the crash. He met me at the door of his home and asked me what I wanted from him. I told him I was writing a book and wanted to talk with him about his daughter who had died in the crash. He snapped at me, "You can write ten books about this crash and I won't read any of them." He then asked me to explain my experience on the day of the crash. When I finished, he looked me in the eye and said, "I have never heard the account of a survivor. You know that we are brothers as a result of this common experience." He then told me of the suffering that he and his wife had gone through since losing another child years prior to the crash. This man had experienced enormous pain, and he freely told me about it. We talked for a long time, and I left his home feeling like I had made a new friend with someone who had been dealt a difficult hand in life.

A woman who lost her fiance looked me up and down and said, "He was so young and so strong, how could this have happened to him and not to you?" Ten years after the crash, she lost a husband after a long and painful illness. The first loss was the most difficult to accept, but both losses left her emotionally drained and alone. She told me that she regularly looked for signals to help her continue with her life. My phone call asking her to meet with me in the same month as the anniversary of the crash represented a signal to keep moving ahead.

Another man, whose sister died in the crash, told me, "This is very personal for our family, and we choose to keep it that way. We are not interested in talking about the crash or joining some association."

The father of a deceased passenger was openly distraught over his daughter's death when I met him for the first time in Houston. He was happy to see me, though, and would grab me and hold onto me and say, "I'm just glad to be able to touch you, knowing that you were on the same plane with my Carla."

Carla Weaver was larger than life to those who knew her. When word of the crash of TAN SAHSA flight #414 reached Houston, the first reaction of her friends and family was that Carla surely survived and might have walked into the jungle.

Carla's father, Carnes, was a crusty and likeable Texas oilman. He told me Carla could have been a "football player" because she had such a strong spirit and always wanted to win. He proudly said, "Carla was stronger than stink on a skunk."

Father and daughter went hunting and fishing together, and a close friend of the family described them saying, that Carla "was his son." Carnes told me, "She was born on Sunday and she was a child of the Lord. I knew she was going to do what she felt was right and there was nothing I could do to stop her."

Carla Weaver was forty-two years old and the oldest of three children. A promising career with the Pennzoil Company was forsaken in the early 1980s when she decided to be a Methodist missionary in Central America. Carla learned Spanish and then took a risk by combining her business acumen with her missionary zeal to start Exitex (exi-outside, tex-Texas) a company that developed and distributed inexpensive, nutritional soy-based food. Her goal was to alleviate hunger by making this food available to governments, non-profits and private institutions serving the poor.

According to Roy Beery, who helped manage Exitex after Carla died, most of the food was sold to Costa Rican institutions until she signed a large contract with the Honduran military to distribute meals in the Contra camps during the 1980's. Carla was committed to "evangelizing the Contra soldiers for the Lord Jesus Christ" according to a friend and went to the camps to personally distribute Bibles to them. When the Sandinistas signed a peace agreement with the Contras in 1989 and set elections for February 1990, Exitex was contracted by the Organization of American States (OAS) to provide meals to repatriated refugees and soldiers returning to Nicaragua from Costa Rica and Honduras.

Carla had ambitious plans to expand her company in order to sell food to China, Turkey and newly formed countries in the former Soviet Union. Her brother, Buddy, who spoke fluent Russian, was a big help to her as the business developed. Among her many accomplishments, Carla was learning to fly and planned to solo on her return to Houston.

She attended the upscale St. John's School in Houston and graduated from Randolph Macon College in Virginia. The Weaver family received a call from then President George Herbert Bush, offering his condolences after the crash.

The last time I saw Carnes Weaver was in Houston in 1999. He told me his heart was broken when Carla died and that he never got over her death. A week after I sat at his bedside talking about Carla and his own life, Carnes died.

Today, Carla's dream for a nutritious emergency food ration program lives on. The United States Department of Agriculture has a list of approved commodities for use by non-profit organizations that work in developing countries. The Exitex Blend (soy fortified rice blend) is on the approved list and has been purchased for overseas programs.

Carla's friend and confidant, Don Workman, who was waiting for her at the Houston Airport on the day of the crash, told me Carla would like to be remembered in the following way.

I set my life upon the Lord and he delivered me.

One man who lost his pregnant wife told me that he had avoided several survivors he knew who lived in the same city, because he couldn't help but feel a pang of jealousy that they had somehow escaped death and his wife had not. "She was so young and so active. It just didn't seem to be fair," he related to me.

A woman in Nicaragua who lost her beloved mother called me an "angel" because I had helped her release years of guilt and anxiety simply by sitting down and talking with her about our experiences related to the crash.

Another woman who lost her daughter told me she had wanted to talk to a survivor since the crash, but it had never been possible. When I called her unexpectedly she told me, "I was shocked and couldn't talk at first. Then I realized that you have come here as a gift from God. My prayers have been answered."

GRIEVING IS NECESSARY

Death is a natural part of life but being incinerated in a sixteen hundred degree oven is cruel. It is not natural. Grieving under these circumstances is emotionally wrenching but essential for those left behind. Psychiatrist George Engel states that "the loss of a loved one is psychologically traumatic to the same extent as being severely wounded or burned."[13] He argues that "grief represents a departure from the state of health and well-being, and just as healing is necessary to bring the wounded body back to full strength, a period of time is also needed to return the mourner to a similar state of equilibrium. Further, being fully functional again does not occur until the mourning process has taken its course."

J. William Worden talks about the tasks of mourning in his book *Grief Counseling and Grief Therapy*. "The first task is to accept the reality of the loss by working through denial that the person is dead. The most difficult step for a surviving family member is to accept that the person is gone and will not return, and just as importantly, that reunion with the person is impossible in this life."

Ten years after the crash, I met Julia Lainez, who lost her only daughter. Life has been merciless to the mother of Vilma Lainez since her daughter perished in the crash of flight #414. She depended on her daughter for her material and emotional needs, and the loss of her support and companionship was devastating. Plagued by physical problems, she could not walk. Making her life more unbearable, thieves had broken into the house several times to rob and terrorize her. They took the jewelry that Vilma had left behind and the money she had been saving for a long anticipated trip to Rome.

Vilma had worked at the National Autónomous University in the Institute of Economic and Social Research for Dianny Pozzo Tarrius, a fellow crash victim. Dianny was the Director of the department, and Vilma was a professor and researcher. Vilma had never married, and had always lived with her mother. She was highly respected for her professional abilities as well as her dedication to the job.

Mother and daughter had a close relationship. When I met Julia Lainez, she wept throughout our conversation and insisted on showing me her daughter's bedroom. It had not been touched since the last night Vilma slept in the house. She was still struggling to accept the death of her daughter.

It is common practice for parents to deal with grief by leaving their children's living space intact. However, the longer the room is left as a living memory, the greater the denial and the longer the postponement of completing the grieving process. It is difficult to move ahead with your own life while memorializing the lost loved one in the home where you live.

Just as dwelling on tangible reminders of the deceased is a form of denial, minimizing the loss by removing all memories of the person is a means of avoiding acceptance of reality. A man and a woman who were both widowed by the crash subsequently married and made a pact never to talk about the experience again. They removed all photos and other reminders of their deceased partners from their home and ignored any mention of them in conversation. In effect, the memories of their spouses were obliterated from their external consciousnesses. This avoidance of reality served as their means of coping with harsh losses.

Until the deceased is finally laid to rest, it is difficult to do anything other than grieve. Rituals such as wakes and burials are ingrained in Latin American culture and are part of the fabric of Catholic tradition. Carrying out these rites after the crash was complicated for many families, because the bodies of the deceased were not easily identified.

A woman who lost her sister told me that she still has doubts about the few disintegrating body parts that she carried out of the morgue and buried. After experiencing the trauma of having a loved one inexplicably snatched from their lives, families were then left with doubt over who they were burying.

The second task is to work through the pain of the loss. Losing a loved one is terribly painful, and a grieving process is important and necessary. Attempting to deny or negate the role of grieving only results in difficulties down the road. In my own case, I postponed grieving because I was intent on returning to a normal life. I did not realize that I needed to grieve.

Another example of working through pain was the woman who lost her sister in the crash and was enlisted by the family to identify the corpse at the morgue. In a traditionally patriarchal society, her brother and then her husband were unable to face the horror of identification, and it was left for her to do. The woman pulled herself together and went to the morgue. Upon entering the woefully small and poorly ventilated facility, she was told by an attendant that she would have to leave if she started crying. The process of identification had been slowed by family members fainting and emotional outbursts. There were too many other people waiting in line outside to get in and the officials wanted to move things along. She spent twenty-four hours in the morgue trying to identify her sister, yet she was not allowed to cry. This was a terribly traumatic experience that forced her to be strong and do her best to identify the sister. The entire family was counting on her.

After emerging from the morgue with some remains of her sister, she then had to make the arrangements for the funeral and burial and was subsequently asked to handle settlement negotiations with the insurance company for the airline. One major responsibility followed another, and the weight of her family's expectations were on her shoulders. To be successful, she was forced to postpone grieving. When she told me her story, tears flowed freely. She was finally allowing herself to heal.

An older woman who lost a daughter and grandchildren never finished grieving. She admitted to me these losses, in effect, had killed her, too. She continued to wear black clothes. In explaining the pain she experienced, she said, "Christmas does not exist for me. It is impossible for me to celebrate." Even more telling was her admission that, "I do not see color, only darkness." It is possible that the loss for this woman was so catastrophic that she did not have the strength nor the desire to work through her pain.

The final task of the healing process is to emotionally relocate the deceased in order to move on with life. Putting a loved one to rest may be the most emotional step in the process, but it's essential to accepting the loss once and for all.

The Catholic Church has a well-established set of grieving rituals. As soon as the dead body is prepared for burial, a twenty-four hour *vela* or *velatorio* (wake) is held by the family. The wake traditionally has been in the home, with an open casket for viewing.

A viewing of the deceased was impossible for many families in this instance, because of the state of the bodies. Nevertheless, wakes in the home still required that the family sit with the dead person during the entire time they were in the house. One woman said to me, "We weren't even sure if it was my father's body inside the coffin, but we had to sit with the body and remain awake as long as it was in the house."

In Honduras, many of the wakes were held in funeral homes in part because the airline paid for the cost of the ritual, and it had become more commonplace in recent years. In Nicaragua, there were few funeral homes, and wakes took place in homes.

The wake serves as an opportunity for family members and friends to take one last look at the deceased and recount the life that person led. Stories and anecdotes about the person are told amidst tears and wailing. In Latin America outward displays of emotion are culturally acceptable and expected. The wake occurs within days of the death and continues for *los nueve dias* (nine consecutive days). Emotions at this point are still raw, if not numb. Seeing the body helps the family confront the reality of the death. Burial follows on the heels of the wake and presents the family and friends with another emotionally challenging moment.

During this period, family members go to church each day and pray for the deceased. Some families in Honduras engaged in the ritual of raising a cross at the church and carrying it to the cemetery on the ninth day.

It is tradition, too, for the family to hold a mass on the birthday of the deceased or on the anniversary of the death. Friends and relations attend out of respect for the family and to offer their support. On the anniversary it is common to eat the food the deceased enjoyed while living. A memorial mass is held each year thereafter for as long as the family continues to live and think about the deceased member. A memorial mass simply means that the deceased is mentioned by the priest during the course of the service.

In some families, custom still dictates that the senior women of the family wear black clothes at least for the first year after the death. A woman who lost her mother told me that she wore black for the first year out of respect, because her mother had always complained that no one would wear black when she died. Thereafter, she rarely wore colorful clothes out of personal preference. In this case, custom reinforced her emotional response.

Another woman told me that her mother continued to grieve by wearing black every day for several years after the death of a daughter. It wasn't until the other daughter gave the mother a stern lecture about learning to live again that the mother threw out the dark clothing and began to lead a normal life.

Throughout the year family members, and in particular mothers of the deceased, visit the gravesite of the loved one. A mother, who was wearing black clothing years after the crash, took me to the cemetery where her daughter is buried. She lived nearby and visited the gravesite daily to ensure that it was clean and adorned with fresh flowers.

It is not uncommon in Latin America for families to sanctify members who died tragically, whether they deserve it or not. The dead family member is often remembered in the most positive terms, regardless of the reality of his or her life. For example, a man who was a womanizer may be spoken of as a good husband, or a drunk might be characterized as a wonderful father.

People find many different ways to help them cope with loss. Families sometimes set up an altar or mini-shrine in the home with photos of the deceased. The altar can include candles, incense and articles of importance from the deceased. One widow told me she goes to the memorial she has set up in the home for her husband each night and talks to him. She told this to me as an explanation for how she copes with his death on an ongoing basis.

"We have a united family and talk all the time about my sister. We keep photos of her throughout the house. She was a star, and we remember her that way," a middle-aged woman told me about her sister.

One man told me he listens to the same music that his son enjoyed. "If it made him happy to hear this music, then it makes me happy," he told me.

An older woman who lost her daughter and two grandchildren had a large headstone made for their collective grave. The black stone has an etching of the three that was made from a photo. It looks like they posed for the headstone. The same drawing hangs on the wall in her living room.

Some of the family members I interviewed consider the Catholic ritual of annual memorial masses an opportunity to celebrate the lives of the loved ones they lost, to remember them in positive terms and give thanks to God through the mass for what they had with that person. They have worked through the pain of grief and have healed, yet going through the ritual of remembering and honoring a loved one is an important aspect of living a balanced life. One family told me about their ritual of going to the gravesite after the memorial mass each year to sing and tell stories about the lost loved one. They have moved on with their lives, but maintain a healthy emotional attachment to the dead family member.

Conversely, I talked with family members who have never been able to reinvest their emotional energy in another relationship. They still carry around the pain of their loss. They live with it every day. A father who lost his daughter and granddaughter told me that he had plans for developing a business with his daughter, but all of that was lost. He regularly felt depressed, and drank whiskey when his pain was strongest. One whiskey led to another and the pain and sadness only worsened as more drinks were consumed. Life has not been easy for him since the crash, and he has turned to writing as a means of processing what happened to him.

Another father told me that, after the crash, he wanted his life to jump ahead ten years. His idea was to fast-forward into another life and away from the memories and pain created by the loss of his wife. It didn't work. He explained that his wife's absence at major family events over the years had only made the graduations, weddings and birthdays more difficult and less joyous.

A mother who lost her son continued to wear his clothes years later. Her adult children considered this to be odd and told her so. She explained to them that the clothing belonged to her dead son, and it made her feel good wearing it.

These different cases confirm my belief that grieving is self-directed. Each of us handles it differently and on our own time. Our grieving is focused inward on what we, the living, have lost including our own fantasies about what life would have been like with the dead person present. Death separates us from all that we hold dear, including ourselves. It is the ultimate of separations.[14]

While rituals around death are important and necessary, I believe they also can serve to reinforce the grief indefinitely. In Honduras and Nicaragua, the greater majority of the population is Catholic. The church is one of the few institutions that offers outlets or support to the bereaved after a loss.

I believe the church does not go far enough. For some people in mourning, they derive strength from their faith and the support of the church. Others are weakened by it emotionally and feel isolated after the death of a family member. Still others reject their faith altogether. In his bestseller, *When Bad Things Happen to Good People*, Rabbi Harold Kushner, takes it a step further by indicting all religions. He says, "Organized religion is doing a poor job of easing the pain. Most religious answers are not intended to ease the pain of the grieving person as to defend and justify God, to persuade us that bad is really good and our misfortune serves

God's greater purpose." In my opinion, the Catholic Church in Latin America could provide useful services to grieving families through grief counseling or support groups for survivors. Educating the public about healthy grieving could be an important contribution to the broader society.

LOSS OF FAITH

A fundamental issue for the any religion is the once obedient faithful questioning God, and the strength of their own beliefs after a catastrophe of this magnitude. Where was God when flight #414 crashed? It is a natural reaction for people victimized by tragedy to doubt the role of God in their lives. Why has this happened to me? What did I do to deserve this fate? I have always been a devout Catholic. What good did it do me?

My conversations revealed that family members of deceased passengers came out on both sides of the issue on faith. Some of them told me how they had lost their faith in God as a result of this tragedy. The refrain I heard was, "My faith has been shattered by this ordeal and I will never get it back." Others I spoke with felt as if their faith had been strengthened by the experience. In fact, it enabled them to cope with the loss of life and build new lives. They believed that God had taken their loved one for a reason and, with God's help, they had hope for the future.

A woman told me that her father, who perished in the crash, had dedicated his life to spreading the word of Christ throughout Nicaragua. He helped build and served as pastor for numerous small evangelical churches mostly in isolated, rural areas. "I don't understand how he could be taken from us after all he has done in the name of the Lord," said Sara Videa Arauz about her father Juan Simon Videa Morales.

He was born in 1924 in Pueblo Nuevo, Nicaragua, and was baptized at age twelve with his parents and brothers. He was pastor for the first time in a place called "El Corozo" near Matagalpa.

The evangelical pastor married Rosita Arauz and had five children: Sara, Nidia, Douglas, Marlene and Juancito. He was known and respected for his tireless efforts to help those less fortunate. In 1968 he was elected National Director for the Assembly of God Church and proceeded to baptize Nicaraguans all over the country. "His funeral procession stretched for seven blocks as friends and admirers came from all over the country to pay their last respects to my father," stated his daughter. She told me that it has been difficult to continue to believe in God after losing her father.

"Without God helping me I would have died from fear," stated Napoleon Rodriguez while recalling what happened in his community on October 21, 1989. When I first met Napoleon, he reminded me that he and his wife and children were survivors too. Flight #414 finished its hellish descent a short distance from his home and could easily have killed the entire Rodriguez family.

"I will never forget what happened that day. It is imprinted on my soul, the fire, the trembling of the earth, the explosions, the screams from inside the plane of men, women and children begging for help..." said Napoleon as his eyes teared up.

He helped as much as he could under the circumstances and, while some of his neighbors from the community of Las Mesitas were accused of stealing luggage, he assisted survivors and guarded their possessions in his house.

"I risked my life that day and some of my neighbors warned me not to get involved, but you know, I am a Christian and I have to help the next person," he said. "At one point I started crying from desperation, but there was nothing I could do," he stated.

Napoleon helps maintain the property where flight #414 crashed. It is now a park with a large memorial to the deceased passengers. He has been instrumental in working with HERMAFAME to build a chapel on the property that will benefit the community of Las Mesitas. His inseparable companion is his son José Luis, who was in his wife, María's womb that day and is now developing into a young man. He proudly announces that his son was the first child born in the community after the crash of flight#414. Napoleon and his wife, María, may have been spared that day to raise their boy. Their faith remains intact.

WHY SOME PEOPLE DIE AND OTHERS LIVE?

Trying to understand why some people on an airplane die and others live is another challenge to their faith. Everyone who has ever experienced survivor's guilt struggles with this issue until they go to their graves. It is an even more profound question for those who have lost a loved one.[15] Other survivors and family members of the deceased I talked with have their own answers or continue to ask the question. One explanation that I like was shared with me by a man who was widowed and left with three young children to raise. He views the world like a huge university, and at certain times we are chosen to join a larger class and are taken away. He believes that one hundred-thirty one passengers on flight #414 joined a larger class in the universe that day.

A physician who lost his wife told me that he was scheduled to join her in Costa Rica. They then planned to return to Honduras together on flight #414. At the last minute, plans changed and he remained in Tegucigalpa. Since the crash, he cannot help but think about why she was chosen to die and not him. He can't find an answer.

Reyna Salazar lost her fifteen year-old daughter, and as a result lost her sanity for close to two years after the crash. Her daughter, Elieth de los Santos Miranda Salzar, was traveling to Miami to visit her brother. She was afraid of flying and had cancelled this trip numerous times. Flight #414 marked her first trip to the United States. The mother was so distraught after the crash that she was barely able to function in any sort of normal manner. She rejected her Catholic faith and wondered why her daughter was taken away and why she was spared. One day she heard a calling from God telling her that she had to accept the loss of her daughter, because he had taken her for other purposes. Once she accepted that her daughter was in God's hands, she was able to regain her sanity and lead a normal life.

One explanation, offered by the expert on death and dying, Elizabeth Kubler-Ross, and others, is that the age of the person who has died is not as important as how fully that life was lived. An eighteen-year-old may have lived a more joyful, peaceful life than an eighty-year-old.[15]

A young man whose father, Miguel Rolando Barahona Figueroa, was approaching retirement before being lost in the crash told me that his dad had lived a rich, full life. "We miss him but we know that he made every day count for himself and for those around him." My meeting with this family was more upbeat than most and the deceased's widow added, "I know that I will join him someday and we will be together again."

It was customary to hear Rolando Barahona's deep, booming voice whenever he appeared at work or entered a room in the morning, "Buenos dias!" October 21, 1989 was no exception, as his colleagues from the United States Agency for International Development's (USAID) Office of Inspector General (OIG) Robert Hebb and Gene Van Dyk were among the first to board and were anxiously waiting for Rolando to make the flight. They relaxed when they heard him greeting other passengers in his customary manner as he made his way onto the plane.

Barahona was on a first name basis with most people he came in contact with. His colleagues described him as "a charmer who got along with everyone." He was the senior national staff member working in the USAID auditor's office in Honduras and was well respected. He had a calming effect on people and occasionally found himself in the role of mediator between staff and management.

Like his colleague, Robert Hebb, Rolando Barahona gave up his life in service to the United States government. He had put in more than thirty years on the job and looked forward to retirement.

The most common refrain that people offered to me as a reason for my survival was that "you were saved for something important" or "you still have work to do on this earth." An astrologist who read my chart and analyzed the date of the plane crash in conjunction with my birth date said to me, "Your work was not done, but the work of the others who died on the plane was finished." She also told me that the deceased were at peace, and that they were expecting me to tell their stories. I find little comfort in tidy explanations like this, but I do not discount them, either.

WHAT REGRETS DO PEOPLE HAVE WHO LOST LOVED ONES?

The loss of someone, with whom you have an emotional and familial connection, is difficult under any circumstances. It becomes even more difficult when the loss is so abrupt and so tragic. A young woman who was a teenager when her mother died told me as she wept uncontrollably, "I didn't get to say goodbye to my mama." A father who lost his daughter and granddaughter told me it was cruel to hear the news on the radio as they were returning home from the airport.

Some surviving family members carry around a load of guilt over their perceived role in what occurred. Georgina Rocha Machado told me that she felt guilty for fleeing to Honduras with her family after the Sandinistas took over Nicaragua. "I didn't see my mother for seven years, and the Sandinistas harassed her because we were considered traitors for leaving the country. If only I hadn't encouraged her to make this trip. She really didn't want to go." Seventy-nine year-old Ana Mercedes Silva Lopez, grandmother and great grandmother from Nicaragua, Ana Mercedes Silva Lopez, was taking her first trip on a plane to visit her daughter.

Another woman told me, "It's my fault, because I convinced my brother to stay an additional week." A daughter told me, "I can't help but feel responsible for the death of my parents. I changed the date of the tickets and feel like I marked them. The truth is that they had to stay an additional week to straighten out paperwork, because they were going to apply for visas in Honduras to go live with another sister in the U.S. I know it's not my fault, but I still feel responsible." Blaming oneself for the loss of another is natural but self-destructive if allowed to persist.

THE STRENGTH OF FAMILY

A hallmark of Latin American culture is the strong family union and network. Extended families live in the same city and children benefit from being raised by aunts, uncles and grandparents in addition to their own parents. In a time of economic or emotional crisis, family members typically come together to help each other and lend support. Never was this more important than after the crash, because so many families and marriages were shattered.

Some who lost a spouse remarried within a year or two of the crash. In many cases there was an attraction between grieving spouses who had been through a common trauma. At the same time, some marriage proposals between widow and widower were rejected, and they have remained single over these many years.

Some spouses were left with young children to raise. One widow told me that she had three older children and a two year old at the time of the crash. She looked at the infant and wondered what would become of her. Today, the mother is convinced that the little girl was there to accompany her through life after the death of her beloved husband and has been her constant companion. The attractive widow received marriage proposals after the crash, but turned them down. She had a household full of children to share life with.

The story of Carlos and Ligia Valle is uplifting. In their case, a Nicaraguan widow and a Honduran widower were happily married with three children each before losing their spouse in the crash. They subsequently met through their church and eventually decided to unite the two families in marriage. It transformed their lives and provided a strong, two-parent family for the six children. Both are positive people and credit their strong faith in God, the ability to avoid blaming others for what happened and their commitment to their children as reasons for leading normal lives after the trauma.

The families of the victims of the 1995 bombing of the Federal Building in Oklahoma City were asked after the tragedy, *How have you managed to get through these past six weeks?* What was the single most important thing in helping you to cope with the loss? The universal answer was the response of "the community." Family, friends, neighbors, church members and even total strangers rallied to their support. They made the point that initially they needed consolation, not explanation. They felt as if they had been singled out by fate, and it was helpful to be reassured that they were still good people who did not deserve what had happened to them.[16] This sort of community support was common in hundreds of households, neighborhoods, offices and churches in Nicaragua and Honduras.

Not all of the survivors or family members of the deceased I contacted were willing to talk with me and to be a part of this experience. For some, the healing process has been longer and more difficult. For others, their experience had been so personal that they were not interested in sharing it with anyone, particularly an outsider. Everyone deals with the trauma of losing a loved one in their unique manner. I respect all approaches, including those who asked me to honor their privacy.

CHAPTER TEN

REMEMBERING THOSE WHO DIED

This pathetic tragedy has shaken the soul of the nation and left behind a deep wound that only the infinite grace and mercy of God can heal...with the passage of time.

Editorial from La Prensa-San Pedro Sula, Honduras October 23, 1989

I made a commitment to all the family members who graciously met with me to tell the stories of their loved ones. It has been an honor to know the husbands, wives, children, parents, grandparents and friends of the deceased of flight #414 whom I have met over the years. It has been a privilege to have an appreciation for what they lost. I found the following anonymous poem one day while scanning the obituaries in the Atlanta Journal-Constitution. It captures the sentiment of almost everyone I have talked with about their loss.

Our heart still aches in sadness and secret tears still flow.

What it meant to love you

No one will ever know.

No farewell words were spoken, no time to say goodbye.

You were gone before we knew it.

And only God knows why.

NICARAGUA UNDER SIEGE

The escalation of violence in Central America during the 1980's was dramatic and had a direct effect on many of the passengers on flight #414. Arms and armaments poured into the region during this period, and it became insecure and dangerous for anyone living there. Nicaragua was under siege. From within the country, rights were suspended and any anti-Sandinista activity was harshly punished. The availability of basic goods was limited, and the devastation of the economy resulted in privations and hardships for most Nicaraguans. Frequent attacks by the Contras and the threat of invasion by U.S. forces created an environment of fear and uncertainty.[17]

It was against this backdrop that seventy Nicaraguans boarded TAN SAHSA flight #414 on October 21, 1989. Most of these passengers were flying with the Honduran airline because the national airline of Nicaragua, Air Nica, was prohibited from flying to the United States due to the economic embargo imposed by the U.S. government in 1985. With few exceptions, the passengers who boarded the plane in Managua were flying that day for reasons that were related to the ongoing instability in the region.

The U.S. consulate in Managua was closed during this period. Nicaraguans were forced to travel to Honduras or other neighboring countries if they wanted a visa to visit the United States. There were Nicaraguans on the plane who had lived in the United States for a number of years, but were investigating the possibility of moving back to their native country. The presidential elections scheduled for February

1990 heralded a potential change of governments and thus a change in the social climate of Nicaragua.

Some passengers were traveling to Honduras or the United States to visit family members who could not return to Nicaragua due to political differences with the Sandinista government. One such passenger who died in the crash was a sixteen-year-old girl who was traveling outside of the country for the first time to visit her older brother in Miami. Her brother had fled the country after the outbreak of hostilities with the Contras, in order to avoid compulsory military duty in the Sandinista Army.

An older couple planned to move to the United States to live with a daughter and had to go to Tegucigalpa to secure visas from the U.S. consulate. They had always driven to Honduras from Nicaragua, but conflicts between the two countries made travel by land difficult and dangerous. They decided to travel on flight #414 instead.

A mother and her two daughters who perished in the crash were traveling to Canada to visit her husband and a son, who had moved there years before as exiles. Another mother was flying for the first time to Honduras to visit her daughters, who were forced to flee the country with their families under cover of night years after the Sandinista takeover.

Each life lost in the crash was important and precious. It was extraordinary, though, that the majority of Hondurans killed in the crash were well known and respected professionals who had been attending different seminars and conferences in Managua and San José. Numerous institutions in Honduras were devastated by the loss of these leaders and technical experts. Hardest hit were the United Nations agencies and the National Autónomous University Honduras that were collaborating on several projects. Thirteen professors from the National Autónomous University lost their lives in the crash. Most of the deceased were working on projects funded by the United Nations.

Nine Honduran professionals traveled to Costa Rica for the final session of a three part course put on by El Instituto Centroamericano de Administracion de Empresas (INCAE). Of the nine participants, six perished in the crash, two survived and one remained in San José for the weekend.

Several of the top forestry experts in the country were on flight #414. Foremost among them was the President of the Board of Directors of the *Colegio de Profesionales Forestales de Honduras* (Honduran Association of Professional Foresters). Another prominent forestry engineer was returning from a conference in San José.

The Honduran government's Minister of Labor had attended from a conference in Managua. He had previously been President Azcona's legal advisor. A colleague of his at the ministry also died in the crash. She was the Director General of Employment for the Ministry of Labor.

Honduras lost its best economists. The most prominent among them worked for the *Banco Central* (Central Bank) and was President of the *Colegio de Economistas* (Honduran Association of Economists). Eight other members of the Association of Economists perished in the crash leaving the Central Bank, the National University and the Ministry of Coordination, Planning and Budget with major vacancies. In addition, a Nicaraguan living in Honduras was the President of the Central American Bank before perishing in the crash.

The *Instituto Hondureño del Café* (Honduran Coffee Institute) lost three key employees who were returning to Honduras from conferences in Managua and San José.

The following is a brief remembrance of the deceased passengers. Some have already been remembered in this book. For those whose families I was unable to reach, I apologize.

JOSÉ RICARDO PEREZ

"The first time I called him 'father' he cried. Legally he was my stepfather, but I came to love him like a father. José Ricardo Perez came into my life when I was six years old. His first present to me was a smile and then a bag of confetti. That night we all hopped on his little green Suzuki motorcycle-he and my mother in front and my sister and me in back-and went to dinner. Months later he married my mother and, for the first time in my life, I had a father," remembers Oscar Flores Lopez.

José was a forestry engineer who had been in San José, Costa Rica for a conference. He worked for the *Centro Agronómico de Investigación y Ensenanza* (The Center for the Investigation and Research of Agronomy). He was well respected in the profession and was a dedicated family man.

Oscar is now a successful reporter for the newspaper El Heraldo in Tegucigalpa. In addition to interviewing me, he wrote an article about his father. "My father didn't drink alcohol and he loved to listen to classical music on Saturday mornings. We were often awakened to him walking through the house shouting Figaro, Figaro, Figaro!"

Ironically one of Oscar's first assignments was to cover the TAN SAHSA crash in October 1989. He remembers his mother, Lucrecia, screaming as she ran out of the bathroom. He knew that his father had been on the plane. Radio reports later confirmed his father's death.

Oscar finished his article with the following, "For me, flight #414 represents a wound that will never heal. The pain will always be in my heart. But I do give thanks to God that I had eleven years with an extraordinary man. There are times when I would like to have him at my side so he could criticize a report of mine or we could buy books together… I would have loved him to know my fiancé or to watch him play with my nephew. They say the hardest thing in life is the final note, and this has not been an exception. Maybe because of that and the emotions that I feel, the only thing that occurs to me to say is, 'Thanks, Dad.'

FRANKLIN DAVIS ZAVALA

"See you in heaven" is how Franklin Davis Zavala used to say goodbye to friends. "He came to visit me in the United States eight months before the crash and it was as if he came to say goodbye to me," related his daughter, Michelle.

A week before the crash of flight #414, Franklin drove out of Tegucigalpa to a small church near the crash site. He gave confession to a priest in the church, and his wife Ligia said that it was almost as if he were preparing for his departure. As far as she knew, Franklin had never gone to that church in his life. There were other signs, too, that he had a premonition or some forewarning of his fate. For example, his work as President of the Central American Bank required regular travel throughout the region and flying was a routine activity that Franklin was relaxed with. For some reason, though, he seemed uncomfortable before making this trip.

Franklin had moved his family to Honduras from Nicaragua several years before the crash as a result of the Sandinista government in his native country. His work for the Central American Bank made it difficult to remain in Nicaragua under a socialist government. Like many families who fled the country, they lost everything they left behind.

Franklin was planning to move his family to the United States in order to seek better opportunities for his children. Subsequent to the crash, his oldest son, Franklin Alfonso, and daughter, Michelle, both graduated from San José State University with engineering degrees. They are happily married and living and working in California.

Ligia told me that her husband wore a pendant around his neck that said he would never die from being burned. As fate would have it, Franklin was one of the few deceased passengers who was not burned.

TOMASA CASTILLO SOTO DEL VALLE

Carlos Valle drove to Toncontin Airport to pick up his pregnant wife, Tomasa, who was returning from a conference in Costa Rica. As they pulled into the parking lot at the airport, Carlos glanced at his watch and said to his three children that Mommy would be landing any minute. His eleven-year-old daughter, Gabriella, turned to him and said, "*No canta Gloria hasta que mireis Momi.*" The translation is, "Don't rejoice until you see Mommy." Gabriella sensed that something was amiss. At just about the time Carlos Valle was parking his car at the airport, flight #414 slammed into the mountainside thirty-seven kilometres away.

The couple was expecting their fourth child, and the news of the crash hit Carlos like a bolt of lightning. He kept waiting for her to show up at the door, expecting a taxi to pull up in front of the house. It wasn't until he was forced to go to the morgue that the full impact of losing his wife and a child so suddenly and so cruelly began to sink in.

Tomasa was a professor of economics at the National Autónomous University of Honduras and had been with eight colleagues at a conference in San José, Costa Rica on economic research. She was a successful and respected professional and a dedicated mother and wife.

MOSTAFA TAVASSOLI

Mostafa was a Honduran of Iranian descent. He worked as a professor at the National Autónomous University. After the crash, his wife took their children to Iran to visit the husband's relatives. They attempted to take possession of the children, but she thwarted them and was able to get out of the country and back to Honduras safely. Mostafa Tavassoli was a well-respected professional.

JOSÉ DE LA CRUZ CACERES

José de la Cruz Caceres worked for the Central Bank of Honduras and was President of the *Colegio de Economistas* (Association of Honduran Economists). He was considered the top economist in Honduras in addition to being a devoted family man. The noted economist was encouraged by colleagues to spend the weekend in San José, but he was anxious to get home to be with his family. José de la Cruz Caceres was survived by his wife, Reina de Caceres, and two sons, Gerardo and Daniel and a daughter, Ligia.

DIANNY POZZO TARRIUS

Dianny Pozzo was the Director of the *Instituto de Investigaciónes Economicas y Sociales de la Universidad Nacional Autónoma de Honduras* (Institute of Economic and Social Research at the National Autónomous University of Honduras. She also worked as a professor of economics. Three of her children, were medical students at the university at that time, Diany Sharon, Alba Esther and Ian Jorge Morales Pozzo.

Dianny had attended the INCAE seminar on economic research in Costa Rica. She was a leader at the university and in the community and was highly respected for her work.

IRMA ROBERTA DIAZ REYES

Irma hated to fly, but as Chief of the Unidad de Docencia e Investigación en Poblacion (Population Research Department) at the National University in Tegucigalpa, she had no choice. She was the first director of the masters program in demographics and the demographic research project she was managing was funded by the United Nations. The seminar she attended in Managua was a U.N. sponsored gathering on population and an opportunity to promote the masters program. Irma had a reputation as a hard worker who was well thought of by her colleagues and other professionals. She never missed work and was never late to the office, a model for others working with her and throughout the university. National University honored her after the crash by naming one of its buildings after her. She was an economist by training, who had worked at the university for twenty-seven years.

RODOLFO ARTURO APLICANO AUGURAL

Rodolfo Aplicano worked for the *Secretaria de Planificacion, Coordinacion y Presupuesto, Secplan.* (Ministry of Planning, Coordination and Budgeting) He had attended the INCAE course in Costa Rica.

MARÍA IVONNE JUAREZ DE OQUELI

"She was an extrovert who was an accomplished professional in her own right," according to her husband Dr. José Trinidad Oqueli, who was the Vice Minister of Public Health for the Honduran government at the time of the crash. María Ivonne Juarez de Oqueli was a Vice Minister in the Honduran Ministry of Finance and was in charge of trademarks and patents. She had attended a meeting in Costa Rica sponsored by the *Organizacion Mundial de Propiedad Industrial* (International Organization of Industrial Property). María was the daughter of the Honduran writer, Santos Juarez Fiallos, and had three children ages fifteen, thirteen and two months at the time of the crash.

ROBERTO ZUNIGA MUÑOZ

"He brightened up everything and everyone around him," said Alba Luz de Zuniga. Roberto Zuniga worked for the Banco Central in Honduras and was considered one of the country's top economists. His dream was to live in the United States with his family and work for the World Bank or the Inter-American Development Bank.

During a conversation in 2000, his wife said, "He was a giving person both to his family and to his community." Roberto had worked for the Honduran Red Cross for a number of years and organized volunteers to support the work of the organization. He was President of the Social Club for the Central Bank of Honduras.

Roberto was returning from Costa Rica, where he attended the INCAE seminar on economic research. As an undergraduate he studied in Chile and then went to the Economics Institute in Boulder, Colorado. Later on, Roberto was sent by the Central Bank of Honduras to get his masters degree in economic development from Vanderbilt University in Nashville, Tennessee.

A widow and four children were left behind, Paulette Marisa, Roberto Ivan, Marilla Janet and Michelle-the youngest was two years old at the time of the crash. His wife, Alba Luz de Zuniga, worked at the Central Bank as secretary to the Vice President for three years after losing her husband. She has successfully raised her four children.

LUIS PORTILLO FLORES

Luis Portillo Flores' engineering students from the Centro Universitario Regional del Norte (Regional University of the North) carried his casket to his grave. Family, friends and students displayed an outpouring of emotion when he was buried in San

Pedro Sula. Luis Portillo Flores was an engineer who had attended the economic research seminar at *INCAE* in San José. He was a well-liked professor who at thirty years of age was the successful Chairman of the Engineering School.

He was born in San Manuel and graduated from National Autónomous University of Honduras. He was survived by his wife, Gladys Aguilar Portillo, and two daughters, Kimberly, four, and Astrid, eight months.

ANA MARÍA TOME DE MERCADO

The San Pedro Sula native Ana María de Mercado was an economist trained at the Catholic University of Chile. She had been in San José, Costa Rica on business for the government of Honduras. Ana María and her husband, Rolando Mercado, both worked for the government's Planning Ministry. She left behind three children- Ana María, seventeen; Paola, fifteen; Patricia, twelve and her husband, Rolando Mercado. The economist had recently moved to Tegucigalpa, where she resided with her family in the neighborhood *El Benque*.

HOSMAN GERARDO TROCHEZ DURON

Hosman was in Managua visiting his ailing father. He worked for the *Instituto de Investigaciónes Agrícolas* (Institute of Agricultural Research). A friend of the family said, "after confirming that his father was all right, Hosman decided to return to Tegucigalpa on flight #414. Family members accompanied him to the airport to see him off. Among them was his fourteen-year-old nephew, Oscar Guerrero Trochez, who begged his uncle not to fly that day."

ROMULO REYES FLORES

Reyes Flores, a Honduran attorney had been living outside his native country as a political exile. He was returning to Honduras for the first time in thirty years on flight #414.

JOSÉ RICARDO FASQUELLE GALINDO

"We had such affection for him that we were planning a birthday celebration at his house in the Jardines de Miraflores in Tegucigalpa," said a colleague from work. October 21 was his birthday and his family was waiting for him at home to celebrate. José Ricardo Fasquelle was a forestry engineer and President of the *Colegio de Ingenieros Forestales de Honduras* (Association of Forestry Engineers of Honduras). He had been in San José to participate in a seminar with the Centro Agronómico Tropical de Investigación y Ensenanza (CATIE). The conference did not conclude until Saturday afternoon but Fasquelle left early in order to celebrate his birthday in Tegucigalpa with his wife, Nery Stevensson, and children.

He was the Director of the *Dirección Agrícola Regional Nororiental (DARNO)* and Sub-Director of the LUPE Project under the Ministry of Natural Resources. The latter project was financed by the United States Agency for International Development (USAID).

MAURICE ALBERT PIERSON CUADRA

"I have so much affection for him. He was always on the side of Nicaraguans," said a friend, who welcomed Pierson's help at the Nicaraguan Assistance Center, a charity office. Maurice Pierson was an architect and civic advocate who lived in South Dade near Miami.

"He left behind a wife, Adela María, five children and a legacy of helping fellow Nicaraguan exiles," said longtime friend Leon Pallais, a Jesuit priest.

Maurice had been visiting his ailing 83-year-old mother in Managua and was intent on making the flight in spite of her protests. According to several survivors who saw him arrive at the last minute, Pierson's car broke down a mile from the airport, and he was forced to make a mad dash for the plane with luggage in hand. He barely made the flight.

In Miami as in Managua, Maurice practiced his profession with distinction. He was the first architect to graduate from Managua's Universidad Centroamericana founded in 1961. Mr. Pierson shared an office with his daughter, Adela María, and was designing a Cayman Islands hotel.

He was born in Nicaragua the second of six sons in Nicaragua to French immigrant Pierre Pierson and native Nicaraguan Virginia Cuadra Pasos. Maurice was fluent in French, English and Spanish and held both French and Nicaraguan citizenship.

Maurice was educated at the Jesuit-run Colegio Centroamericana in Granada and then studied architecture at Notre Dame University. More recently, he earned a master's degree in urban planning at the University of Miami.

A member of his country's Conservative Party, Maurice opposed the dictatorship of Anastasio Somoza. Along with Pedro Chamorro, the late newspaper publisher, Maurice spent several months in prison after the Conservatives' failed 1959 invasion at Olama y Mollejones in Chontales province.

The year before the crash, he helped organize a picnic at a West Dade park, giving several thousand exiled Nicaraguans a chance to show their appreciation to their new community. He was also a director of the Centro Asistencial Nicaraguense, a social service agency for Nicaraguan refugees.

GIACONDA JAZMIN VEGA BALTODANO DE HUECK

Jazmin lived in Miami with her daughter and only child who was thirteen at the time of the crash. She was returning home early to help her daughter prepare for a school function. She had accompanied her sister's oldest daughter back to Nicaragua and stayed a few days for a visit with her family in Managua. As a result of changing her flight at the last minute, Jazmin was on the waiting list and was the second to last person to be called onto the plane. Possibly for this reason, she did not appear on any of the passenger lists that TAN SAHSA Airline originally distributed.

"She had a special affinity for the lepers in Nicaragua and always did what she could to help them," related her sister, Janette. In their last moments together, Jazmin gave money to Janette and asked her to buy towels and food for the lepers in Managua. When they were finally able to identify Jazmin's body in Honduras after the crash, the only belonging of hers that they found were some stamps of the patron saint for lepers that she had been carrying with her.

ALFONSO GENARO WONG VALLE and MARUCA JARQUIN DE WONG VALLE

"It was love at first sight for my father. He had just graduated from the University of Texas and was driving through the streets of Managua in his new car. It was a graduation present. He spotted my mother trying to cross the street and was so taken with her that he got out of his car and made sure she crossed safely. After that he pursued her until they were finally married in 1948," explained daughter, Claudia Crow. Alfonso Wong Valle was a highly respected bacteriologist in Managua and ran the Laboratorio Wong Valle for many years. Maruca Jarquin de Wong Valle was a dedicated wife and mother. They successfully raised six children Alfonso, Eduardo, Vanessa, Vicky, Alejandro and Claudia.

"Alfonso took pride in his flawless English and had great affection for his Texas alma mater. His commitment to Nicaraguans was unwavering and he made numerous contributions of his time and resources over the years to the Nicaraguan Red Cross," said Claudia. He established the Nicaraguan Blood Bank and was Director until the Sandinista government removed him. "My mother was well-liked due to her no-nonsense, straightforward approach to life. She was always willing to help out or support friends in any way necessary," related Claudia.

Alfonso was a devoted father who ensured that his children received the best possible educational opportunities. Through his hard work, the children studied in top universities in the United States and Europe. Maruca was as devoted to her grandchildren as she was to her children. "She spoiled them with special treats and was happy to rock them to sleep at night," said Claudia.

She was hard working and energetic and enjoyed helping others. As if raising six children was not enough, Maruca regularly put aside food, clothing and medicine for people who were less fortunate. She had numerous *aijados* (god children) which was testimony to the respect that people of all backgrounds had for her.

Alfonso Wong Valle had always been nervous before flying but was calm the day he boarded flight #414 with his wife Maruca. The couple was traveling to the United States to visit their daughter, Claudia, and her family, in Atlanta, Georgia. They had enjoyed a happy marriage that came to an end that day after forty-one years.

CONNIE MONTEALEGRE

Sergio Montealegre said his mother, Connie, was flying to Miami from Managua to see her grandchildren. "She just felt the urge to be with them," he said. "Look what happened!"

Born in Arizona and raised in Chicago, she married a Nicaraguan attorney, Sergio Montealegre, and adopted the country. For twenty-eight years she worked as Manager of the commissary at the U.S Embassy in Managua. "She always loved Nicaragua," he said. "And she wanted to be buried there."

HUMBERTO JOSÉ CALDERA RAMIREZ AND IVETTE HORTENSE SALOMON BERNARDEZ DE CALDERA

Dr. Humberto Caldera was well known in Managua for having tended to generations of Nicaraguan children. He was considered one of the country's best pediatricians. The flight marked a special occasion for the pediatric surgeon and his wife Ivette, who held a dual French/Nicaraguan citizenship. "They were on their way to a wedding in Miami" said their daughter, Beatriz Caldera. Whose was it? She answered with a sad voice: "Mine."

FRANCISCO ENRIQUE DELGADILLO SILVA AND ERNESTINA ANTONIA AGUIRRE MARTINEZ DE DELGADILLO

The Nicaraguan couple was returning from Managua where they had been looking into the possibility of moving back to their country. They had lived in Miami in exile for a number of years and were attracted back to Nicaragua as the peace process was taking hold in the country.

JUAN GEORGES GAVINET

Juan was a French citizen.

BERNARD GEORGES LEVALLOIS AND MODESTA JUANA HERNANDEZ ABURTO DE LEVALOIS

Bernard Georges Levallois was a French citizen and his wife, Juana Hernandez, was a naturalized French citizen and still held Nicaraguan citizenship.

MARÍA ANGELA PINEDA PONCE

Maria was the niece of the Nicaraguan politician, Rafael Pineda Ponce-President of CCEPL. She was *Directora General de Empleos* (Director General of Jobs) in the *Ministerio de Trabajo* (Ministry of Labor) and had accompanied the Minister of Labor Armando Blanco Paniagua to the regional meeting of the Organization of American States (OAS). She was a resident of Colonia Victor F. Ardon in Tegucigalpa and had worked for the Ministry of Labor since 1985. She was survived by her husband, Alfonso Mejia Ochoa, and two sons, Fabricio, 15, and Enrique Mejia, 13 years of age at the time of the crash.

CAMILO RENE CASTELLON ESTRADA AND IRENE GRACIA ARGUELLO VILLA DE CASTELLON

"They were tired of living in the United States and had just visited Nicaragua for the first time in many years to explore the possibility of moving back after 10 years in exile," said Rene Castellon Jr. about his father and mother, Rene and Irene Castellon. The elder Castellon was working in Miami as a security firm employee. "The news punched me," said the son. "They thought they might move back," he said.

LESBIA MARINA VALLADARES CANALES

"She was the star of the family," said her sister. A highly successful professional among successful professionals. The youngest of four sisters who never shied away from leadership. Lesbia Valladares was always the best student in her class from primary school through graduate school in biology. She had become chief of the department of biology at the National Autónomous University. In that capacity, she was conducting research into an antitoxic serum for snakebites. Prior to the crash of flight #414, Lesbia had been working on a United Nations funded project on Development and Population with a focus on the Honduran birthrate. Poverty in Honduras, particularly as it affected children, was a concern of hers. She didn't attend conferences; she led the conferences. By age 30, Lesbia was recognized internationally for her many contributions to health and population issues.

CESAR AUGUSTO MONTES MANTILLA

"The last time I talked with him was Thursday, October 19. Cesar called me to tell me he would return on Sunday. He said that San José was beautiful and not too expensive," said his father Cesar Montes Lagos. He was an exceptional student throughout school and got a degree in Business Administration at the University of Los Andes in Bogotá, Colombia, before studying law in Honduras. His first job out of law school was with the United States Embassy working for then U.S. Ambassador John Negroponte. Cesar subsequently went to American University in Washington, D.C. for a post-graduate degree in International Law.

"He had a bright future, was a natural leader and was smart enough, handsome enough and charismatic enough to be a future president of Honduras. Whatever he would have ultimately pursued, there is no doubt he would have continued to be successful," said his father. "Cesar's biggest fear was to die by being burned beyond recognition," said his sister Alcira.

He was a sportsman who worked out regularly and loved all sports. Some of his father's fondest memories of Cesar were watching football or baseball games together and drawing on his son's extensive knowledge of the players and the game.

Cesar had been in San José, Costa Rica where he attended a conference on Non-Discriminatory Practices in the Workplace put on by the United Nations. He participated as a delegate from the *Consejo Hondureño de la Empresa Privada* (Honduran Association of Private Enterprise) in the seminar that included representatives of government, employers' associations and labor union members. The seminar concluded on Friday, and Montes had planned to remain in Costa Rica until Sunday. He attended the seminar with María del Rosario Ulloa, a delegate from the Honduras *Ministerio de Trabajo* (Ministry of Labor) who also perished in the crash.

MARÍA DEL ROSARIO ULLOA

Maria was returning from San José, Costa Rica with Cesar Montes where the two of them participated in a conference on Non-Discriminatory Practices in the Workplace that was put on by the United Nations office-International Labor Organization (Organizacion Internacional del Trabajo-OIT). She had been married to Jacinto Diaz, who died in an automobile accident outside of Comayagua. María had worked for the Ministry of Labor since June 1983. She lived in Colonia Las Colinas in Tegucigalpa with her two sons, Eduardo Alfredo, 9, and José Aparicio, 4 years of age at the time of the crash.

TEDDY OGILVIE NORMAN BODDEN

The entire island of Roatan in Honduras was effected by his death. Teddy Norman was a highly respected member of the community of

Jonesville where he was born. He was the owner of fishing boats that he was working in Lake Nicaragua. His boats had been seized by the Nicaraguan government and he was in the process of trying to secure their release with the help of his attorney, Ramón Sanchez Borba, who survived the crash of flight #414. Norman was on his way home to spend the weekend in Honduras before returning to Nicaragua. He was married to Katy and had two children, a son, 10, and a daughter, 5.

ARMANDO BLANCO PANIAGUA

Just days after the crash, the streets around the offices of the Ministry of Labor were full of people from all strata of Honduran society to pay their respects to Armando Blanco Paniagua-the Minister of Labor for the Government of Honduras who was returning to Honduras from Nicaragua where he attended a regional meeting of the Organization of American States (OAS). His body was first taken to his house, then moved to the *Catedral Metropolitana* (Metropolitan Cathedral) and from there for a short time to the Ministry of Labor by petition of the employees.

A good friend and political colleague, Beto Reina, spoke at his burial and said, "He was recognized as a gentleman without fault, a great brother, a great son, a great father and a great friend. He has gone to the other side on a new mission in the universe." The *Ministro de Hacienda* (Minister of Housing) said, "This is a heavy blow for the party, for the nation and for all of us."

Blanco Paniagua was born in La Ceiba and was married to María Isabel Pineda. They had three children-María Isabel, Armando and María Mercedes. He was an active member of the Liberal Party and previously held positions as Magistrate of the Court of Appeals of Comayagua and was President of the *Banco Municipal Autónomo (BANMA)*. He was highly respected throughout Honduran society and people took his death very hard.

FRANCISCA HERNANDEZ DE CANALES

Francisca worked for the Pan American Health Organization (Organización Panamericana de la Salud (OPS)). She was a nurse who also worked for the Universidad Nacional Autónoma de Honduras.

AUGUSTO RAFAEL CARCAMO ZAVALA

"He told me that he was a Seventh Day Adventist and Saturday is a day for church members to dedicate to rest and meditation," related friend, Rodriguez Chacón, of deceased passenger Augusto Rafael Carcamo Zavala. He also told me that, "He was not afraid of air accidents because he believed in God." Augusto Rafael Carcamo was returning from a regional seminar on cacao that was put on by the Centro Agronómico Tropical de Investigación Especializada (CATIE).

"We had planned to return to Honduras on Sunday, but our flight was changed to Saturday afternoon so Rafael must have decided to go ahead and take the earlier SAHSA flight," said Rodriguez. He was shocked to find out that his friend and traveling partner, Rafael Carcamo Zavala, died in the crash of flight #414. Rodriguez Chacón stated that the previous day Rafael had purchased toys in Turrialba to take to his young children in La Ceiba where he resided. Evidently, Carcamo Zavala had promised his wife that he would return to La Ceiba, in order to attend Saturday services of the Seventh Day Adventist Church in their neighborhood.

He was born and raised in La Ceiba and worked for the *Instituto Nacional Agrario* (National Agrarian Institute) in San Juan. He was married to Nilda Oliva and had three children Augusto, 8, Cristel, 5, and Alba Belicia, 3.

JOSÉ ANGEL CASTELLANOS

Castellanos was an extension worker for the Honduran government's *Ministerio de Recursos Naturales* (Ministry of Natural Resources). He had attended a regional seminar on cacao that was put on by the Centro Agronómico Tropical de Investigación Especializada (CATIE). He represented the *Asociacion de Productores de Cacao* (Association of Cacao Producers) and had been in San José since Wednesday. José Angel Castellanos was married to Ruth Zapata Castellanos. They had three children José Angel, 4, Carlos Alberto, 2, and Roberto Emilio, two months.

CARLOS ALBERTO BONILLA BUESO

He was from Santa Rita, Copan in Western Honduras. Bonilla Bueso was considered one of the top experts in the country for the design and cultivation of coffee plants. He graduated from the Centro Universitario del Litoral Atlantico with a degree in agronomy. Bonilla Bueso had been working for the Honduran Institute of Coffee (Instituto Hondureño del Café-IHCAFE) since 1981. Married to Dilcia Suyapa Reyes, he had been in Nicaragua attending a number of courses in his specialty with other coffee growers. He had an active schedule and only planned to be in Honduras for the weekend. On Monday October 23, he was scheduled to fly to the Dominican Republic for more training.

OMAR GUILLERMO ZAVALA ARIA

Omar was born in the town of Minas de Oro, Comayagua, Honduras. He studied at the Universidad Nacional Autónoma de Honduras and graduated with a degree in economics. A single man, he had plans to marry in the coming months. He had worked for the Honduran Institute of Coffee since 1987, and his parents Miguel Rafael Zavala Sandoval y Gloria María Arias de Zavala both worked for IHCAFE in the central office.

DAGOBERTO GUILLEN MENDEZ

Guillen would have celebrated his 28th birthday on October 28. The coffee growers in the area of Comayagua were devastated by the news of his death. In recent years he had worked tirelessly with the growers to help them improve their production. Like many of the fallen passengers of flight #414, Dagoberto's birthday was in October.

He started working at the Honduran Institute of Coffee in 1986 and had a degree in agronomy. His primary work was as a trainer at the IHCAFE training center. Born in Las Liconas, Comayagua, Honduras, Guillen Mendez had recently married Yamileth Cabrera. He had been in Costa Rica the previous week with his colleague, Zavala Arias, attending a course on economic analysis that was put on by PromeCafe of the government of Costa Rica.

SELMA IVONNE SIERRA

The attractive flight attendant from La Ceiba was married in July 1989 and had just found out that she was pregnant. According to a friend, Selma was a close friend of her workmate and fellow flight attendant, Luis Alberto Colindres. It was their habit to sit in the rear galley of the plane. Her husband worked for the *Dirección Nacional de Investigación* (National Office of Investigation).

ERIKA WILLIAMS

From the time she found out that Captain Raul Argueta would be in charge of the flight from Costa Rica to Honduras, Erika Williams complained to the purser that she was uncomfortable flying with Argueta. "She insisted that she had had a premonition and something bad was going to happen," said Nivia Umanzor in a October 23, 1999 interview in La Tribuna. Williams complained that Captain Argueta liked flying into turbulence and had no regard for the personal safety of the flight attendants, who were the ones affected by his flying style.

Erika Williams was sitting in the rear galley and survived the crash. Purser Nivia Umanzor remembers talking to her on the mountainside and urging her to hang on. Ms. Williams was still alive when she was taken away from the crash site. She died at the Centro Médico of a heart attack at 5 P.M. on Saturday.

She was originally from El Corpus, Choluteca, and was the mother of a ten year old son and a daughter of five months. Her husband, Wilfredo Banegas, was a flight captain for TAN SAHSA Airline.

LUIS ALBERTO COLINDRES

Luis Alberto was a TAN SAHSA flight attendant who had worked on the same Boeing 727-200 the previous day flying from Honduras to Houston and then back to Costa Rica. He was nervous the night before the crash and called his wife by phone around midnight. For some reason he couldn't sleep. He was the oldest of six children-three boys and three girls. He was scheduled to continue on to Houston on October 21, but never made it to Tegucigalpa.

He planned to buy a house in the near future and was expecting a holiday bonus for the high volume of international flights he worked during the year.

MARCO ESTEBAN FIGUEROA

"He would never have risked his life flying on a plane in bad condition," said his brother. Family members of Flight Engineer Marco Esteban Figueroa insisted that the aircraft had been well maintained and the crash was not the result of mechanical failure.

Marco Esteban survived the crash according to Nivia Umanzor, but neither she nor the pilots were able to get him out before the plane exploded. He had worked for the airline for twenty years and was a specialist in turbine engines as a result of advanced studies in West Germany. At the time of the crash, Marco Esteban doubled as the Sub-Director of Maintenance for TAN SAHSA. He was married to Alma Yolanda Gomez and left three children, Alma Yolani (10), Marco Alejandro (7) and Carlos José (3 months).

GREGORY VINCENT PAGLIA

He was a Sergeant for the United States Marine Corps stationed in Managua, Nicaragua at that time. Gregory was born on July 1, 1963 and was from New Castle, Pennsylvania.

CHARLES ANTHONY FREDERICH

Friederich was involved in a pro bono human rights project in Nicaragua along with crash survivor, Deborah Lea Browning. He was a first year associate at Arnold & Porter and graduated magna cum laude from Harvard Law School in 1987. Along with fellow attorney Browning, the two had been on a week long fact finding mission involving voter registration which was sponsored by the DC based International Human Rights Law Group (IHRLG).

A native of Long Island, N.Y. and father of two, he was known as Tony to his friends and had survived a plane crash previously in 1984. At that time, Tony was returning to the U.S. from Spain where he had spent a year working on his senior thesis. Apparently Friederich was among approximately 300 passengers on a plane that crashed outside of Madrid killing more than half of those on board. According to his brother Mark Carson-Selman, "Tony was among a few who walked away from the crash without sustaining any injuries."

ROBERT HEBB

"He was an easy going person who was well liked by all those who knew him," said Gene Van Dyk a colleague and crash survivor. Robert Hebb grew up in rural Maryland and went overseas for the first time in 1986 when he was assigned to the Office of Inspector General for the United States Agency for International Development in Honduras.

Prior to the assignment, Hebb studied and struggled with learning Spanish at the Foreign Service Institute. There he met Gene Van Dyk and Shelly Schwartz, whom he later worked with in Central America. Gene told me, "Language did not come easily to Bob. However, once he moved to Honduras everything seemed to fall together. His language skills improved more than most of the other U.S. staff."

'Bob was single and led an active social life. He enjoyed living abroad and had a number of Spanish speaking girlfriends. This no doubt contributed to his improved language skills. He was known for his tolerance for chili sauce and his ability to drink straight scotch on the rocks. Amazingly, after a late evening on the town, Robert was always ready to go to work at the crack of dawn," related Gene Van Dyk.

In November 2001, Robert Hebb was honored by the American Foreign Service Association along with nine other State Department employees who died abroad serving the United States. (State Magazine, November 2001, United States Department of State)

In a subsequent ceremony in May 2002, marking Foreign Affairs Day the Secretary of State delivered a message from President George W. Bush and unveiled the plaque that carries the name of Robert Hebb. His final comment was "May they always be in our memory."

MIGUEL ROLANDO BARAHONA
FANNY ARACELY SANCHEZ BULMES
CHARLES KENDALL MORROW

Charles was from Grandview, Missouri USA

MICHAEL TERRENCE O'SHEA

Michael was from Costa Rica.

DANIEL HARRY YURISTA

"He just had this acute sense of how important it is for people around the world to get to know one another and be fair with one another," said Dan Yurista's wife Kathy. "He went to Nicaragua because this was the chance for him to help a country that had been devastated by Contra wars, revolutions and natural disasters."

Daniel Yurista was not supposed to be on flight #414. He was returning home a week late after a five-week journey to Nicaragua. He drove a converted school bus with other farm activists as part of the Farmer to Farmer dairy and friendship project. The trip took longer than expected and Yurista extended his stay in Nicaragua for an additional week. The final week of the trip was spent near Matiguas, Nicaragua, where the Farmer to Farmer group was attempting to assist the Nicaraguan people in establishing a productive dairy cooperative.

Yurista drove a school bus from his home town of Prairie Farm, Wisconsin, to Nicaragua to deliver the vehicle and supplies and to begin working with the members of the cooperative. Kathy Yurista spoke to the media as a means of trying to make sense out of what happened to Dan and to their lives. She said, "He was always taking care of other people and helping out, and sometimes things didn't get done around here," referring to the sixty-acre dairy farm where the Yuristas lived with their three children, Peter, Marta, and Sadie.

With his wife Kathy, Yurista was active in the Wisconsin Farm Unity Alliance, fighting with non-violent methods to stop farm foreclosures, the use of Bovine Growth Hormone and the destruction of the family farm due to low farm prices. "You could always count on Dan being there," said friend Cindy Theorin. "We do many things as a community, like fundraising projects or just getting our own work done. It just won't be the same without Dan."

Yurista's specific mission in Nicaragua was to help in the assessment of the possibility of using draft power for parts of the farming operation. Pete Edstrom, friend and member of Farmer to Farmer, pointed out that Dan was particularly suited to that role. "Dan was not a 'model farmer' in the usual sense of the word. But that's not what you need in a Third World country. You need someone who knows how to make use of what is available, using only the technologies that can be adapted to the conditions in a cost effective way. Dan practiced those principles at home. He wasted nothing. He made do and lived within his means. He could make horses work with him, not for him. It was the same with people. He was a team player, a pleasure to work with." Yurista's background as a skilled tradesman, his carpentry skills and his practical working knowledge of dairying were other qualifications that made him a valuable part of the effort according to Edstrom.

He had strong convictions that he lived out every day of his life. Daniel Yurista left his convictions in Central America.

EDUARDO APODACA ARCE and ESTHER MARÍA APODACA

"They were devoted to us and they were devoted to education," said daughter Margaret. "They touched many lives in the music world and through education."

Eduardo Apodaca and his wife María Esther Apodaca were traveling together from San José, Costa Rica back to their home base in Tegucigalpa, Honduras. Eduardo was an employee of the Cal Poly Foundation that was involved in producing educational materials for secondary schools and community colleges. Apodaca was Program Director for the foundation's vocational education production and was assigned to work in Honduras in May of 1988 to help develop textbooks and materials for school children.

The project was part of a contract between the Cal Poly Foundation and the United States Agency for International Development. According to a spokesperson for the Cal Poly Foundation, the textbooks would have been the first specifically designed for Honduran school children. The Apodacas planned to return to San Luis Obispo, California in 1990.

Al Amaral, Executive Director of the Cal Poly Foundation, described Mr. Apodaca as having a special affinity for schoolchildren. "Eduardo was an extremely talented, dedicated individual," said Amaral.

Eduardo and María Apodaca were natives of Texas. They met at the University of Texas where both were studying to become teachers. After graduation, María Apodaca taught for seven years in El Paso, Texas where she was named Teacher of the Year. She also taught in Indio, California before giving up her career to devote her time to her family.

Mr. Apodaca started his teaching career at Ysleta High School in Texas as an art and Spanish teacher. He moved his family to California in 1968 and taught in Indio and Eagle Mountain.

A daughter, Margaret Apodaca, said her father was a pioneer in bringing bilingual education to California and directed the state's bilingual education project in the 1970's. He was President of the San Luis Obispo County Youth Symphony and a youth soccer coach for many years.

Mrs. Apodaca taught the couple's four children classical music at home. According to the daughter, the couple's last years in Honduras together were happy ones. They were publishing games and helping poor children get an education.

I have a strong image of the couple, because they first caught my eye when I was standing behind them in line waiting to check in at the airport in San José, Costa Rica. Later in the waiting area they were sitting across from me. The Apodacas were close to each other, holding hands and dozing as we waited for the announcement to board the plane. In those moments before boarding flight #414, the Apodacas looked happy, content and very much in love.

EVAN LOCKWOOD ANTHONY

He was a used car dealer from Houston, Texas, who was en route to Honduras on business. His wife, Irma Anthony, had to travel to Tegucigalpa to identify and return the body to the US. He was listed as a Nicaraguan on the official TAN SAHSA passengers list.

CARLOS A. EGAN

A tall, handsome Argentinian who lived and worked in the U.S. was engaged to marry a Nicaraguan dancer, Gloria Bacon. He had been in Nicaragua visiting his fiancé and planning their marriage. Egan took out a life insurance policy before leaving Nicaragua. He was a professor at Williams College in Massachusetts and Carlton College in Minnesota. The couple planned to move to Massachusetts after their marriage.

CARMEN COLEMA DIAZ

Carmen was a Peruvian traveling to Honduras to provide technical support to a United Nations supported educational project in Comayagua. As a United Nations employee, she worked for the International Labour Organization. She was one of three U.N. functionaries who died on October 21, 1989.

DANIEL RODRIGUEZ OSORIO

Daniel was a Chilean national on his way to the United States, where he worked for the United Nations. He was a consultant to the U.N. Regional Employment Program for Latin America and the Caribbean.

JESUS HERRERA LLANQUE

Jesus was a recently arrived Bolivian volunteer for the United Nations who had been working in Honduras for only two months. He was working on the Population Training and Investigation Project that was under the direction of the faculty of Economic Science at the National Autónomous University.

He was making plans to move his wife, Isabel, and two children, Andrea and Pamela to Tegucigalpa. Jesus was born on December 25 and died at the age of 33 years. Magaly and I met Jesus' wife and daughters in La Paz, Bolivia in 2005 after Isabel saw me being interviewed about the book on television.

FRANCISCO JAVIER IRANETA GOICO

Francisco was a Spaniard from Navarra working in Nicaragua as an agricultural specialist. He had been contracted by the Sandinista government and was buried in Nicaragua following the wishes of his family.

MARÍA DEL VALLE LOZANO MARTINEZ

"Her mother requested a Christian burial in her native Logranes region of Spain. I plan to honor that request," said Ali Velasquea, husband of María del Valle Lozano. She was the secretary for the Spanish Ambassador to Nicaragua for twelve years. María was married to Ali Velasquez, who went to Honduras to identify the remains of his wife. They had been married for fourteen years and had two children: Ali Javier, 11 years old, and Inés de María, 8 years old.

HIKKA HELENA SARJAMO

Hikka was a citizen of Finland.

YUK KUEN WONG

Yuk was a British citizen from Hong Kong.

CARL JEAN NELIS

Carl was a citizen of Belgium.

NILS AKE KAULSSON and JAN ANDERS EDY JOHANSSON

Nils and Jan were Swedish businessmen in the region scouting out opportunities. Their bodies were identified and returned to their country by functionaries of the Swedish government.

MIKHAIL STAROUCHIV

Mikhail was a citizen of what was still the USSR (Union of Soviet Socialist Republics).

ZDENEK KLIPA

Zdenek was a native of Chechoslovakia.

MARIO RODRIGUEZ CUBERO

Mario was a consultant to the President of Costa Rica, Oscar Arias. His son, found out about his father's death when he went to the airport in San José the following day to catch a flight to Mexico.

ERNESTO DOLORES SEQUEIRA BLANCO

Ernesto was the Director of the Health Center in the Nicaraguan City of Bluefields. He was a legislative candidate for the Sandinista Party (Frente Sandinista) for the upcoming elections.

MARÍA CONSUELO BUITRAGO DEL ROSAL DE NOVOA

Ms. Buitrago del Rosal was a high official in the Nicaraguan Ministry of Health for the Sandinista government. She was on her way to the United States for a medical gathering.

ALFONSO GERMAN

Alfonso was a Nicaraguan physician.

JOSÉ IGNACIO BALTODANO

There was a long and profound silence among all the employees at the Managua International Airport for José Ignacio Baltodano, the well-known manager of the TAN SAHSA operations in Nicaragua. He had worked at the airport for a number of years and was considered a human relations expert. Baltodano knew everyone and was met on his last trip back to his native Nicaragua by a group of his closest friends. They walked out on the runway with his wife to receive the casket.

The popular manager was on his way to Houston to celebrate the birthday of one of his brothers. It was one of the perks of the job he could travel free of charge. José Ignacio had joked with a friend some days before the crash that if he died, he would like a 727 airplane to be named after him.

MARÍA ELENA VILCHES NOLASCO, ARIELA MARÍA RODRIGUEZ VILCHES AND ARIANA VALERIA RODRIGUEZ VILCHES

María Elena Vilches and her two children were on their way to Canada to visit her husband and an eight-year-old son. She was from Somoto, Nicaragua and was traveling with two daughters, Ariela María, 9 years old, and Ariana Valeria, 2 years old. Her husband had fled Nicaragua to Canada after the Sandinistas took power in the late 1970's.

She had worked for the principal newspaper in Managua, *La Prensa*, since 1985 as an accountant. María Elena had prepared for her trip to Canada for months and was traveling with her good friend and colleague from La Prensa, Martha Lorena Ramirez.

MARTHA LORENA RAMIREZ CASTILLO DE VILLALOBOS, JOSÉ ALBERTO VILLALOBOS RAMIREZ AND CINTYA YESENIA VILLALOBOS RAMIREZ

The entire family went to the airport to see Martha and her children off. They prayed for the safe arrival of the travelers and the children were excited about seeing their father for the first time in a year. She was traveling to Canada to visit her husband, Jorge Antonio Villalobos. Martha Lorena Ramirez decided to travel with her good friend María Elena Vilches along with her children, José Alberto Villalobos, 9 years, and Cintya Jessenia Villalobos, 6 years. She worked for a year for the accounting department for the Nicaraguan paper, La Prensa. José Alberto was the final passenger to be identified at the morgue in Tegucigalpa. Surviving members of the family included Martha's mother, Dona Elba Castillo, and five brothers.

ANA MERCEDES SILVA LOPEZ

Ana was a mother, grandmother and great grandmother from Nicaragua taking the first plane flight in her life to visit daughter, Georgina Rocha Machado, and her family in Honduras. She lived with another daughter, Yolanda, in the Managua neighborhood Colonia de Centro America. The trip for Ana Mercedes signified the first time in seven years she would be able to see her daughter, Georgina, who had left Nicaragua with her husband and children after the Sandinista victory.

ANA CAROLINA BRENES ALVAREZ

She was one of the last to arrive at the airport and board the plane. Before entering the plane she made a phone call to her mother and told her, "Even though I have to sit in the tail of the plane, I am going." It was her second trip to Miami in a short period of time. She had attended the wedding of a cousin just eight days previously and was returning for a vacation. Ana Carolina Brenes worked for a travel agency and had the opportunity to fly regularly. She told her sister, Dr. Patricia Brenes, before boarding flight #414 to "take care of my mother and don't leave her alone."

Ana Carolina was relaxed before her previous trip to Miami but this time something didn't feel right. According to her sister, she was chewing her fingernails and was visibly nervous. The sisters had stayed together the night before and both were uncomfortable with flight #414.

MARÍA DE LA CONCEPCION CASTILLO PICADO, ZELA DIAZ CASTILLO AND ELBA GANINA SANCHEZ DIAZ

Grandmother María, granddaughter Elba and her aunt Zela were traveling together.

FRANCISCO ESPINOZA LOZA

"My father talked about visiting his brother in New York so many times over the years that we grew tired of hearing about it," related his daughter Fatima Espinoza. With his mind made up, Francisco Espinoza booked flight #414 as the first leg of the trip to finally see his brother in the United States. He tried to convince his only daughter to go with him, but she declined.

Francisco was an air condition repairman for the United States Embassy in Managua. He left a wife and sixteen-year-old daughter behind.

"Wife and daughter believed that Nicaraguan attorneys had taken advantage of them and paid out as much in compensation as they chose to instead of what they were obligated to pay. Virtually all of the compensation money was spent on his wife's medical bills who suffered from complications due to diabetes," said Fatima.

Fatima lamented to me the fact that they had to deal with "dirty attorneys." She would have preferred avoiding the whole thing because "they weren't going to return my father's life." Wife and daughter felt like they had no choice in the matter because Francisco was the breadwinner for the small family.

JACINTO DAVID ABDALAH ALEMAN

Jacinto was the owner of a bus company called Autobuses ABDALAH.

ELIETH DE LOS SANTOS MIRANDA SALAZAR

"She had just turned fifteen and was full of joy," said her mother Reyna Salazar. She was the youngest of seven children and was on her way to Miami to visit four brothers. Elieth had cancelled the trip numerous times and did not like the idea of traveling to another country. She was in her second year of high school and planned to stay a month in the United States.

AUXILIADORA DEL CARMEN NARVADEZ LOPEZ

Auxiliadora was known as "La gordita."

FRANCISCO HUMBERTO TAPIA VARQUERO

Francisco was a well-known coffee producer from Masatepe, Nicaragua. He was on his way to Florida to attend a series of conferences related to coffee plants and production. Tapia had a degree in agronomy according to his brother-in-law Rogelio Ramirez Mercado.

RAQUEL BALTODANO ORTEGA

"I wanted to remember her as she was," said David Baltodano about his sister Raquel Baltodano Ortega. He chose not to go to Tegucigalpa to identify the cadaver and refused to look at her body when she was returned to Nicaragua. The day Raquel's casket arrived in Managua the airport was full of people who were there to show support, solidarity for the Baltodano family. Raquel was the sister of David Baltodano, an editorial assistant for the newspaper *La Prensa* in Managua.

The night before the flight, the family prepared a large dinner to send her off to the United States where she had lived for a year-and-a-half. "Raquel was a positive person by nature and was considered to be the life of the party. On the occasion of the farewell dinner, though, she was sad and dejected," said brother David.

Raquel worked for a family in Connecticut caring for four young children. She was a member of a Christian group called, *Misión Cristiana Verbo.*

RAQUEL MATEO RODRIGUEZ and EDMUNDO AYALA AVILA

"Isn't it strange, it's always the best one, the favorite daughter," said Carmen Mateo about her big sister Raquel who was lost on flight #414. Mateo was taking an English course in Goshen, Indiana when she got word of the crash and had to borrow a car to drive to Miami to take a plane to Honduras. "My life has stopped. I haven't changed clothes since yesterday," said the small curly-haired woman with an eleven-year-old son in tow. Mateo said that she was committed to returning to Honduras to raise her sister's three children.

Raquel Mateo was returning to Tegucigalpa from Costa Rica with her husband Edmundo Ayala Avila. She was the sister of reporter Milton Mateo and worked as a professor at the *Instituto Central Vicente Caceres.*

MAGALY SORIANO FIALLOS DE LONERGAN

The authorities, who were searching the crash site for personal belongings of the passengers, found a lemon in the purse of Magaly Soriano that was sliced open at one end in the shape of a cross. There were numerous pins stuck into the fruit to form the cross.

OFFICIAL TAN SAHSA PASSENGER LIST

The official list of passengers and crew members for Flight #414 was published by TAN SAHSA on October 24, 1989 in a number of Honduran newspapers.

Passengers Originating in San José, Costa Rica

Augusto Rafael Carcamo Zavala	José Angel Castellanos
Carmen Colema Diaz	Eugene Van Dyk
José Ricardo Fasquelle Galindo	María del Rosario Ulloa Buezo
Eduardo Apodaca Arce	Jannette Irazorry
Curtis Reed Schaeffer	Mary Carla Weaver
Omar Guillermo Zavala	Miguel Rolando Barahona Figueroa
Francisco Hernandez Reyes	Martha Chavarria Rodriguez
Raquel Mateo Rodriguez	Ronald Devereux
Helen Devereux	Charles Morrow
Dagoberto Guillen Mendez	Cesar Augusto Montes Mantilla
Alfredo Portillo Flores	Dianny Pozzo Rarrius
Vilma Esmeralda Lainez	Fanny Aracely Sanchez Bulnes

Roberto Zuniga Muñoz	Hernan Madrid Turcios
Juan Evenor Lopez Scott	Tomasa Castillo Soto de Valle
Alfonso Franklin Davis Zavala	Edmundo Ayala Avila
José Ricardo Perez Munguia	Mostafa Tavassoli
Mario Rodriguez Gubero	Robert Hebb
María Ivonne Juarez de Oqueli	José de la Cruz Caceres
Michael Terence Oshea	Ester María Apodaca

Passengers Originating in Managua, Nicaragua

Laura Arauz Ortiz	José Ignacio Baltodano
Victor Manuel Sanchez Valerio	Cinthia Yesenia Villalobos Ramirez
José Alberto Villalobos Ramirez	Ariela María Rodriguez Vilches
María Elena Viches Nolasco	Delfa María Fajardo Parrales
Ariana Valeria Vilches	María Joséfa Mendoza Cabrera
Katy Mercedes Concepcion Korea Torres	Joséfa Auxiliadora Torres Mendoza de Castillo
Harry Antonio Vega Ibarra	Carlos Eduardo Vega Reyes
Yasmina del Socorro Reyes Martinez de Vega	Ivett Hortense Salomon Bernardez de Caldera
Alfonso Genaro Wong Valle	Marin Consuelo Bultrago del Rosal de Novoa
Humberto José Caldera Ramirez	María Delfia Jarquin Saenz de Wong Valle
Umina Abdeiah Aleman	Vivian Fernandez Garcia de Pellas
Patricia Leonor Torres Chavez	Tatiana Elizabeth Torres Chavez
Carlos Alberto Lopez Cruz	Leonor Mari Chavez Moran de Torres
Pedro Montoya Leiva	Jacinto David Abdalah Aleman

Marina Castellon Lopez de Montoya	Francisco Espinoza Loza
Francisco Humberto Tapia Varquero	Magaly Soriano Fiallos de Lonergan
Cesar Octavio Escobar Lopez	Camilo Rene Castellon Estrada
Irene Garcia Arguello de Castellon	Ernestina Antonia Aguirre Martinez de Delgadillo
Luis Alfonso de la Rocha Chow	Juan Ismael Lopez Quintana
Marta Lorena Orosco Matamoros	Margarita de los Angeles Abea Talavera
Francisco Javier Molina	María del Rosario Icaza Icaza Vda. de Vigil
Gioconda Jazmin Vega Baltodano de Hueck	Francisca Rosario Ubeda Gonzales
Francisco Enrique Delgadillo Silva	Carl Jean Nells
Daniel Rodriguez Osorio	María de la Concepcion Castillo Picado
Maurice Albert Pierson Cuadra	Juan Simon Videa Morales
Zela Diaz Castillo	Ana del Carmen Centeno Cano de Flores
José Angel Flores Rivera	Ana Carolina Brenes Alvarez
Martha Lorena Ramirez Castillo de Villalobos	Ana Mercedes Silva Lopez

Modesta Juana Hernandez Aburto de Levalois	Placida Aurora Barrantes Gutierrez
Purificacion Rivera de Rizzo	Francisco Javier Iraneta Goicoa
Vigarny Gonzalez Montiel	Bernard Georges Levallois
Romulo Reyes Flores	Connie A. de Montealegro
Charles Anthony Friedrich	Evan Lockwood Anthony
Juean Georges Gavinet	Deborah Lea Browning
Gregory Vincent Paglia	Nils Ake Kaulsson
Jesus Herrera Llanque	Zdenek Klipa
Daniel Harry Yurista	Rodolfo Arturo Aplicano Aguilar
Mikhail Starquchiv	Ramon Eulalio Sanchez Borba
María Angela Pineda Ponce	Ana María Tome Altamirano de Mercado
Armando Blanco Paniagua	Irma Roberta Diaz Reyes
Hosman Gerardo Trochez de Duron	Hikka Helena Sarjamo
Lesbia Marina Valladares Canales	Carlos Francisco Pellas Chamorro
Yuk Kuen Wong	Carlos Alberto Bonilla Bueso
Carlos A. Egan	Teddy Oglivie Norman Bodden

Jan Anders Eddy Johansson	Elieth de los Santos Miranda Salazar
Raquel Baltodano Baltodano	Ernesto Dolores Sequeira Blanco
Aurora Pineda Ruiz de Molina	Elba Ganina Sanchez Diaz
Axuliadora del Carmen Narvadez Lopez	José Luis de la Rocha Diaz
Erick Antonio Brenes Bojorge	José Roger Zavala Zuniga
Emma Leonor Abarca Toruno de Sequeira	Blanca Rosa Hasbun de Zarruk

TAN SAHSA CREW MEMBERS

Captain-	Raul Argueta
First Officer-	Reinero Canales
Flight Engineer-	Marco Esteban Figueroa
Flight Attendants-	Nivea Umanzor-Purser
	Ericka Williams
	Guiomar Lizzeth Nuñez
	Luis Colindres Luna
	Selma Yvonne Sierra Leiva

SURVIVORS

Honduras:
Nivea Umanzor
Reinero Canales
Guiomar Nuñez
Raul E. Argueta
Hernan Madrid
Evenor Lopez

USA:
Jean Van Dyk
Curtis Reed Schaeffer
Deborah Lea Browning

Australia:
Helen Devereux
Ronald Devereux

Nicaragua:
Carlos Pellas
Vivian de Pellas
Francisca Rosario Ubeda Gonzalez

Paraguay:
Ramon Sanchez Borba

CHAPTER ELEVEN

THE INVESTIGATION

"This was the most preventable air accident I have ever seen, it should not have happened."

-John Grayson, Houston attorney who successfully
represented twenty-five Honduran families against
TAN SAHSA and Continental Airlines

In October 1999, I was sliding into my seat on a plane in Miami and preparing to fly to Tegucigalpa, Honduras. This was my first flight back to Toncontin International Airport since the crash ten years earlier. An airline official asked for our attention over the intercom. My nerves were already on edge, and I was not prepared to hear an American Airlines representative say, "Sorry folks, but we will be delayed for at least fifteen minutes. We are looking for a pilot who can fly into

Tegucigalpa because not just any pilot can fly there. If we don't find one, we may have to cancel the flight."

Oh my God! I thought. I couldn't believe what I had just heard. Did they have to give us all that information? I knew first-hand that Toncontin was a notoriously dangerous airport, but did it have to be advertised to the passengers? Spare me the details, please.

I found out later that it is now standard policy for U.S. carriers flying into Toncontin to only allow flight captains, not first officers, to pilot the craft. American Airlines is even stricter—requiring that only captains who have flown to Honduras within the past three months be allowed to fly into Tegucigalpa.

After regaining my composure, I realized that I was being tested. The flight to Tegucigalpa was my first venture into Central America to conduct research and begin documenting the crash of flight #414 and its impact. I debated stepping off the plane and returning to Atlanta. The door was still open, and I could have escaped the plane and the flight.

I was just beginning my journey, and calling it off before it got started would have simplified my life. "Steady, Curt steady," I kept telling myself. I anxiously took my seat. The pilot finally appeared and flew us to Tegucigalpa. It was a routine flight.

TONCONTIN INTERNATIONAL AIRPORT

The airport in Honduras' capital city of Tegucigalpa, **Toncontin International Airport**, is set deeply into a valley that makes entry and exit difficult. It has always been considered one of the most dangerous airports in the world. In the 1950s and 1960s, Pan American Airlines refused to fly there and designated San Pedro Sula, the second largest city in the country, as the international point of entry to Honduras. Recently, the History Channel ranked Toncontin as the second most dangerous airport in the world.

Toncontin is surrounded by mountains and has only one runway, which runs north and south. The runway is short and sits on a plateau, with mountains at the north end and a cliff at the south end. The result is that a pilot must bring the plane down under enough power to get over the mountains and immediately cut back the power in order to drop the plane on the runway early enough so it can be stopped before reaching the cliff at the other end. There is little room for mistakes.

The one and only landing strip at Toncontin International Airport

Philip Schleit, the first attorney for TAN Airline, described flying into Tegucigalpa for the first time in 1951 aboard a cargo plane:

"The C-46 was full of cargo and as the only passenger I was sitting in the jump seat in the cockpit with the two pilots. To land at Toncontin, one must actually ascend from a valley to the uphill end of the runway. In ascending from the valley, the aircraft must be eased up very slowly, close to stall speed, to avoid overflying the threshold or having too much ground speed to stop on that downhill runway. Pilot Forsblade alternately gunned and throttled back the engines to shoehorn the air-craft up into the airport for a perfect landing. The runway was invisible until we reached the top of the valley, then it was time to set down, im-mediately! It was explained to me that landing at Toncontin was "like a bird flying up to land on top of a flagpole."[18]

Since 1989, there have been half a dozen accidents at the Tegucigalpa airport. Worst among them was the crash of a U.S. military C-130 on April 1, 1996, as the pilot was making his first-ever landing at Toncontin. According to U.S. investigators, the plane came in too high and fast, and the pilot didn't put on his flaps fully to brake on the short runway. Three U.S. servicemen on board were killed; seven oth-ers scrambled from the wreckage before it exploded.

A former TAN SAHSA pilot had numerous scares at Toncontin. He says, "Honduras for decades has ignored the central problem of Tegucigalpa's airport, its geography." He described landing a 737 at Toncontin in 1997.

"Descending steeply and banking sharply--it is always a tricky land-ing. Dead ahead lies Toncontin International Airport in the heart of Tegucigalpa, Honduras. To my right, camel-backed mountains, so close I could hit them with a rock. To my left, a teeming city, near enough for passengers to see people eating inside their hillside homes. In front of me, a short landing strip with no radar, no instrument landing sys-tem, not even runway lights. If I land perfectly, I will clear the airport fence by about ten feet. If I come in a little too fast, or misjudge the approach, I could easily spill the Boeing 737 into a deep ravine at the end of the runway."[19]

The dangerous conditions at Toncontin International Airport were not responsible for the crash of flight #414, but the knowledge of these conditions should have made the most experienced pilot cautious dur-ing approach. Additionally, the southern route from Managua was no-torious for bad weather and a challenging approach (mountains have to be cleared before descending quickly and sharply to the airport).

Ex-Chief of the Honduran Air Force, Walter Lopez Reyes, made a public statement after the crash, saying that "Toncontin International Airport represents insecurity for all travelers." He postulated that Tegucigalpa required a new airport and that it would have to be located well outside of town. He confirmed that the geography in and around the capital was not suitable for the construction of a new airport that is safer than Toncontin.

In an interview three days after the crash, Honduran President José Azcona admitted that Toncontin Airport was "dangerous for residents of Teguigalpa and anyone who flies in or out of the capital." Azcona said it is a shame that there is not a more reliable and secure airport.

Some months after the crash, I called the National Transportation Safety Board (NTSB) and requested a copy of the report on the investigation of what was initially considered a plane collision with a mountain. I sought the report to satisfy my curiosity. I was still in the throes of rehabilitation, but was anxious to see the results of the investigation. My condition at the time and rumors about pilot negligence were motivation enough to want to know the truth about the crash of flight #414. I continued to wonder about how a plane that seemed to be flying normally could suddenly slam into a mountainside ninety seconds before landing.

The investigation and resulting report were carried out by a commission appointed by the President of Honduras under the direction of the *Organizacion de Aviacion Civil* (Civil Aeronautics Board), the top aviation authority in the country. The United States government's National Transportation Safety Board (NTSB) provided technical assistance and advice to the Honduran body. In a crash that involves a foreign carrier in another country, the NTSB has two primary responsibilities. The first responsibility is for the manufacturer of the aircraft (in this case Boeing) to investigate the possibility of "product deficiency." The second responsibility is to send in representatives who provide technical assistance and advice to the investigating body.

The NTSB has no authority on foreign soil with a foreign carrier and can only make comments to the final report. It is a requirement, though, that the comments either be incorporated into the report or attached to it. Bob MacIntosh, an NTSB employee I spoke with, had a personal story to share about flying into Tegucigalpa. He was on a SAHSA flight in 1974 when the 737 aircraft slid off the end of the runway at Toncontin. The passengers were not hurt, but it was a close call that he has never forgotten.[20]

In the aftermath of the crash, the President of Honduras reassured the public that the investigation would be thorough and promised to make the findings available. He surprised many by weighing in on the issue of culpability for the crash. President Azcona essentially absolved the pilots of any guilt before the commission was able to assume its responsibilities. In the interview, he stated that bad weather was the determining factor in the crash, not pilot negligence or mechanical failure.[21]

President Daniel Ortega of Nicaragua responded to the enormous loss of Nicaraguan lives sustained in the crash by calling for a full and unbiased investigation. Ortega pledged to a shaken Nicaraguan public that the truth would come out about the crash.

THE INVESTIGATION REPORT

The report of the Investigating Commission was issued on November 28, 1989 by the Civil Aeronautics Board of the Ministry of Communications, Public Works and Transportation of the Government of Honduras. The NTSB sent me a copy, but initially, it was not made public in Honduras or Nicaragua. Neither survivors nor family members of the deceased were granted access to the findings. Some family members did eventually get copies of the report through their attorneys in the United States and key portions of the report appeared in Honduran dailies.

The investigation report specified the following mistakes made by the pilots:

1. "The Captain did not conduct a briefing before the landing."

(*This is standard procedure between the captain and the control tower following a checklist designed for use by pilots flying the Boeing 727.*)

2. "The ground proximity warning system (GPWS) was not operating at the moment of impact. There are strong indications that the captain disconnected the GPWS and removed its circuit breakers."

(*The GPWS is an important safety measure that is activated when the aircraft is descending too quickly and is approaching land. A voice gives a verbal warning to the crew.*)

3. "The Investigating Commission could not determine exactly why the crew members descended below the critical altitudes without any of them expressing or protesting the same."

(*The captain and the first officer both have an altimeter and a radar altimeter. The former measures absolute altitude and the latter measures height above ground. This means that, between them, the two pilots had access to four measures of altitude.*)

4. The issue of pilot fatigue was raised in the report as a possible contributing factor, "The crew, especially the Captain, had not complied with the rest requirements; there may have been some flight fatigue." A great deal has been written recently about pilot fatigue and its potential impact upon aviators' performance, "resulting in impaired vigilance, judgement, situational awareness and crew coordination."[22]

In the book *Broken Wings–A Flight Attendant's Journey*, the author makes the case that flight attendants regularly visit the cockpit not out of boredom or to be friendly with the pilots, but to "make sure the boys are awake and with it." It is interesting, too, that analyses of confidential reports to NASA's Aviation Safety Reporting System indicate that about twenty-one percent of all reported aircraft incidents are fatigue related. Research confirms too that air incidents are more likely to occur in the early morning hours.[23] TAN SAHSA #414 crashed at 7:50 A.M.

The final conclusion of the investigation report is an indictment of the pilots. The reference to adverse weather conditions was defined earlier in the report as being cold, wet, cloudy and windy.

"The probable causes of the accident were that the crew did not strictly comply with the procedure and profile of the instrumental descent published in the approach chart, for which they had received authorization from the Controller (VOR/DME 01) with respect to the altitudes and distances established, aggravated by the adverse weather conditions at the time when the approach was being made."[24]

Shortly after the crash, rumors circulated that the pilots had been partying the night before and were actually intoxicated when they arrived at the airport in San José. One rumor claimed that the pilots were not prepared to fly that day and may have been out carousing until early in the morning. I was also told that the pilots were drinking during our flight and that two stewardesses were in the cockpit with them at the time of the crash. I had no way of knowing if any of these rumors were true, but I desperately wanted to believe them. I wanted to blame someone for this tragedy and enough blame was cast on the pilots by the investigative report to make the rumors at least plausible.

Nivia Umanzor, the purser, told me emphatically that the flight crew did not drink alcoholic beverages the night before the crash. She said that it was raining in San José and the entire crew had stayed in their hotel rooms, ordering out pizza and soft drinks from Pizza Hut. She acknowledged that her account ran counter to rumors about the flight crew. She was clear, however, that the rumors were false.

The investigation report was critical of the pilots for not maintaining a "sterile cockpit" after descending below 10,000 feet. A "sterile cockpit" requires pilots to communicate only with each other and with the control tower about the approach and landing. No extraneous conversation about anything else or with anyone else is permitted. The pilots' conversation (as confirmed by the black box transcript) was not focused on the approach of the plane to Toncontin International Airport, and a flight attendant was in the cockpit during a portion of the approach period.[25]

THE PUBLIC FIGHTS BACK

Cesar Montes Lagos, a Honduran insurance adjuster, lost his oldest son, Cesar Augusto Montes, in the tragedy. On his own initiative, he launched a valiant effort to prosecute the captain and the first officer for their negligent behavior that resulted in the crash of TAN SAHSA flight #414. In his book, *Crimen Sin Castigo* (*Crime Without Punishment*), Mr. Montes describes his efforts to bring the pilots to justice, using the findings of the investigation report as the basis for the charge of homicide.

The pilots were indicted on the charge of homicide and spent twenty-four hours in the Central Penitentiary in Tegucigalpa on November 23, 1989, a month after the crash. Both the captain and the first officer maintained their innocence to the press, saying that they had followed all the required procedures for the approach to Toncontin. The two were released on bail the following day and were then absolved of all wrongdoing by Judge Ruben Dario Nuñez on April 24, 1990. He found that there was insufficient proof to find the pilots guilty of homicide. All charges against them were dismissed.

Undaunted, Mr. Montes immediately took the case to the First Court of Appeals in Tegucigalpa, where it was reviewed by three magistrates. While meeting with the magistrates prior to deliberations, Mr. Montes discovered that they had been provided copies of the investigation report that were altered to cast the pilots and the airline in a more favorable light. Worse yet, the black box transcript was not included in the official report. Montes immediately delivered copies of the full, original report that he had secured in the United States. The magistrates refused to receive Montes' report on the basis that they were obligated to make use of the official report delivered to them by the Civil Aeronautics Board. The report had been tampered with, but there was nothing that Mr. Montes or anyone else could do to rectify the situation.

On June 26, 1990, two of the three magistrates ruled in favor of the pilots and absolved them of all responsibility for the crash, the deaths of 131 passengers and the injuries of the other thirteen survivors. The decision essentially released TAN SAHSA Airline from any criminal culpability.

It is rare in any criminal justice system for judicial decisions to be rendered so swiftly and so decisively, particularly when the deaths of so many people are involved. Nevertheless, the First Court of Appeals chose to render a decision that was apparently based on a falsified report. As Mr. Montes concluded in his book, "justice in Honduras, in this case, was compromised by the corruption of the state." It brought international discredit upon the country of Honduras. Mr. Montes concluded by stating, "Verifying the truth and then remaining silent is to be an accomplice to the worst crime in the history of the country."

THE IDEOLOGICAL BARRIERS WERE BROKEN

The crash of flight #414 was the worst air catastrophe in the history of Central America. Condolences came in from all over the world, including the Pope, the Secretary General of the United Nations, Javier Perez de Cuellar, President George Herbert Bush of the United States and other presidents from the region. The loss was painful and profound for the countries of Nicaragua and Honduras. One hundred and four of the deceased passengers hailed from the two Central American republics.

Three days of national mourning were declared by Presidents José Azcona and Daniel Ortega. For a brief period of time, the two governments were able to set aside their political differences and cooperate.

Honduras and Nicaragua share a border and historically have been like first cousins that fall in and out of favor with each other. At the time of the crash, relations between the two countries were deeply strained. Through much of the 1980s, the Sandinista revolution in Nicaragua and the aggressive opposition by the United States government drove a wedge between Honduras and Nicaragua. The Honduran government supported U.S. government policy by giving refuge to the CIA created anti-Sandinista guerillas known as the Contras on its southern border. In addition, there was a buildup of U.S. troops and military facilities in Honduras. The Contras (contra means against or opposite in English) made frequent strikes into Northern Nicaragua to terrorize and kill Nicaraguans who were suspected of being Sandinista sympathizers. These actions were designed to disrupt Nicaragua with the intention of overthrowing the Sandinista government.

Sandinista rebels defeated Anastasio Somoza and his *Guardia Nacional* (National Guard troops) on July 19, 1979. The Somoza family had controlled Nicaragua economically, politically and militarily since the 1930s. When the Sandinistas took control, the majority of people lived in the countryside, where only 5 percent of the children completed sixth grade. The average life expectancy was fifty-three years, and the main causes of death were preventable diseases like diarrhea and tuberculosis. Two-thirds of children under five years old suffered from malnutrition. Eighty percent of the country's houses did not have running water and approximately 60 percent had no electricity. Most Nicaraguans lived in small shacks with dirt floors.[26]

From the start, Washington was leery of the Sandinista government and charged that the new rebel junta received support from the Soviet Union via the communist regime in Cuba and the leftist guerillas in El Salvador under the Frente Farabundo Marti de Liberacion Nacional (FMLN). The fears of the U.S. government were confirmed over time and Nicaragua turned out to be one of the last cold war battlefields with the U.S. created opposition forces fighting to bring down the Soviet-supported Sandinista government.

By 1981, Honduras had become the nucleus of U.S. foreign policy in Central America. In exchange for large increases in military and economic aid, Honduras signed on as an ally with the U.S. government to help in the fight against the Sandinistas.

The Contras consisted of former Somoza national Guard troops, disaffected Nicaraguans and mercenaries. They set up camps in southern Honduras and were provided with weaponry and provisions by the Reagan Administration. The United States government helped turn Honduras into an "armed camp." U.S. financed construction included building or improving eleven airstrips, two sophisticated radar stations, several base camps and training facilities, combat ready helicopter refueling pads and a large-scale command and logistics center at Palmerola Air Base. U.S. military and economic assistance to Honduras was $31.4 million in 1979 but reached $282.6 million by 1985.[27]

Contra attacks on key Nicaraguan facilities and infrastructure were initiated in early 1982 forcing the Sandinista government to declare a state of emergency and dig in. Hostilities continued throughout the remainder of the decade with the Sandinistas forced into a defensive posture of defending Nicaragua from a well-armed and trained guerilla army that seemingly struck at will and just as quickly melted into the mountains and retreated to safety across the border in to Honduras.

Damages and loss of life were enormous for the Nicaraguans. In most cases Nicaraguans were killing Nicaraguans.

In 1987, Oscar Arias, President of Costa Rica, cobbled together a regional peace plan that called for a cease-fire timetable for the region's guerilla wars, an international verification commission for the cease-fires, negotiations with guerilla groups, free elections, freedom of the press and a lifting of the states of emergency in all countries in the region. Arias eventually won a Nobel Prize for brokering the regional peace plan. Hostilities between the Contras and the Sandinistas continued for several years after the presidents of Costa Rica, El Salvador, Guatemala, Honduras and Nicaragua signed the Arias Plan.

Prior to the crash of flight #414, the Sandinista government had agreed to presidential elections that were scheduled for February 1990. The Sandinista leader and president of the country, Daniel Ortega, was pitted against Violeta Chamorro. Doña Violeta was the, widow of Pedro Chamorro--newspaper owner and critic of the Somoza family whose assassination in 1978 sparked the revolt against the regime. She had been a member of the original ruling junta after Somoza was deposed but quit over disagreements with the Sandinistas on how to run the country. The election was thought to be a true test of the popularity of the Sandinista regime after ten years of ruling Nicaragua that included the struggle with the Contras resulting in 40,000 deaths. The crash of flight #414 added to the national grief and further numbed a nation that had grown accustomed to quick, brutal and inexplicable loss of life.

HONDURAS' ROLE IN AVIATION HISTORY

Ironically, Honduras and TAN Airline had played a central role in the development of aviation in Latin America and had a spotless safety record until 1989. The introduction of air travel in the 1920's and 30's in the region proved it to be a successful means of transportation due to the geography and the proximity of countries to each other and to the United States. Rugged mountains, dense jungles, swamps and erratic weather patterns made development of railroads and highways difficult and expensive.

Initially air travel was accessible to only a handful of wealthy people throughout the region. Some argued that investment in commercial and cargo airlines was done at the expense of developing infrastructure. Others made the case that if you could fly slaughtered cattle from the lowlands to urban populations in the mountains at little cost, what motivation was there for building a highway? The choice between eight hours in a jeep over rough, dusty roads or thirty minutes in a plane was an easy one. Cash-strapped governments were not inclined to spend scarce resources on infrastructure that they could ill afford to build or maintain.

TAN Airline (Transportes Aereos Nacionales) was founded in Honduras in the early 1950s by a North American aviation pioneer, C.N. Shelton. Shelton had been ferrying people and cargo around the region since the late 1920s[28] and started the fledgling airline with one plane and a loan from Madame Chiang Kai-shek. The plane was a C-46 cargo with four seats for passengers. Shelton's goal was for TAN to be the first airline in Latin America to "make air travel affordable to the general public." He was successful and opened routes throughout the region and to the United States.

After Shelton died in 1965, his daughter, Patsy Shelton Spohrer, bought TAN Airline at auction and became the first female airline president in the world. She eventually sold her controlling interest in TAN to General Oswaldo Lopez Arellano, a former dictator of Honduras and a former TAN pilot. It was during this period that TAN Airline developed a close association with Honduras' other main carrier, SAHSA.

General Lopez Arellano was the majority owner of TAN Airline when the crash occurred. At that time, the airline flew throughout Central America and to Mexico City, Houston, New Orleans and Miami from Honduras with three Boeing 737s and one Boeing 727.

The crash of flight #414 was the first in a series of problems that beset the airline and started it on a downward spiral. A year after the crash of flight #414, at virtually the same spot on Cerro de Hula, a TAN cargo plane went down and two crewmembers were lost.

It is ironic, too, that Boeing designed the 727 to service smaller airports with shorter runways than those used by its predecessor, the 707. The 727 was an ideal aircraft for use in Central America and particularly for Toncontin. The tail of the 727 was designed to allow the aircraft to climb fast, fly fast and descend fast, without excessive vibrations.

The 727-200 was introduced in December 1967 with an increased gross weight and a twenty foot-longer fuselage. The 727-200 that crashed on October 21, 1989, was leased from Continental Airlines. The aircraft was manufactured in 1968 and was the 579th model produced by Boeing. According to the National Transportation Safety Board investigators, there was no record of any critical maintenance during a ten-day overhaul period (October 9-October 19, 1989) immediately prior to the crash. The engines had all been removed in recent years for routine maintenance and the investigators found no structural problems with the aircraft. The plane was in good shape and received a clean bill of health from the investigators. The rumors about mechanical problems and a malfunctioning aircraft were false.

In the early 1990s, concern over lax and dangerous safety practices in many countries led the Federal Aviation Administration (FAA) to assess aviation systems in thirty countries, including Honduras. The FAA conducted the Honduras assessment in 1993 and found that the government's civil aviation authority did not comply with the International Civil Aviation Organization (ICAO) aviation safety oversight standards for operations conducted to and from the United States.

Honduras was among nine countries (Belize, Dominican Republic, Gambia, Ghana, Nicaragua, Paraguay, Uruguay and Zaire) that were found to have unsafe aviation systems. This finding was the basis for banning TAN SAHSA Airline from operating flights in the United States. Among other things, the assessment looked at compliance with all air safety guidelines, and particularly focused on pilot training, aircraft maintenance and air carrier certification. The FAA decision proved to be the final nail in the coffin for an airline that thrived throughout the 1980s, until the crash of flight #414. After a long and proud history of safety and accessible, affordable service, TAN Airline went out of business in 1995 under a cloud of shame and disgrace.

THE IMPORTANCE OF ASSIGNING BLAME

The behavior of the pilots cannot be casually dismissed as carelessness, inattention or a momentary lapse in concentration. The fact is that the plane crashed as a result of their negligence. Houston attorney, John Grayson, who represented twenty-five Honduran families in a successful suit (Evenor Lopez-Scott et.al. v TAN SAHSA, Continental et.al.), told me, "This was the most preventable air accident I have ever seen. It should not have happened. Grayson confirmed that First Officer Canales admitted under oath that the "primary cause of the crash was failure to maintain proper altitude." He admitted "they did not follow standard approach procedures," and he "knew it while it was happening." Canales chose to say nothing because, in his words, "co-pilots do not challenge the captain."[29]

When you have gone through a trauma of this magnitude, you want to believe that someone was at fault, that someone can be blamed. It is a lot easier to focus your anger and frustration on another person(s) than on the weather or a mechanical failure. In the case of the pilots, it was rumored shortly after the crash that they had not only avoided prosecution in Honduras, but that they were flying again. I had no way of confirming any of these rumors.

At that point, I wanted to believe the rumors because they gave me a place to focus my enmity, an enmity born from the painful and painstaking process of burn treatment and the knowledge that so many people had suffered and died needlessly. Blaming the pilots and directing my hatred toward them was a temporary salve for my wounded body and psyche.

Directly related to the issue of assigning blame was the position of Lloyd's of London wich was the insurance company for TAN SAHSA-on the limits of liability. The Warsaw Convention is an agreement between air carriers and governments of countries where those carriers operate. It was created in 1929 to unify "certain rules relating to international transportation by air" by setting benchmarks for airlines and courts to follow. Most notable among these is the limitation of liability that establishes a maximum amount of money to be paid out to any consumer of the air carriers' services.

The 1929 limitation of liability or damage cap per passenger was $8,300. It was raised to $16,000 in 1955 and then to $75,000 in 1958. Clearly it was to my advantage and to the benefit of all survivors and family members of deceased passengers for the maximum required compensation to be waived. As I understood it, though, the Warsaw Convention can only be waived if there is culpability on the part of the "carrier" or "any agent of the carrier acting within the scope of his employment." The Warsaw Convention is designed to protect airlines from excessive costs for accidents that may well have been beyond their control. However, if the airline is found to be responsible for what occurred, the limitation is lifted and the airline is liable for an undefined amount of money.

There is no limitation if it can be proven that the airline or its employees were guilty of willful misconduct. This is difficult to prove, because it basically means that not only were mistakes made, but they were deliberate or intentional. Was it possible to prove that the Captain and First Officer of TAN SAHSA flight #414 were guilty of willful misconduct? Did they voluntarily or intentionally make mistakes that caused the plane to crash?

In a landmark ruling involving the articles of the Warsaw Convention, the United States District Court for the Southern District of New York set forth a standard for willful misconduct:

"It is common ground that 'willful misconduct' goes far beyond any negligence, even gross or culpable negligence, and involves a person doing or omitting to do that which is not only negligent but which he knows and appreciates is wrong, and is done or omitted regardless of the consequences, not caring what the result of his carelessness may be."[30]

Close to a year after the crash I received a call from my attorney in Miami with the news that TAN SAHSA Airlines was concerned enough over the issue of culpability that they were willing to waive the Warsaw Convention limitation or damage cap of $75,000 and negotiate through their insurance company. This admission by the airline confirmed the findings of the Investigation Report, and in my mind confirmed the rumors about the flight crew. Apparently, the airline believed that the evidence proved that "willful misconduct" had been committed by the pilots who were "acting as agents of the carrier within the scope of their employment."

Within a month after the crash, my father and my brother, Alan, both attorneys, put together a legal team to represent my claim. While discussing the case with my father, I said to him, "Dad, I am not interested in a settlement with the airline. The only thing I want is an hour in a closed room with the two pilots who walked away from the crash without a scratch. I hate these guys."

He reacted angrily by saying, "You need to think rationally and let go of this nonsense. Now I don't want to hear any more talk about the pilots." My father was a man of few words, and when he spoke he got right to the point. I felt like a little kid who had said something stupid, but I truly loathed the pilots for what had happened. It was a loathing I could not expect others to understand. It was a loathing that would take me years to excise from my emotions.

I thought I was thinking rationally. What could be more rational than wanting to face the accused of a crime that killed 131 people and left thirteen survivors, myself included, in different states of pain and suffering? Of course this is not the way it works, but from a mental health point of view, my healing process may well have accelerated if I had had the opportunity to face the pilots within the first year or two of the crash. I have no idea what I would have said to them, nor how I would have acted. In all fairness to my father, it is possible I would have done something irrational.

My interest in the pilots' guilt lay dormant for many years. However, after nine years, I was suddenly curious about what the other survivors looked like including the pilots. I wanted to know how they had lived since the crash, what they had to say about the crash and how it occurred.

In September 1999, I twice interviewed Nivia Umanzor, the purser. In both interviews, she contended that First Officer Reinero Canales knew that the plane was too low, but chose to say nothing. She made the same statement to La Tribuna reporter Oscar Flores Lopez in an interview published on October 23, 1999, a month after I talked with her. She stated:

"The Captain [Raul Argueta] looked at his instruments while flying, and the First Officer looked at other instruments. What the captain saw, according to him, was correct, but one of the instruments was off [not functioning properly]. The First Officer saw the altimeter, something called the ground altimeter, that indicated we were dangerously close to the ground."

"Should he have known?" I asked.

"He knew the altitude of the plane from the altimeter, but he nevertheless said nothing to the captain. He went to Houston to testify, because the lawyers used the statements and he testified there. I saw his testimony."

"He said that?"

"He said that he knew... that for four minutes he knew that the plane was going to crash."

"Explain to me," I prompted, "What happened between the captain and the First Officer in Managua?"

"I was the one who heard them arguing, and I believe they were arguing about the fuel," replied Nivia.

"They had to fill the tanks in Managua because there was no fuel, or the fuel was expensive in Tegucigalpa?"

"Yes, and I heard them fighting about that. I don't remember very much, but the one who was angrier and arguing was the first officer. And I believe that Reinero [first officer] was angry during the flight [to Tegucigalpa]. Perhaps it was for that reason that he said nothing to the captain."

"Did you ever talk to the First Officer Canales after the crash?

"Yes, I talked with him, and he explained that he never said anything to the pilot because they had been so angry with each other."

"He said that!"

"He said that to me. After returning from Houston, we were convinced that he was responsible for not telling the captain how things were, that we were too low. I ran into him at a birthday for our children. We saw each other in gatherings like that, and I felt very bad when I saw him. I began to cry and stamp my feet and I didn't want to see him there. Then he came to my house looking for me and said to me, "Why do you get upset every time you see me?" I told him, "because you saw that the plane was going to crash and you didn't say anything. Why didn't you say something? Look at the number of deaths, the people crying, the number of orphans, mothers that won't see their children again. Then he said, 'Look, you saw that we were angry with each other.'"

***

I had a hard time believing this story after hearing it the first time. It was so incredible that I had Nivia repeat it for a second time on tape during a visit to the crash site with another survivor, Ramon Sanchez Borba. I wanted to believe her, but the story was so astonishing that I filed it away until I saw it confirmed in a newspaper interview in Tegucigalpa a month later.

How can a simple disagreement lead to the death of innocent people? If true, in my opinion, Canales was a deranged person who was both suicidal and homicidal. He apparently was devoid of any sense of responsibility for the passengers and the crew.

The Houston litigation against TAN SAHSA and Continental Airlines revealed additional information that is at once startling but consistent with the other findings. It turns out that the U.S. investigators (NTSB, FAA, and Boeing) were so concerned about what the pilots told them about the crash, that they requested a psychologist from Washington to conduct a follow-up interview. The psychologist concluded that the pilots needed reconditioning and training to get away from the "cultural" problem of a subordinate never challenging the superior officer. The respect for hierarchy was reinforced in this case by pilots who had military backgrounds and were never able to accept that they were no longer in the military. Specifically, First Officer Canales admitted that he knew the aircraft was too low, but chose to say nothing under the guise of not challenging his superior, Captain Argueta.[31]

A final footnote adds further fuel to the fire. The aircraft was owned by Continental Airlines and had been leased to TAN SAHSA. The lease, which was written by attorneys for Continental, required that daily and weekly maintenance reports be faxed to Continental's office in Houston. The attorney who wrote the lease testified that Continental wanted to know the maintenance condition of the aircraft at all times. The maintenance records indicated that the ground proximity warning system (GPWS) was not working. Continental did not read the reports or ignored this information even though the GPWS is on the FAA Minimum Equipment List and must always be used unless permission is granted by the FAA. The records clearly showed that the GPWS had not been used on this plane for several flights, and it turned out that the pilots were disarming the system by pulling its circuit breaker. The pilots testified that they did not want to be bothered by the loud noise made by the GPWS when the plane got too close to land. Both airlines attempted to demonstrate that the warning system would not have activated soon enough to allow the pilots to pull out of their descent and avoid the mountain. Attorney John Grayson was able to prove in a Houston courtroom that, had the pilots received a GPWS warning, they could have pulled the plane up in time and avoided crashing into Cerro de Hula.

The captain and the first officer were experienced pilots, but were relatively new to the Boeing 727 aircraft. Captain Raul Argueta had logged 20,018 hours flying for the airline and had received his qualification to fly the B-727 in April 1989-just over six months prior to the crash of flight #414. He had logged 344 hours on the B-727. First Officer Reinero Canales qualified to fly the B-727 aircraft in March 1989 and had logged 436 hours flying the B-727-200 out of a total 6,653 flying hours.[32]

In my opinion, the pilots were not evil men and had no evil intent on October 21, 1989. They were irresponsible in how they carried out their professional duties and committed "gross negligence" as it regards the safety of the crew and the passengers. They were not evil men, but they committed an evil act.

FDR Data Based Final Phase of Flight Profile to Impact
B-727 TAN/SAHSA Flight 414, 21 October 1989

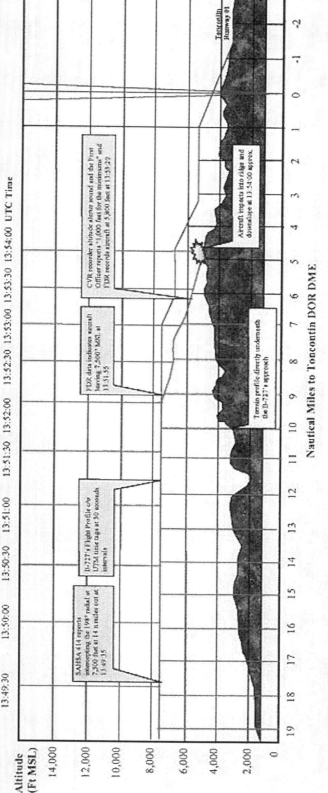

Source: Four Institute Geografico Nacional
Final Report on the TAN/SAHSA Flight 414 Boeing 727 Accident by DGAC, Honduras
A.I.R Inc.'s FDR Data Reproduction & Analysis & CVR Transcript Analysis

CHAPTER TWELVE

MY HEALING

Take your life in your own hands and what happens?
A terrible thing: no one to blame.

                                        Erika Jong

I initiated this journey of research, introspection and writing in 1998, because I was still aware of my own unfinished business, my lingering inner conflicts. Too many personal issues associated with the crash of flight #414 remained unresolved, and this initiative was my personal commitment to do something about it.

THE PILOTS

Foremost among the unresolved conflicts was my continuing rage toward the pilots who I held fully responsible for the crash. In October 2000, I was still struggling with my anger toward them when I flew to Honduras. My plan was to continue my research and to expressly attempt to locate and talk with the pilots. I was determined to find them.

Upon arrival, I called Nivia Umanzor, the purser for Flight # 414 to see if she could help me. She explained that she had talked with Captain Argueta the previous year after being interviewed in the local Tegucigalpa paper, *La Tribuna*. In that interview, Nivia had made some positive comments about the Captain, and he had called to thank her. She in turn asked him to make a public statement about what occurred on October 21, 1989. He responded to her by saying that it was too late for that sort of thing. Nivia and I agreed that it is never too late, particularly since plenty of people affected by the crash could benefit from a public disclosure by the captain.

Nivia gave me the name *Colonia Pinares de Ulluoa*, where she thought Captain Argueta lived. I decided to look for him. At the time I was staying with an old friend, who offered me his jeep and driver, Manuel, to make the search. It was a bit like of a long shot, but I decided to pursue the captain. We drove half an hour out of town north and turned at the sign for Colonia Pinares de Ulluoa. A guard let us through, and we drove into a small community of upscale new homes.

I asked a homeowner working in his yard if he knew Captain Argueta. He said he knew everyone in the community and there was no one by that name. He suggested we continue down the road to another community called *Residencias Tatumbla*. At this point I felt like there was nothing to lose, so we pushed on.

We followed a dirt road for a couple of miles, and the ruts deepened while the road became increasingly narrow as it wound around a mountainside. I was struck by the beauty and isolation of the heavily wooded area. We finally came upon a sign over the road with the name *Tatumbla* on it. As we entered the community, it was obvious that the small residential development had seen better times. Many of the homes were boarded up and had not been maintained in years. Houses were in disrepair, with doors hanging on hinges. Yards were overgrown. There was still a semblance of a community, though, with some of the homes occupied.

A few people were working around their residences, and we came across several children playing by the roadside. We stopped, and I asked them if they knew where Raul Argueta lived. A little boy no older than ten years shouted out, "Yes, he lives right over in those woods. It's the first house. We saw him this morning."

Just like that we found the pilot's home. I immediately felt anxious over the prospect of seeing this guy. We proceeded along the road into the thick woods and quickly came upon the first and only house for as far as we could see. There was a ten-foot high black wooden door that formed part of a cement block fence with barbed wire on top of it. This was it. We had arrived at Captain Argueta's home.

Loud music was blaring from what sounded like a radio in the house. After ringing the doorbell with no response, Manuel and I made as much noise as we could possibly generate. Banging on the door, honking the horn of the jeep and screaming the name of the pilot did not rouse anyone from behind the impregnable wall. I finally decided to leave a note for Captain Argueta, telling him that I wanted to meet with him and to please call me in Tegucigalpa. I honestly did not think anything would materialize, and chalked it up to an interesting but fruitless afternoon adventure in the Honduran countryside.

Not long after returning to my friend's home, the phone rang. The caller identified himself as Guillermo Argueta, the son of the pilot. He said that he was glad to hear from me and began talking about how difficult it had been for the family since the crash. He said his father did not remember anything after the plane crashed and used words like "*marginado*" (person on the fringe of society), "*ocultado*" (in hiding) and "*recuparse*" (recover from) to describe his father and the life he had led since the crash. He said it was always hard this time of the year, anniversary of the tragedy, and that his father usually left town to avoid hearing about the crash. He seemed intent on somehow setting the record straight with me.

Guillermo offered to get together under the pretext of determining whether or not it would be appropriate for his father to subsequently meet with me. I told him my interest was to meet his father, and that I was documenting the experience of the crash. I also told him that there were positive stories coming from survivors and families of deceased passengers about how they have gotten on with their lives. We finally agreed to meet in two days. I was surprised and excited by this opportunity to get more insight into the character of the captain and his behavior on the day of the crash.

At the appointed spot, I was picked up by a young man in his late twenties, well dressed in a suit and driving a late model pickup truck. Guillermo suggested we go to TGI Friday's in a nearby shopping mall. We spent an hour together and never lacked for things to discuss. I purposely did not take my tape recorder, not wanting to scare him off.

As I stared into the eyes of the pilot's son, I felt a mixture of anger and angst, driven by a genuine desire to know the truth. The last time I saw his father, we were fleeing the scene of a horrific plane crash that we both survived. For eleven years I had been carrying around a deep-seated hatred for his father, who by all accounts was negligent in his duties and responsible for the crash.

Listening to Guillermo relay his father's version of the story did not convince me of the captain's innocence, but I did slowly feel my bitterness fading as the young man made a case for his father, Captain Argueta, who had ended his career that day.

The young attorney explained that his father had suffered a great deal by not being able to fly again. He had flown for twenty-five years and had logged approximately twenty-five thousand hours. Captain Argueta was forty-five years old at the time of the crash and lost his license to fly.

I asked what life had been like for his father, and Guillermo explained that there had been a number of lawsuits brought against him in the United States and Honduras. He said that it had been difficult for his father to put the crash behind him, particularly because of all the "false rumors" about the pilots drinking and partying the night before. Guillermo said that his father was a very disciplined person who was always careful about preparing for flights and carrying out his responsibilities as a captain.

When I pressed him about what actually happened to flight #414, Guillermo said that his father testified several times in lawsuits that he descended on the basis of the instruments (DME) altitude reading. According to Guillermo, the instrument was broken and the reading was incorrect, which resulted in the plane being too low and crashing into the mountainside. This story is consistent with Nivia's account.

He said that to this day, his father does not remember the crash itself, and that he was found wandering around the crash site in a daze saying that he had to help the passengers. This story is also consistent with the accounts of other survivors.

Guillermo asked what happened from my perspective, and I related my experience from the time of impact to our arrival at the Hospital Escuela in Tegucigalpa. Guillermo was curious about what other survivors and family members of the deceased said about his father. I explained that most people I had talked to believed that the crewmembers had been drinking the night before, and that virtually all of us who were associated with this tragedy held the airline, the captain and the first officer responsible for what happened.

I told Guillermo, "A lot of people are still hurting from the crash and the impact it had on their lives. They are looking for some sort of *alivio o consuelo* (relief or consolation). Your father could help people and probably help himself by making an official statement explaining what happened from his point of view." He responded by saying, "That will occur when the time is right, but now is not that time." With some emotion in my voice I said, "When will that time arrive?"

Guillermo answered me, "It will depend on a number of circumstances." These circumstances were never explained to me, and it is likely that Captain Argueta will never make a statement of any kind about the crash.

I then asked Guillermo, "How has your father coped with the stress of the crash, the resulting lawsuits and criticism? He responded by saying, "My father is very sensitive to criticism. That is why he doesn't listen to the news or look at the newspapers on and around the anniversary of the crash. It is just too painful a subject for him to hear or talk about. He did go to therapy after the crash and has benefited from strong family support over the years."

Guillermo Argueta seemed somewhat relieved to have talked with me about the crash and its impact upon his father. He said that it would be possible to meet with his father at some point in the future, but again couldn't say when or how. He asked how I had found the house and said that no one had ever showed up at their door before. He said the family was surprised by my visit and concerned over someone locating the isolated home.

This young man reacted as any son would react to a real or perceived threat to his father. He defended him. I respected Guillermo for taking the time to meet with me and thanked him for being so forthcoming during our time together. We exchanged addresses, but I really didn't expect to see Guillermo or his father in the future.

While walking away from our meeting, I felt a certain relief for the first time since the crash. My rational side always told me to let go of these overwhelming feelings of hatred and vengeance toward the captain and the first officer, but realistically I was never able to. How could I? There was too much pain and suffering for me and for so many others to simply dismiss the pilots' irresponsibility. I did not know how to let go, and it seemed perfectly natural to feel so strongly about something that hurt me so deeply. This one-hour meeting had allowed me to express some of my frustrations and anger in a civilized manner. I felt momentarily relieved.

On this same trip I traveled to San Pedro Sula, the second largest city in Honduras situated in the Northwestern part of the country. My primary interest in making the trip was to meet with two Honduran survivors of flight #414, Evenor Lopez and Hernan Madrid, who lived in San Pedro. My secondary reason for making the trip was to look for First Officer Reinero Canales.

While eating lunch with fellow survivors Lopez and Madrid, I mentioned my interest in talking with Canales. Lopez said that he moved in the same social circles and ran into the first officer on occasion. I was surprised and pressed him, "But doesn't it bother you to see this guy, knowing what happened and all the pain and suffering that you went through?"

He responded matter of factly, "No, it really doesn't. We aren't good friends, but I see him and we speak to each other."

I had to go further, "What about your wife, who lost her first husband in the crash?" Lopez responded, "No, no she has no interest in seeing or talking with Canales. In her opinion he is a bad person, but I don't feel that way."

I couldn't understand how Evenor Lopez, who once tried to jump from his hospital window in Houston because the pain from his burns was so excruciating, could be so accepting of a person I considered to be a criminal. He clearly had evolved into a more open person than I.

Evenor wanted to show me where he lived which happened to be near Canales' house. We stopped at the home of the first officer and knocked on the door of the large house surrounded by a high wall topped off with shards of broken glass. No one answered the door, and I felt nervous standing there on the sidewalk expecting Canales to poke his head out the door at any moment. What would I say, and how would I respond when I saw him? Alas, there was nothing to worry about. No one was home.

I had spent the previous week in Nicaragua, accompanied by Magaly, my daughter, Alexa, and my mother, Paula. They were great support to me and Magaly provided excellent guidance to the many emotionally wrought, heart-wrenching interviews. Her training as a psychotherapist provided insight and facilitation skills when they were needed most.

When the crash occurred, Magaly was a financial analyst for International Planned Parenthood Federation. (IPPF) She had a masters of business administration and worked with IPPF affiliates in Latin America and the Caribbean to improve their management capacity. After we moved to Atlanta in 1993, she pursued a masters degree in psychology and by the late 1990s was counseling the chronically mentally ill for a county mental health center.

After meeting with the two survivors and numerous other people in Honduras and Nicaragua, I flew back to Atlanta. It was time to return to normalcy in my life and attempt to process all that I had learned. I was exhausted, emotionally drained from two weeks of research. At the same time, I was satisfied because so many people had been willing to meet with me and had been so open about their own experiences and feelings over what had befallen them. My journey was far from over, but I felt as if it was headed in the right direction.

Upon returning to Atlanta, I was talking to Magaly about my experiences in Honduras. I told her about my meeting with the son of the captain. It was apparent to her that I felt better about the situation in general, but still harbored a lot of anger toward the pilots. She challenged me to confront my rage toward the pilots by writing a letter to them. Magaly was right, I was still angry and felt helpless and powerless that there was no recourse for dealing with the perpetrators of the crime. Talking to the captain's son in Honduras was a step toward letting go of my anger and hatred, but I wasn't there yet. The letter was never sent to them. Simply writing it was a therapeutic exercise.

Dear Raul and Reinero:

I have wanted to communicate with the two of you since I first recovered from the burns that I sustained in the crash of TAN SAHSA flight #414. You both were responsible for this tragedy. I continue to hold out hope that someday I will meet with each of you, but up to this point that has not been possible. My primary interest in writing to you is to express to you how I feel about what occurred on October 21, 1989, when the Boeing 727 that we were traveling in together crashed in the area of Cerro de Hula upon approach to Toncontin International Airport in Tegucigalpa.

Like any crime, the victims have to live with the impact of what the perpetrator carried out. In my case, dealing with the burns on my body was simply one small part of the impact of your hideous crime. I have had to constantly think about and, yes, relive that crash in my conscious hours each day and through my dreams. A trauma of this magnitude never goes away, and I trust you have experienced your own pain and suffering over the years.

I am now very familiar with what happened to the other passengers who were on board flight #414--how so many of them died unfairly in the most horrible, and torturous manner possible. They burned alive. I have heard the stories about family members bidding a father and mother, a young daughter or a sister farewell at the airport and then finding out less than an hour later that their loved one was dead. They then had to embark on an even more traumatic undertaking of identifying a burned corpse or pieces of a corpse in a stinking, inadequate hellhole of a morgue. The sorrow and distress inflicted upon these innocent people--the survivors, the deceased and the family members of deceased--is all a result of your negligent behavior. The evidence is clear about this and there is no discussion of who is responsible. The two of you are responsible! The two of you are guilty!

Now that I have said that and feel somewhat relieved, I implore you both to make a public statement about what happened from your point of view. After years of silence, the most cowardly silence, it is time to tell your stories as you experienced the crash that day. Only you know exactly what happened in that cockpit and why the plane crashed. You need to share your experience with the world, most importantly, with those of us who were affected directly by this tragedy. I ask you to make this information public as one way to help us all heal. I believe that coming out and making your own statements will help you both feel some relief from the anguish you must carry around and from the blood of the dead passengers that is on your hands for life. May you both meet your just ends for the crimes you have committed.

Sincerely,

Curt Schaeffer

As the year progressed, I found that my fury towards the pilots would not go away. I knew it would not disappear as if nothing had ever happened to me, but somehow I wanted that to happen. I had this rather naïve magic wand notion about going face-to-face with the pilots. I thought that if I were able to meet them and talk with them that everything would be all right. Only then would I be able to let go of my negative feelings.

I returned to Honduras in October 2001, in pursuit of the pilots once again. I tried to reach both the captain and the first officer by phone. To my amazement, I got through to the First Officer, Reinero Canales, on my first try from my hotel in Tegucigalpa. He was in his office and seemed to be as surprised to hear from me as I was to actually talk with him. He was cordial, but there was an edge to his voice. He told me to call him when I got to San Pedro later that week. Even though I still harbored an intense dislike for this man, there was a certain calming effect to talking with him, hearing his voice, and knowing that he was a person just like me, with all his defects and complexes.

Shortly after talking to First Officer Canales, I got a call from his attorney, Veronica Rodriguez. She wanted to know who I was and why I wanted to talk with her client. She was acting as his representative, and I felt a cloud of disappointment take over my mind as I realized that a reunion with Canales would be impossible. I told her I was writing an account of the crash, what had happened through the eyes of the survivors and how people affected by it had healed over the years.

The attorney explained that it was very difficult for Canales to talk about the crash and that he would prefer not to meet with me. She said that she had advised him not to talk with me and was very concerned about what I might put in print about Canales and the crash. I explained that all I wanted to do was meet him, say hello and talk for a few minutes. I also told her that talking with others about the crash had helped me begin to let go of my pain and sadness and to ultimately feel better about myself and my life. She said she understood and that Canales would call me if he felt like talking. Her call was a clear warning not to bother her client. As I hung up the phone, it occurred to me that maybe it was best to drop this pursuit of the pilots.

Canales' reaction should have been expected. I believe it is typical of someone who has committed a crime not to want to own up to it. Paranoia of lawsuits, fear of physical injury and having to relive what occurred must constantly shadow Canales. He cannot possibly live in peace, and refusing to talk about what happened is simply one more decision to suppress feelings that must contribute to his own personal hell. Someone like me shows up and Pandora's box is opened again, like it or not. He has to be a tangle of nerves, guilt and depression.

I discussed the possibility of meeting Canales in San Pedro Sula with my Honduran friends. They were interested in my encounter with the first officer, but strongly advised against further pursuit of either the first officer or the captain. What was the point? What was to be gained from all of this? In a way, this let me off the hook. I had pursued the captain and the first officer as far as I could and finally accepted the fact that I would not have to face the accused. I was relieved.

After meeting with the son of Captain Argueta the year before, I had begun to think about the value of face-to-face encounter between the victim and the perpetrator of a crime. I knew this had been used as a therapeutic technique over the years to help the victim who was traumatized by the acts of the criminal. Was it helpful and healing for me to have this encounter with the son of the captain? I think so. Did I sleep better as a result of this encounter, or was I just fooling myself?

I felt a sense of relief afterwards and was sleeping more soundly after years of fitful slumber.

Finally feeling some sense of relief was liberating. I found it more than coincidental that I started encountering articles on the subject of healing in the newspaper. These articles jumped off the page at me. They spoke to me because I had experienced similar inner turmoil and was looking for relief too.

The articles covered a range of experiences and emotions, but all of them came back to the issues of letting go of anger and dealing with your own sense of rage and revenge. There were Jews struggling to be tolerant of Germans who had been born since World War II; a young man faced the truck driver who was responsible for a fiery crash that burned him on eighty-five percent of his body at two years of age; the Cuban Bay of Pigs veterans from the United States and Cuba met in Havana forty years after the bloody invasion to recount experiences and reconcile their differences; a man who lost his daughter in the Oklahoma City bombing let go of his deep-seated hatred of Timothy McVeigh by visiting McVeigh's father; the veterans of both sides of Colombia's guerilla wars who have formed a peace and reconciliation group--former rebels and soldiers who were gravely injured but committed to setting aside animosities and resentments in the interest of peace. There were also South Africans who participated in their country's truth and reconciliation process when Archbishop Desmond Tutu said, "Forgiving and being reconciled are not about pretending that things are other than they are."

What did all these people have in common with me, and why were these articles grabbing my attention? I kept a file of the articles and started thinking about their significance, while discussing the issue of healing with friends and family members.

The connection was obvious. A line out of the Bay of Pigs reunion partially captured how I thought I would feel if given the chance to meet the captain and first officer. In the article, Fidel Castro had just introduced Cuban officers, CIA men and anti-Castro brigadistas to each other. One of them said, "In that instant, I realized that all my hate and remorse was gone." That was after forty years of carrying around strong feelings and emotions. In a matter of seconds they dissipated, as the former enemies came together in a human encounter.

In a subsequent discussion about my experiences in pursuing the pilots, a friend challenged me by asking, "Do you really need to forgive these guys? Why can't you just get on with your life and forget about them?"

I could more readily forgive the pilots of flight #414 if they made some gesture of contrition. Neither the captain nor the first officer had been willing to say anything about what occurred.

Doug Jones, the prosecutor in the Bobby Frank Cherry trial for the bombing of the Birmingham Baptist Church that killed four young girls in 1963 said, "For there to be true forgiveness, it has to come from both sides." I think he is right, and I am still waiting for the pilots to say something. Forgiving the perpetrators of a painful trauma that has defined your life is difficult and complicated. In my case, forgiving the pilots could take the rest of my life.

Would I feel any better if the pilots were behind bars for a period of time? Probably not, although at least I would know where they were and how to visit them. But after seeing where both pilots currently live (behind high walls trimmed with barbed wire and broken glass) and after talking to their representatives (Argueta's son and Canales' lawyer), it is clear that they live in self-imposed jails. They are suffering and will continue to suffer from their fatal mistakes. Remaining silent about what occurred on October 21, 1989, will only exacerbate their torment. Chances are that the pilots look over their shoulders every time they go out in public.

What about revenge? Did the families who lost loved ones in the Oklahoma City bombing feel better after Timothy McVeigh was executed? Some said that yes, it was satisfying to know that he was dead. Others said no, it would not bring back those who perished and only served to perpetuate the very things that were at the root of the act in the first place-hatred and revenge. We all deal with our pain differently and one person's relief may represent further suffering for another. There are no absolutes when it comes to pain and its impact on our lives.

The pain of losing a loved one never goes away regardless of the willingness to forgive. The struggle with one's own pain is important, though, because it allows you to climb out of your own morass and live life more fully. Each day can be a little bit better for you and for those around you. You can never fully excise it from your being.

THE PILOTS ARE GUILTY!

During my October 2001 visit to Honduras, I was interviewed by a reporter for one of the top daily newspapers in Tegucigalpa-*El Heraldo*. The reporter, Oscar Flores, lost his father in the crash of flight #414. We were both survivors struggling with our emotional pain that day as we sat across from each other trying to make sense of what had happened and how we felt about it. The interview was more difficult for me to sit through than I had expected. It turned out to be a therapy session as Oscar asked hard questions about what had occurred and how I felt about it. I was stunned at one point when he asked, "Why didn't you go back to the plane to look for survivors?" The following is an excerpt from Flores' article.

I still think about that (closing his eyes)." Editor's note: Schaeffer puts both hands on his head and breathes deeply. "I don't know, maybe because of the shock or because I thought that everyone had my same luck and escaped. I never imagined that there would be so few survivors.

Do you feel bad that perhaps you could have saved someone?

Yes, yes...it is something that I ask myself (on the verge of tears).

I had always assumed that the other passengers escaped on the other side of the fuselage, since I was alone in the field. But the questions did force me to wonder if I could have returned to the aircraft to help. I was badly burned but able to walk. I do remember the fuselage being engulfed in flames and the pop, pop, pop sound of explosions as I came to in my seat in the field. I saw no sign of life and assumed that the other passengers had escaped on the other side of the plane, out of my sight. I was also in shock and probably not thinking clearly about all of the possibilities. Over the years I have thought many times of why I did not go back up the hill to the plane from the road once I came in contact with survivors.

Toward the end of the interview he asked, "Can you forgive the pilots?"

Without hesitation I answered, "No."

This question came after more than an hour of emotionally charged give and take. Had he asked me that question another time, under different circumstances, I might have said "yes," but not that day. My emotional pain was at its height and reliving the crash with the son of a deceased passenger did not put me in a forgiving mood.

The headlines the following day screamed out, "Pilotos tuvieron la culpa" ("The Pilots are Guilty!") I had exacted my revenge and maybe even a measure of justice by telling my story publicly in Spanish at the scene of the crime. Unknowingly, I had struck back at the pilots, perhaps where it hurt them most, in the realm of public opinion. Webster's defines revenge as "an opportunity to retaliate or gain satisfaction" and justice as "the administering of deserved punishment or reward." By responding to a last-minute request for an interview, I had unconsciously taken my revenge against the pilots and at the same time meted out some justice by confirming publicly what everyone had known for years--the pilots were guilty of the crime!

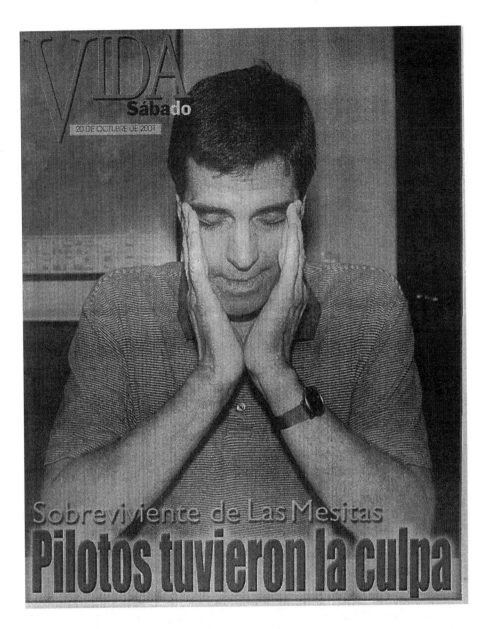

VIDA
Sábado
20 DE OCTUBRE DE 2001

Sobreviviente de Las Mesitas
Pilotos tuvieron la culpa

Was this enough for me? Was my appetite for striking out at the pilots satisfied? Probably not. I expected the trauma to remain in my psyche for life, but each encounter, each shred of understanding, each acknowledgement or healing moment helped me let go a bit more.

THE COUNTRY WAS TO BLAME

Before returning to the United States in October 2000, I attended the anniversary mass that is held each year at the crash site. October 21 dawned cloudy and cool in Tegucigalpa. There was a light wind and a fresh feel in the air. During the course of the morning the clouds dissipated and the sun shone brightly. I was up early and off to a local radio station to be interviewed about the air crash and my survival. I remained anxious about going out to the crash site.

My friend, Salvatore Pinzino, offered to take me to the mass on this anniversary of the disaster. The weather we encountered in the mountains changed dramatically once we climbed out of the city. The sky was cloudy and there was a strong wind with occasional rain spitting at us. It was cold, and I was glad to have taken a coat. I couldn't help but think that this was the way it was on the morning of the crash, when I shivered while begging for a blanket.

Sal and I walked up the long stone steps that lead to the memorial on the hillside above the road. HERMAFAME had purchased this property and erected a beautiful monument on the crash site that displayed a tablet with the names of the deceased passengers.

As I reached the top of the stairs, I was greeted by Mauricio Montes, who lost his brother in the crash. Then a microphone was shoved in my face by a radio broadcaster. He asked me how I felt as a survivor attending the mass. At this moment I looked directly at the long list of names of those who perished in the crash and began to cry. I told the reporter that I felt very emotional and was pleased to be able to attend the ceremony with the others who were there.

A priest was commencing the mass, and I quickly calculated that there were more than one hundred people in attendance. Included were a number of local residents from the immediate area and a youth chorus from a church in Tegucigalpa. I was upset throughout the service and had trouble following the ceremony. There were plenty of distractions, including the booming voices of two broadcasters and the constant arrival of people. A newspaper reporter kept following me around asking for an interview.

The priest spoke for some time about how people should not loose their faith because of a disaster like this. He explained that God does not decide who lives and who dies, rather that man makes that decision particularly as it relates to death due to accidents.

One of the more powerful moments of the mass was when the priest invited anyone who chose to call out the name of a loved one who had perished in the crash. One person after another shouted out the name of a brother or sister or father or son or husband. Each time a name was called, it felt like an electric shock zapped my body. It was dramatic and emotional.

The priest asked the assembled how many of us wanted to take communion. A small group of us chose to do so. I don't go to church very often and never take communion when I do. On this day it felt like the right thing to do. I wanted to participate fully with these people with whom I now realized a common bond.

After the mass, some of the people in attendance introduced themselves to me, and I embraced a number of those I knew from previous encounters. There was great fellowship among us all, and tears flowed freely. A woman who lost her daughter in the crash said to me, "Isn't this a beautiful place to die." The comment stopped me cold. Well, yes, *Cerro de Hula* was a beautiful place. I had never thought of it as a place of beauty, but she was right. Once again, it took the comment of someone who had suffered far more than I had to open my eyes to what was around me.

I remained on the mountainside with Carlos Valle, Ligia Davis and Lucrecia Perez. All three had lost their spouses in the crash and were active members of HERMAFAME. They took responsibility for hiring the priest and organizing and publicizing the mass each year. We walked around the property and inspected recently initiated construction of a small chapel. This was a joint effort of the people living in the local community, *Las Tablitas*, and the members of the association. The local community had never had a place to worship under a roof, and they appeared to be motivated to build one.

As we were walking down the steps to the cars, a boy of about eight years stopped us and told us that his mother wanted to offer us food she had prepared that morning. We walked through some brush and over to a nearby house that we later learned did not exist at the time of the crash. A short, plump woman with a broad smile emerged from the house and asked us to sit down. She served us corn tamales and fresh cheese. The food was delicious after standing in the cold wind for several hours. It was satisfying to sit there on the mountain-side and break bread with people from the area.

Carlos and Ligia invited us to eat lunch with their family at a restau-rant on the road back to Tegucigalpa. The handsome couple was ac-companied by four of their teenage children who had clearly benefited from their parents marriage after the crash.

For years I had hated Honduras and its people for the simple fact that the crash occurred in the country. My experiences on this day were begin-ning to change my mind. It was irrational to hate a country and its popula-tion over the willful misconduct of a couple of pilots. It was not the fault of all Hondurans that this crash had occurred, nor that the campesinos ignored me and other pleas for help near the crash site, nor that the airline did such a poor job of assisting survivors and then tried to make it difficult for families of the deceased to collect their rightful settlement.

All of these things had contributed to my strong dislike for Honduras. This dislike gave me a place to focus my anger; a place to focus my frustration over not being able to do anything about the crash; a place to focus my guilt over having survived something that killed one hundred thirty-one people; and a place to focus my pain, the inexplicable pain that comes from a trauma like this. A pain I had carried around since the crash occurred.

As we ate *pupusas* (corn tortillas with black beans and cheese) and drank cold Honduran beer, the cloud-enshrouded *Cerro de Hula* was visible from the window of the restaurant. On this day we couldn't escape the reality of flight #414. At one point during the lunch, Ligia Valle turned to me and said, "You have been reborn in Honduras and are now an honorary citizen of the country." I was immediately thrown off balance by this simple but cogent remark. She was right. I had gained a new lease on life in Honduras and should be thankful, not scornful, toward the country. Ligia helped me turn my attitude around. The beautiful smile on her face and the warmth of the group around the table helped me make peace with the country and its people.

THE CAMPESINOS

Since the day of the crash, I had been upset over the behavior of the Honduran campesinos at the crash site. The image of me standing on wobbly legs next to my seat and screaming for help while the laborers harvested corn remained fresh in my mind. I couldn't erase it. I continued to blame them as if they were somehow responsible for what had happened to me. The many accounts of looting the crash site and even robbing the personal effects from the dead passengers played and replayed in my mind.

When family members of the passengers drove to the crash site that fateful morning, they found their access blocked by police and soldiers. The area had not been officially cordoned off, and most of them were able to talk their way past the roadblock or simply walk around it and up the mountainside. In short order, they found the charred and broken remains of the aircraft. They also found more than one hundred people sifting through luggage, papers, personal belongings and body parts.

It was reported by the Tegucigalpa dailies that soldiers were seen sorting clothing, children stuffed toys and clothes into bags, and a firefighter slipped away with a suitcase under his overcoat. Wallets and billfolds disappeared.

Information about the crash was made even more macabre by local newspaper reporters who picked up passengers' wallets, inventoried the contents and then wrote about what they found. A television station recovered wedding photos among the debris and assumed it was a couple that had died in the crash. The photos actually belonged to an older woman who perished. Her daughter and son-in-law were aghast to see their wedding photos on the evening news, along with a report of their demise.

When the National Transportation Safety Board team arrived at the crash site three days after the plane went down, they were surprised to see local people sitting on seats from the aircraft in the front yards of their homes. As they approached the aircraft by foot, the team members found a man on a horse trying to pull one of the jet engines from the crash site down the mountainside with a rope tied to the horn of his saddle. Fortunately for everyone, he was unsuccessful.[33]

What would motivate people to loot the belongings of the deceased on a cold, windswept mountainside? How could someone steal the ring off a severed hand or swipe the watch from a charred arm or open luggage and pilfer it or walk off with parts of the aircraft?

Since time immemorial, people from varied cultures have taken advantage of the misfortune of the few by stealing their possessions. I believe the best explanation for this is because the items of value were there, suddenly accessible to a lot of people.

But I could not stop wondering about these acts.

Regardless of why people steal from the dead, most of us are shocked by this behavior and have a hard time understanding it. Claiming the goods from a wrecked ship as they wash ashore amidst dead bodies is practically a birthright in some parts of the world.

Pillaging the bodies of dead soldiers on battlefields has occurred for thousands of years. Theft under these circumstances may be motivated by issues or emotions that have nothing to do with poverty.

Hondurans denounced the thievery at the crash site so graphically captured by the press. Newspaper photos of people running from the crash site with their arms full of personal effects or carrying away a suitcase created a public uproar and spurred President Azcona to send police into homes on Cerro de Hula to look for stolen items. Several people were arrested and charged with theft. Those who lived in the immediate area of the crash, like Napoleon Rodriguez, insisted that they helped the survivors and did not rob from the dead. To his credit, Rodriguez carried luggage into his home for safekeeping and then turned it all over to the authorities.

Adding poverty to the mix complicated the issue of thievery. Flight #414 crashed in an area populated by poor, subsistence farmers who were adept at surviving with little land, income, nutrition, health or education. Residents owned small plots of land that produced some of the food they consumed during the year, but not enough to feed a family. Income was seasonal, based on the availability of work either locally or in other parts of the country. Crops produced on the land were set aside for consumption but were sold in times of crisis. Diet was limited, because most nutritious foods were too expensive to purchase. Children started working hard at an early age and were fortunate if they completed the sixth grade in public school. For the most part, the residents of the area lived outside the economy and struggled their entire lives to eke out a living.[33]

Looking back on my own experience, prior to the crash, I traveled and lived in Latin America for close to twenty years. Over that period of time, I had cameras stolen, tires lifted from my jeep, money taken from different briefcases, numerous jacks and crowbars and a host of other possessions swiped. These were all acts of petty theft. I used to joke to friends about the "gentlemen thieves" who would steal my briefcase from under my nose and then leave it for me to find twenty minutes later without the money and calculator, but everything else intact. At one point, the jacks were disappearing from my jeep as quickly as I replaced them. I knew exactly where to go in the marketplace to buy them back, and one day was waiting for the thief when he arrived to fence my jack. We practically knew each other by that time.

I found all of this annoying, but usually amusing since no one was hurt. In the grander scheme of things, it was the price one pays for being careless and living in poverty-stricken countries.

Is poverty an excuse for thievery? My middle class Western values automatically scream no, it is not. I can't accept criminal behavior, but I have grown to understand it in a fatalistic context where having enough to feed yourself and your family is a daily challenge. It is the worst kind of pressure that poor parents have to endure. What are we going to feed the children today? How can I pay for medicine for my sick infant? Should I sell our few animals to pay off debt and eat adequately for a week or two? Do I leave my family alone this winter to work in the lowlands? Living with this sort of pressure on a regular basis can drive good men and women to abuse alcohol, to become violent and to steal.

Most of us experience many challenges during the course of our lives. Losing a job through downsizing, the death of a family member, fire or flooding of a home are not unusual occurrences for Americans. We live through these events and are often prepared to resolve the impact by falling back on savings, collecting insurance or relying on help from a family member.

Living in poverty means that these events are even more dramatic, because there are so few resources or services for dealing with them to ensure survival. Rational economic decisions are made to cope with crises such as giving up on non-productive land and moving to the city; choosing to eat seed intended for planting because the family is hungry; or soliciting help from a non-governmental organization because the government has proven to be inept in helping out.

People living in poverty have a small margin for error and are prone to take advantage of a rare occurrence like a plane falling out of the sky in their neighborhood. The crash of flight #414 presented an economic opportunity for many people, who descended upon the largely unguarded crash site. As Moritz Thomsen said in his book *Living Poor*, "Poverty makes a thief of a man who doesn't have monumental character."[34]

The campesinos who were harvesting corn on the adjacent hillside from the crash can be viewed similarly. For years the image of these men harvesting corn while a Boeing 727 burned up in front of them upset me. Whenever I thought about my futile attempts to get their attention, I remained incredulous. Why didn't they help me or others?

In October 2001, I interviewed a campesino who lived in the area and gained some insight into the behavior of the men on the hillside. These men were *peones* (landless peasants) who worked whenever and wherever they could as day laborers. A daily wage at that time varied from $1.50 to $2.50. [33] They were at the bottom of the social scale in a poor country--the poorest of the poor. The workers that day had been hired from outside the community to come in and harvest the corn by the owner of the land near where my seat landed. The owner was not a wealthy man, but preferred paying the peones a minimum wage than doing the backbreaking work himself.

The only assets these men had were their health and their unskilled labor. Both allowed them to provide for their families as long as they could find work and muster the energy to carry it out. They lived mostly on beans and tortillas. On this particular day, the laborers had a paying job and nothing was going to distract them from finishing the work. They made an economic decision to continue to work and not get involved with the aftermath of the crash. It is entirely possible, too, that given their social status, they were less inclined to get involved than the local residents.

These explanations were logical and effectively assuaged my once strong feelings about being left to fend for myself on the mountainside after the crash. In retrospect, nothing would have changed had these laborers helped me. I still would have wound up on the dirt road below the crashed plane, I still would have gone into Tegucigalpa in the back of a truck and I still would have been burned on 25% of my body. My angst and unhappiness was really about being victimized by a plane crash and not the inattention of a group of laborers.

A final note of irony to my conflict over the behavior of the Hondurans at the crash site occurred just a week after the crash. A campesino walked into the CARE office in Tegucigalpa and handed over my briefcase to the receptionist. He had found it at the crash site. This was truly an act of kindness that demonstrated the good will of the people of the area. Yes, there had been looting and theft from the dead, but a local man took the time to return my briefcase to the CARE office intact. It still contained my passport, birthday presents for Magaly, all my papers and a camera. This man had "monumental character."

- She offered me a glass of water after the crash

My process of struggling to understand and let go of my inner conflicts started the day of the crash and took thirteen years to run its course. I have come to realize that for many years I carried two personalities as a means of dealing with my anger and unhappiness over being the victim of a plane crash. My external personality was the calm and collected survivor. I was always in control and happy and projected this image to the outside world. I continued to fly and enjoyed demonstrating a fearless image to the world. I had gone through a horrible experience but not to worry—everything was fine.

My other personality or my shadow personality was an enraged victim who was plagued by nightmares of being on fire, fear of flying, shying away from intimacy and vulnerability and a desire to exact some form of revenge or payback for those who were responsible for the crash of flight #414. Until I embarked on this journey of research and writing, I shared my shadow personality with no one—including those closest to me. I thought it was easier and more comfortable for me to project a calm and controlled personality while dealing with my shadow on my own terms with no interference from others.

Prior to starting this journey, restlessness and searching for something I didn't understand were characteristics of my shadow personality. We moved six times in ten years. After every move I continued looking for new homes or apartments to move to. I became an expert in packing up our belongings as if this was a normal condition. Three different times over the years I was promoted to senior management positions at CARE only to walk away from the opportunities. I never allowed myself to have a career or truly taste success professionally even though I had ample prospects.

I believe that I became a less ambitious person after the crash. I set my family and my own well being as priorities and not how much money I made nor how much power I wielded. I came to the conclusion that my ultimate goal in life was to make a difference in my little community and enjoy myself doing it. After all that I had been through, it really was a simple conclusion to reach.

CHAPTER THIRTEEN

THE END OF THE JOURNEY?

What is to give light must endure burning.

-Viktor Frankel

We may never know exactly what happened on October 21, 1989. After reading and rereading the only official report, talking to attorneys and attempting to meet with the surviving pilots from the crash, it has become clear to me that it does not matter. I no longer have this insatiable need to know the truth. Knowing the exact circumstances of the crash will not change anything nor will it necessarily help anyone affected by the disaster. The plain facts are that 131 people died and the surviving 15 passengers suffered varying degrees of burns, fractures and psychological traumas.

Through my journey of introspection over the last five years, I finally came face to face with my principal inner conflict—trying to heal by blaming others. The journey would not be complete until I resolved this conflict, this unyielding sore on my mind, on my psyche. I blamed Honduras and Hondurans, I blamed the airline, I blamed the campesinos and I blamed the pilots.

I now understand my determination to find fault with others for what happened to me. Those of us who feel as if we have been traumatized by something beyond our control want and need to be able to blame someone. It is much easier to explain or justify, in your own mind, something that has gone awry if you can focus the blame on another person. In the case of flight #414, blaming the pilots has been convenient for me, but it has also proven to be a curse. When I found out that the pilots were probably responsible for the crash, it angered me, but somehow I felt relieved. This news provided me with an identifiable target at which to aim my rage. There is greater satisfaction in blaming another person for something that has hurt you than blaming the weather or a mechanical failure. But then what? They are to blame, but that does not change what happened. The pilots spent one night in jail and that is the sum total of their formal punishment. I am sure they have suffered, but at this point it no longer matters to me. I am no longer interested in wasting time thinking or worrying about them.

I find myself approaching the end of the journey. After discussing the crash and its impact with so many people over the years, I find myself talked out and suddenly, losing passion for the subject. I have experienced a breakthrough, a relieving myself of the burden of grief and survivor guilt over the deaths of so many.

This breakthrough was the result of challenging myself through this journey and then being challenged by Magaly. After repeated attempts to find and confront the pilots, Magaly asked me why I was giving them so much attention when this was always about me. She pulled out a quote from Rabbi Harold Kushner that best made her point, "What I try to teach people is that forgiveness is a favor we do for ourselves, not a favor we do to the person who has injured us. It's a way of cleansing ourselves of bitterness. It's a way of saying, 'I don't like the person you turned me into when I spend all day being angry at you.'"[35]

Magaly helped me realize that survival is a rare and precious gift. It was finally time to let go of my bitterness and angst over what had happened and enjoy the gift by focusing on myself and my family. It was time to rid myself of the shadow.

My journey has taken me to Central America numerous times and has put me in touch with many people who were affected by the plane crash. My own family has been with me throughout, particularly Magaly, who stood by my side from the day of the crash and never wavered. She has not allowed me to be depressed over the horror of it all and has been a strong and consistent guide. Without her brightly shining light and insight, I may well have slipped into the abyss of self-pity.

There are no guarantees in life. I am convinced though that the best way to heal is to be true to yourself and those you love. By focusing on the pilots, I allowed hatred and bitterness to occupy too much space in my heart. Life continues, and at some point we have to learn from negative experiences without allowing them to consume us. It is really about caring for yourself, loving yourself and those closest to you. If you can do that, everything else in life becomes clearer.

I am no longer emotionally invested in the crash experience and what it represented to my life for so many years. I am finally letting it go after coming to terms with my own grieving. Disinvesting myself of the emotional burden does not mean the experience simply disappeared from my psyche though.

It has taken me years to begin to put the experience of my survival behind me. I have achieved this by embracing the experience and integrating it into who I am. I recognize that I have learned from the experience and am a stronger person from it. I have let go of my anger and no longer blame others for what happened to me. I know I cannot forget the trauma of living through this hellish experience and the resulting burn treatment, nor do I want to. It has defined me as a person. It helps explain who I am. Knowing me without being aware of my survival of the plane crash is not really knowing me.

For many years, I labored with the belief that if I talked about the experience often enough it would somehow go away. It didn't begin to go away until I changed my focus from the negative impact of the crash to what I had to look forward to every day. There was no changing the fact that I survived a plane crash, but I came to understand that I could change my attitude toward the experience.

In the case of flight #414, like many human tragedies, there are questions that cannot be answered. I can't explain why I survived and a number of children perished, but I will always ask myself the question. I can't explain the actions of the pilots or the airline, but I will always wonder about it. I can't explain why I occasionally find myself staring into space or experiencing feelings that leave me short of breath or tight in the chest.

As a survivor, who narrowly escaped death, it never occurred to me that I needed to grieve, to experience the pain of grief. I was alive. What was there to grieve? Why should I complicate my life? I did not know anyone on board flight #414.

I did not realize it at the time, but I was closely linked if not bonded to all the passengers. The loss of life profoundly affected me. One minute I was surrounded by other passengers and the next I was thrown out of the plane, and they were dead. I couldn't disassociate myself from the deceased.

I had plenty of other reasons to grieve that had nothing to do with death. In a matter of seconds my entire future had been thrown into doubt. Again, without understanding it, I was grieving over all the changes in my life. It was going to take years to fully regain my health and be active. My ability to return to work and provide for myself and my family was questionable. I wasn't sure if and when I would be able to fly again, and I knew enough about psychology to appreciate the mental health challenges before me.

All of these primary and secondary reasons for grieving contributed to the intense sadness I felt after the crash. It was an unconscious form of grieving. I didn't understand at the time why I would break down and weep uncontrollably from one moment to the next. Now it is clear. I was grieving and grieving was a necessary step towards healing.

Ultimately, my challenge has been to learn to live with the trauma of surviving a plane crash, not to ignore it, not to forget about it and certainly not to wrap it up and put it on the shelf as some sort of finished product. I know I will live with it for the rest of my life.

Life is rooted in change. We are constantly evolving as people, but the basis of who we are is our collective life experiences, good and bad. Confronting death helped me focus on the here and now and to truly celebrate life for its meaning. The crash experience gave me the wherewithal to live differently and to take risks, to be more spontaneous.

Most importantly, though, I have come to appreciate how fortunate I am to be alive, to have a wonderful wife and daughter, as well as extended family and the friendship of numerous people. I truly feel like each day offers me one more bonus in the game of life.

Waking up on the mountainside in Honduras was my first break, and life has offered me nothing but surprises and new challenges since then. A survivor of any tragedy, particularly a tragedy that has taken so many lives, cannot help but feel fortunate and very blessed. My attitude towards this defining experience is that my glass is half full, not half empty. For whatever reason, I survived a catastrophic plane crash with my physical and mental health largely intact. I would not recommend this experience to anyone, but in many ways it was the best thing that ever happened to me. I am thankful every day for being on this earth.

The beauty of "Cerro De Hula"

NOTES

NOTES - CHAPTER TWO

[1] p. 40 La Prensa, Managua, Nicaragua October 22, 1989

[2] p. 41 Tiempo Nacional, Tegucigalpa, October 23, 1989.

NOTES - CHAPTER THREE

[3] p. 59 Severe Burns, A Family Guide to Medical and Emotional Recovery, Andrew M. Munster, Johns Hopkins University Press, Baltimore, 1993.

[4] p. 60 The Wound Care Information Network-Phases of Wound Healing, The Wound Expert, www.wellness.ucdavis.edu.html

[5] p. 61 www.Burn.html

NOTES – CHAPTER FOUR

[6] p. 65 Burn Center Information Booklet, University of Miami Jackson Memorial Hospital, Nursing and Patient Education, 1986.

[7] p. 67 "The burn nurses are those very special people whom a burn patient tends to hate on a daily basis. It's hard to understand that the people doing all those painful procedures aren't there to cause pain but to help you heal. Burn nurses also have an unusual way of making you feel safe in what I often viewed as hell on earth. Throughout nightmares, loneliness, fear and a never-ending stream of questions a nurse is there…24 hours a day." Caroline C. Rouen, Severe Burns, p. 4.

NOTES – CHAPTER FIVE

[8] p.82 Post-Traumatic Stress Disorder, The American Psychiatric Association, www.amerrescue.org/ptsd.htm, 8/16/99

NOTES – CHAPTER SIX

[9] p. 90 Curtis Schaeffer Report, Comprehensive Rehabilitation Consultants, New York, 5/22/90

[10] p. 91 Curtis Schaeffer Record, Dr. Susan Shapiro, New York, September 1990

NOTES-CHAPTER NINE

[11] p. 139 For example, the Honduran government passed a land reform decree in 1975 that was designed to redistribute 600,000 hectares of land to 120,000 campesino families within five years. Most of the families are still waiting for their land. Worse yet is the conduct of the institutions. After the crash of flight #414, the Honduran court system, the Civil Aeronautic Board and the office of the Presidency demonstrated a reckless disregard for the truth and engaged in a pattern of lies and deception toward the public that are detailed in Chapter 6.

[12] p. 141 (El Heraldo-Nacionales p. 44, October 26, 1989)

[13] p. 149 George Engel, essay entitled Psychosomatic Medicine, 1961.

[14] p. 155 J. William Worden, Grief Counseling and Grief Therapy, Springer Publishing Company, New York, 1991

[15] p. 159 Elizabeth Kubler-Ross, Death The Final Stage of Growth, Simon and Schuster, 1975.

[16] p. 162 Harold S. Kushner, When Bad Things Happen to Good People, 1981.

NOTES-CHAPTER TEN

[17] p. 164 The Death of Ben Linder, The Story of a North American in Sandinista Nicaragua, Joan Kruckewitt, Seven Stories Press, 1999.

NOTES-CHAPTER ELEVEN

[18] p. 204 Shelton's Barefoot Airlines, Philip Schleit, Max Graphics, 1982.

[19] p. 205 'Danger on Wings-Latin America Has Antiquated Airports, Spotty Radar Coverage, called Latin America: Trouble in the Skies-Sun Sentinel Ft. Lauderdale, Florida, 1997.

[20] p. 206 Interview with Bob McIntosh-NTSB, Washington, D.C. July 27, 2001

[21] p. 207 Tiempo Nacional Tegucigalpa, Honduras October 25, 1989, p. 3

[22] p. 208 Central America Report, August 22, 1986; data from Economic Commission on Latin America (ECLA)

[23] p. 208 The Death of Ben Linder, Joan Kruckewitt, 1999.

[24] p. 208 J.A. Caldwell, "Fatigue in the Aviation Environment: An Overview of the Causes and Effects As Well As

[25] p 209 Recommended Countermeasures." In: Aviation, Space and Environmental Medicine, March 1993

[26] p. 212 P.H. Gander, "Age, Circadian Rhythms, and Sleep Loss in Flight Crews." In: Aviation, Space, and Environmental Medicine, March 1993

[27] p. 212 Report of the Investigating Commission Concerning the Accident Involving Boeing Aircraft SAHSA 727-200, Registration N-88705

[28] p. 216 Black box transcript in Spanish with English translation from Report of the Investigating Commission

[29] p. 217 Shelton and the founder of TACA (Transportes Aereos Centroamericanos) Airlines, a New Zealander by the name of Lowell Yerex, were hired by the Honduran government in 1932 to help put down a popular uprising. Their work consisted of reconnaissance flights and occasionally dropping a homemade bomb from the plane. At one point Yerex landed his plane on a grassy strip at a spot called Cerro de Hule, a

mountain ridge outside of Tegucigalpa. Yerex was shot in the eye by an insurgent but managed to escape. 57 years later TAN SAHSA flight #414 crashed in the same spot. The uprising was eventually put down and Shelton and Yerex were amply paid for their work. Yerex was subsequently contracted to set up the Honduran Air Force.

[30] p. 221 Phone interview with John Grayson, 9/13/02

[31] p. 221 Westlaw Document Retrieval-(149 F.3d 127) Brink's Ltd. V South African Airways, No. 94 Civ. 1902, 1995 WL 225602 S.D.N.Y. April 17, 1995

[32] p. 221 Phone Interview with NTSB Team Member Greg Phillips 8/13/02

NOTES – CHAPTER TWELVE

[33] p. 245 Don't Be Afraid Gringo-A Honduran Woman Speaks From the Heart, The Story of Elvia Alvarado, Translated and Edited by Medea Benjamin, Harper Perennial, 1987.

[34] p. 246 Living Poor-Peace Corps Chronicles, Moritz Thompson, 1969.

NOTES – CHAPTER THIRTEEN

[35] p. 251 Don't Be Afraid Gringo.

Made in the USA
Charleston, SC
06 January 2015